The DLM Early Childhood EXPRESS

Teacher's Edition

Unit 5
Amazing Animals

Nell Duke • Douglas Clements • Julie Sarama • William Teale

 Wright Group

The McGraw·Hill Companies

Authors

Nell Duke
Professor of Teacher Education and Educational Psychology and Co-Director of the Literacy Achievement Research Center Michigan State University, East Lansing, MI

Douglas H. Clements
Professor of Early Childhood and Mathematics Education University at Buffalo, State University of New York, New York

Julie Sarama
Associate Professor of Mathematics Education University at Buffalo, State University of New York, New York

William Teale
Professor of Education University of Illinois at Chicago, Chicago, IL

Contributing Authors

Kim Brenneman, PhD
Assistant Research Professor of Psychology at Rutgers University, National Institute for Early Education Research Rutgers University, New Brunswick, NJ

Peggy Cerna
Early Childhood Consultant Austin, TX

Dan Cieloha
Educator and President of the Partnership for Interactive Learning Oakland, CA

Paula Jones
Early Childhood Consultant Lubbock, TX

Bobbie Sparks
Educator and K-12 Science Consultant Houston, TX

The McGraw-Hill Companies

www.WrightGroup.com

Wright Group

Acknowledgment

Building Blocks was supported in part by the National Science Foundation under Grant No. ESI-9730804, "Building Blocks— Foundations for Mathematical Thinking, Pre-Kindergarten to Grade 2: Research-based Materials Development" to Douglas H. Clements and Julie Sarama. The curriculum was also based partly upon work supported in part by the Institute of Educational Sciences (U.S. Dept. of Education, under the Interagency Education Research Initiative, or IERI, a collaboration of the IES, NSF, and NICHHD) under Grant No. R305K05157, "Scaling Trajectories and Technologies" and by the IERI through a National Science Foundation NSF Grant No. REC-0228440, "Scaling Up the Implementation of a Pre-Kindergarten Mathematics Curricula: Teaching for Understanding with Trajectories and Technologies." Any opinions, findings, and conclusions or recommendations expressed in this material are those of the authors and do not necessarily reflect the views of the funding agencies.

Reviewers

Tonda Brown, *Pre-K Specialist*, Austin ISD; Deanne Colley, *Family Involvement Facilitator*, Northwest ISD; Anita Uphaus, *Retired Early Childhood Director*, Austin ISD; Cathy Ambridge, *Reading Specialist*, Klein ISD; Margaret Jordan, *PreK Special Education Teacher*, McMullen Booth Elementary; Niki Rogers, *Adjunct Professor of Psychology/ Child Development*, Concordia University Wisconsin

Table of Contents

Getting Started

Getting Started with *The DLM Early Childhood Express*

The DLM Early Childhood Express is a holistic, child-centered program that nurtures each child by offering carefully selected and carefully sequenced learning experiences. It provides a wealth of materials and ideas to foster the social-emotional, intellectual, and physical development of children. At the same time, it nurtures the natural curiosity and sense of self that can serve as the foundation for a lifetime of learning.

The lesson format is designed to present information in a way that makes it easy for children to learn. Intelligence is, in large part, our ability to see patterns and build relationships out of those patterns, which is why *DLM* is focused on helping children see the patterns in what they are learning. It builds an understanding of how newly taught material resembles what children already know. Then it takes the differences in the new material and helps the children convert them into new understanding.

Each of the eight Teacher Edition Unit's in *DLM* are centered on an Essential Question relating to the unit's theme. Each week has its own more specific focus question. By focusing on essential questions, children are better able to connect their existing knowledge of the world with the new concepts and ideas they are learning at school. Routines at the beginning and end of each day help children focus on the learning process, reflect on new concepts, and make important connections. The lessons are designed to allow children to apply what they have learned.

Social and Emotional Development

Social-emotional development is addressed everyday through positive reinforcement, interactive activities, and engaging songs.

Language and Communication

All lessons are focused on language acquisition, which includes oral language development and vocabulary activities.

Emergent Literacy: Reading

Children develop literacy skills for reading through exposure to multiple read-aloud selections each day and through daily phonological awareness and letter recognition activities.

Emergent Literacy: Writing

Children develop writing skills through daily writing activities and during Center Time.

Mathematics

The math strand is based on **Building Blocks,** the result of NSF-funded research, and is designed to develop children's early mathematical knowledge through various individual and group activities.

Science

Children explore scientific concepts and methods during weekly science-focused, large-group activities, and Center Time activities.

Social Studies

Children explore Social Studies concepts during weekly social studies-focused, large-group activities, and Center Time activities.

Fine Arts

Children are exposed to art, dance, and music through a variety of weekly activities and the Creativity Center.

Physical Development

DLM is designed to allow children active time for outdoor play during the day, in addition to daily and weekly movement activities.

Technology Applications

Technology is integrated throughout each week with the use of online math activities, computer time, and other digital resources.

English Language Learners

Today's classrooms are very diverse. *The DLM Early Childhood Express* addresses this diversity by providing lessons in both English and Spanish. The program also offers strategies to assist English Language Learners at multiple levels of proficiency.

Flexible Scheduling

With *The DLM Early Childhood Express*, it's easy to fit lessons into your day.

Typical Full-Day Schedule

10 min	Opening Routines
15 min	Language Time
60-90 min	Center Time
15 min	Snack Time
15 min	Literacy Time
20 min	Active Play (outdoors if possible)
30 min	Lunch
15 min	Math Time
	Rest
15 min	Circle Time: Social and Emotional Development
20 min	Circle Time: Content Connection
30 min	Center Time
25 min	Active Play (outdoors if possible)
15 min	Let's Say Good-Bye

Typical Half-Day Schedule

10 min	Opening Routines
15 min	Language Time
60 min	Center Time
15 min	Snack Time
15 min	Circle Time (Literacy, Math, or Social and Emotional Development)
30 min	Active Play (outdoors if possible)
20 min	Circle Time (Content Connection, Literacy, Math, or Social and Emotional Development)
15 min	Let's Say Good-Bye

Welcome to *The DLM Early Childhood Express.*

Add your own ideas. Mix and match activities. Our program is designed to offer you a variety of activities on which to build a full year of exciting and creative lessons.

Happy learning to you and the children in your care!

Themes and Literature

With **The DLM Early Childhood Express,** children develop concrete skills through experiences with music, art, storytelling, hands-on activities and teacher-directed lessons that, in addition to skills development, emphasize practice and reflection. Every four weeks, children are introduced to a new theme organized around an essential question.

Literature selections and cross-curricular content are linked to the theme to help children reinforce lesson concepts. Children hear and discuss an additional read-aloud selection from the *Teacher Treasure Book* at the beginning and end of each day. At the end of each unit, children take home a *My Theme Library Book* reader of their own.

Unit 1: All About Pre-K
Why is school important?

	Focus Question	Literature
Week 1	What happens at school?	Welcome to School Bienvenidos a la escuela
Week 2	What happens in our classroom?	Yellowbelly and Plum Go to School Barrigota y Pipón van a la escuela
Week 3	What makes a good friend?	Max and Mo's First Day at School Max y Mo van a la escuela
Week 4	How can we play and learn together?	Amelia's Show and Tell Fiesta/Amelia y la fiesta de "muestra y cuenta"
Unit Wrap-Up	**My Library Book**	How Can I Learn at School? ¿Cómo puedo aprender en la escuela?

Unit 2: All About Me
What makes me special?

	Focus Question	Literature
Week 1	Who am I?	All About Me Todo sobre mí
Week 2	What are my feelings?	Lots of Feelings Montones de sentimientos
Week 3	What do the parts of my body do?	Eyes, Nose, Fingers, and Toes Ojos, nariz, dedos y pies
Week 4	What is a family?	Jonathan and His Mommy Juan y su mamá
Unit Wrap-Up	**My Library Book**	What Makes Us Special? ¿Qué nos hace especiales?

Unit 3: My Community
What is a community?

	Focus Question	Literature
Week 1	What are the parts of a community?	In the Community En la comunidad
Week 2	Hoe does a community help me?	Rush Hour, Hora pico
Week 3	Who helps the community?	Quinito's Neighborhood
Week 4	How can I help my community?	Flower Garden Un jardín de flores
Unit Wrap-Up	**My Library Book**	In My Community Mi comunidad

Unit 4: Let's Investigate
How can I learn more about things?

	Focus Question	Literature
Week 1	How can I learn by observing?	Let's Investigate Soy detective
Week 2	How can I use tools to investiagte?	I Like Making Tamales Me gusta hacer tamales
Week 3	How can I compare things?	Nature Spy Espía de la naturaleza
Week 4	How do objects move?	What Do Wheels Do All Day? ¿Qué hacen las ruedas todo el día?
Unit Wrap-Up	**My Library Book**	How Can We Investigate? ¿Cómo podemos investigar?

Unit 5: Amazing Animals
What is amazing about animals?

	Focus Question	Literature
Week 1	What are animals like?	Amazing Animals Animales asombrosos
Week 2	Where do animals live and what do they eat?	Castles, Caves, and Honeycombs Castillos, cuevas y panales
Week 3	How are animals the same and different?	Who Is the Beast? Quien es la bestia?
Week 4	How do animals move?	Move! ¡A moverse!
Unit Wrap-Up	My Library Book	Hello, Animals! ¡Hola, animales!

Unit 6: Growing and Changing
How do living things grow and change?

	Focus Question	Literature
Week 1	How do animals grow and change?	Growing and Changing Creciendo y cambiando
Week 2	How do plants grow and change?	I Am a Peach Yo soy el durazno
Week 3	How do people grow and change?	I'm Growing! Estoy creciendo!
Week 4	How do living things grow and change?	My Garden Mi jardin
Unit Wrap-Up	My Library Book	Growing Up Creciendo

Unit 7: The Earth and Sky
What can I learn about the earth and the sky?

	Focus Question	Literature
Week 1	What can I learn about the earth and the sky?	The Earth and Sky La Tierra y el cielo
Week 2	What weather can I observe each day?	Who Likes Rain? ¿A quién le gusta la lluvia?
Week 3	What can I learn about day and night?	Matthew and the Color of the Sky Matias y el color del cielo
Week 4	Why is caring for the earth and sky important?	Ada, Once Again! ¡Otra vez Ada!
Unit Wrap-Up	My Library Book	Good Morning, Earth! ¡Buenos días, Tierra!

Unit 8: Healthy Food/Healthy Body
Why is healthy food and exercise good for me?

	Focus Question	Literature
Week 1	What are good healthy habits?	Staying Healthy Mantente sano
Week 2	What kinds of foods are healthy?	Growing Vegetable Soup A sembrar sopa de verduras
Week 3	Why is exercise important?	Rise and Exercise! A ejercitarse, ¡uno, dos, tres!
Week 4	How can I stay healthy?	Jamal's Busy Day El intenso día de Jamal
Unit Wrap-Up	My Library Book	Healthy Kids Niños sanos

Tools for Teaching

The *DLM Early Childhood Express* is packed full of the components you'll need to teach each theme and enrich your classroom. The *Teacher Treasure Package* is the heart of the program, because it contains all the necessary materials. Plus, the *Teacher's Treasure Book* contains all the fun components that you'll love to teach. The *Literature Package* contains all the stories and books you need to support children's developing literacy. You'll find letter tiles, counters, and puppets in the *Manipulative Package* to connect hands-on learning skills with meaningful play.

Teacher Treasure Package

This package contains all the essential tools for the teacher such as the *Teacher's Treasure Book, Teacher's Editions*, technology, and other resources no teacher would want to be without!

*Alphabet Wall Cards
(English and Spanish)*

*ABC Picture Cards
(English and Spanish)*

*Sequence Cards
(English and Spanish)*

*Oral Language Development Cards
(English and Spanish)*

*Photo Library
CD-ROM*

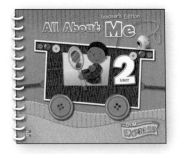

▲ Each lesson's instruction uses a variety of cards to help children learn. **Alphabet Wall Cards** and **ABC Picture Cards** help build letter recognition and phonemic awareness. **Oral Language Development Cards** teach new vocabulary, and are especially helpful when working with English Language Learners. **Sequencing Cards** help children learn how to order events and the vocabulary associated with time and sequence.

▲ There is one bilingual **Teacher's Edition** for each four-week theme. It provides the focus questions for each lesson as well as plans for centers and suggestions for classroom management.

▶ The bilingual **Teacher's Treasure Book** features 500+ pages of the things you love most about teaching Early Childhood, such as songs, traditional read alouds, folk tales, finger plays, and flannelboard stories with patterns.

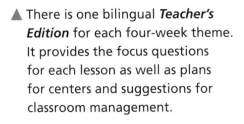
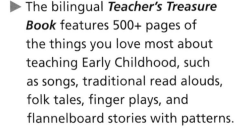

▶ An **ABC Take-Home Book** with blackline masters is provided for each letter of the English and Spanish alphabets.

*ABC Take-Home Book
(English and Spanish)*

▶ Flip charts and their Audio CDs support the activities in each lesson. Children practice literacy and music skills using the **Rhymes and Chants Flip Chart,** which supports oral language development and phonological awareness in both English and Spanish. An Audio CD is included and provides a recording of every rhyme or chant. The **Making Good Choices Flip Chart** provides illustrations to allow students to explore social and emotional development concepts while facilitating classroom activities and discussion. 15 lively songs recorded in both English and Spanish address key social emotional development themes such as: joining in, helping others, being fair, teasing, bullying, and much more. The **Math and Science Flip Chart** is a demonstration tool that addresses weekly math and science concepts through photos and illustrations.

▶ Other key resources include a **Research & Professional Development Guide,** and a bilingual **Home Connections Resource Guide** which provides weekly letters home and take-home story books.

Building Blocks

Building Blocks, the result of NSF-funded research, develops young children's mathematical thinking using their bodies, manipulatives, paper, and computers.

Building Blocks online management system guides children through research-based learning trajectories. These activities-through-trajectories connect children's informal knowledge to more formal school mathematics. The result is a mathematical curriculum that is not only motivating for children but also comprehensive.

▶ **DLMExpressOnline.com** includes the following:

- e-Books of student and teacher materials

- Audio recordings of the **My Library** and **Literature Books** (Big/Little) in English and Spanish

- Teacher planning tools and assessment support

Tools for Teaching

Literature Package

This package contains the literature referenced in the program. Packages are available in several variations so you can choose the package that best meets the needs of your classroom. The literature used in the program includes expository selections, traditional stories, and emergent readers for students. All literature is available in English or Spanish.

▶ *My Library Books* are take-home readers for children to continue their exploration of unit themes. (English and Spanish)

Baby animals need help to grow big and strong. Baby animals need a safe place to live.

▶ *Concept Big Books* are nonfiction selections that introduce the essential questions for each unit and help children make connections between their background knowledge and unit themes. (English and Spanish)

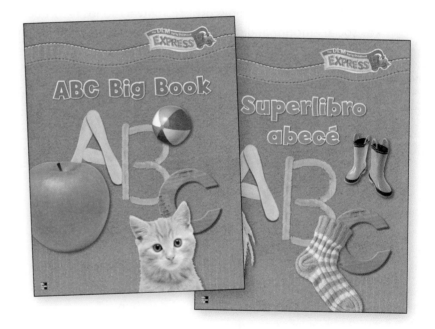

▶ The *ABC Big Book* helps children develop phonemic awareness and letter recognition. (English and Spanish)

▶ The **Big Books** and **Little Books** reinforce each week's theme and the unit theme. Selections include stories originally written in Spanish, as well as those written in English.

▶ The stories in the **Big Books and Little Books** are recorded on the **Listening Library Audio CDs**. They are available in English and Spanish.

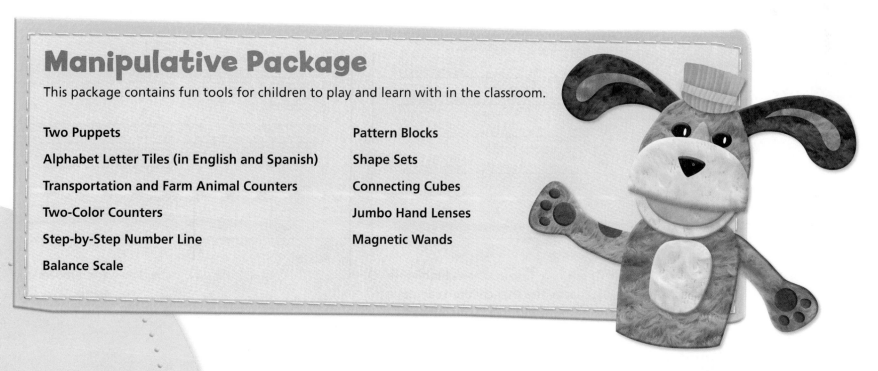

Manipulative Package

This package contains fun tools for children to play and learn with in the classroom.

Two Puppets

Alphabet Letter Tiles (in English and Spanish)

Transportation and Farm Animal Counters

Two-Color Counters

Step-by-Step Number Line

Balance Scale

Pattern Blocks

Shape Sets

Connecting Cubes

Jumbo Hand Lenses

Magnetic Wands

A Typical Weekly Lesson Plan

Each week of *The DLM Early Childhood Express* is organized the same way to provide children with the structure and routines they crave. Each week begins with a weekly opener that introduces the focus question for the week and includes a review of the week's Learning Goals, the Materials and Resources needed for the week, a Daily Planner, and a plan for the Learning Centers children will use throughout the week.

Each day's lesson includes large-group Circle Time and small-group Center Time. Each day includes Literacy, Math, and Social and Emotional Development activities during Circle Time. On Day 1, children explore Science. On Days 2 and 4, they work on more in-depth math lessons. On Day 3, Social Studies is the focus. Fine Art or Music/Movement activities take place during Circle Time on Day 5.

○ You will find the **Program Materials** and **Other Materials** needed for each day on the Materials and Resources page.

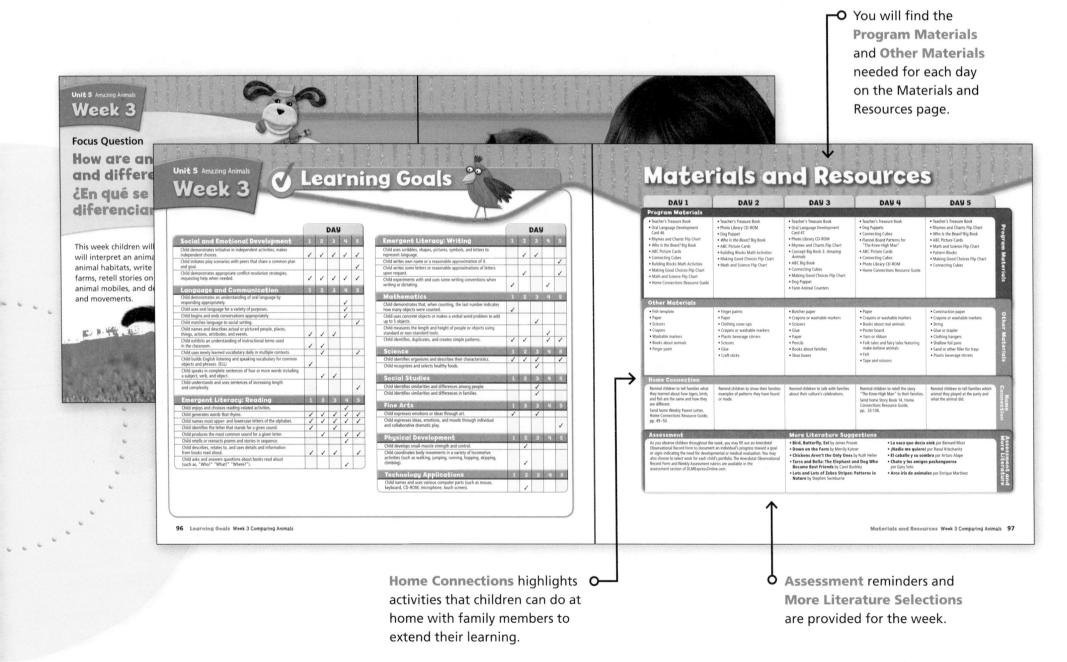

Home Connections highlights activities that children can do at home with family members to extend their learning.

Assessment reminders and **More Literature Selections** are provided for the week.

The **Daily Planner** provides a Week-at-a-Glance view of the daily structure and lesson topics for each week.

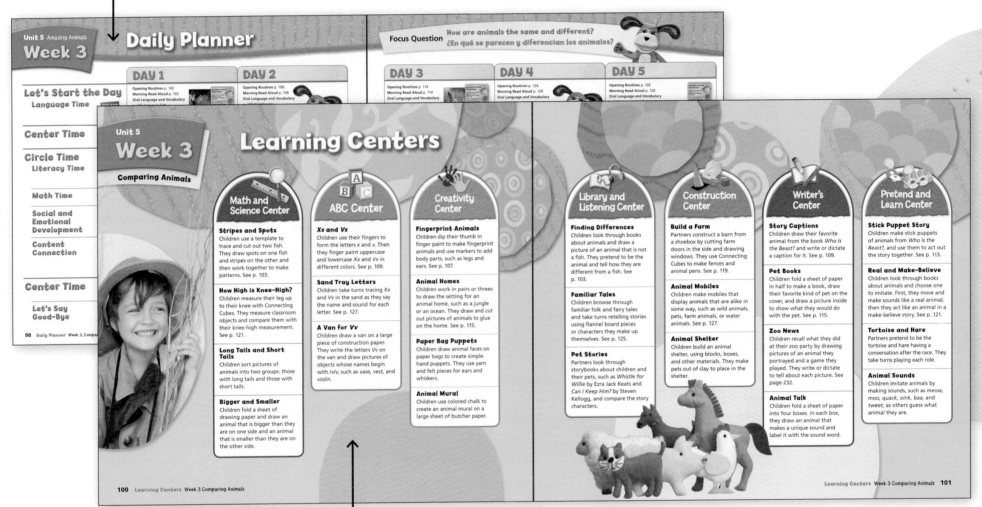

Learning Centers should be used throughout the week during Center Time. This page provides an overview of center activities to set up for children. Additional information about some center activities is provided in the daily lessons. The Learning Centers are intended to remain open for the entire week. These centers provide the opportunity for children to explore a wide range of curricular areas.

Lesson Overview

Our **Teacher's Editions** are organized by theme, week, and day. Each day's lesson is covered in six page spreads. The lessons integrate learning from the skill domain areas of: Social Emotional Development, Language and Communication, Emergent Literacy Reading and Writing, Mathematics, Science, Social Studies, Fine Arts, Physical Development, and Technology.

Each day begins with **Opening Routines** and a **Read Aloud** selection. This structured time helps children settle into their day.

The **Learning Goals** met by the lesson are listed on each page.

Observational Checks at point of use help to focus learning. These informal assessment questions help to ensure children are meeting lesson objectives.

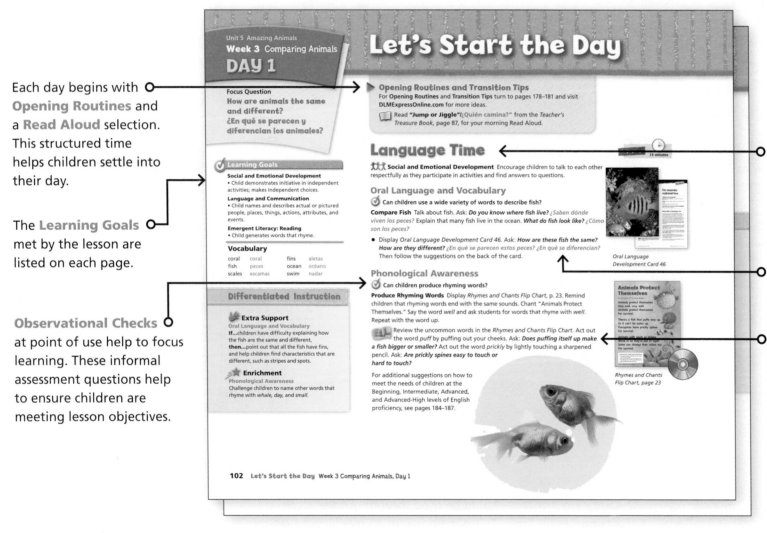

Language Time is the first large-group activity of the day. It includes Oral Language and Vocabulary Development as well as Phonological Awareness activities.

Instructional questions are provided in both **English and Spanish.**

Tips for working with **English Language Learners** are shown at point of use throughout the lessons. Teaching strategies are provided to help children of of all language backgrounds and abilities meet the lesson objectives.

Center Time provides additional information for teacher-guided small-group activities and suggestions for independent activities children will complete during weekly Center Rotation.

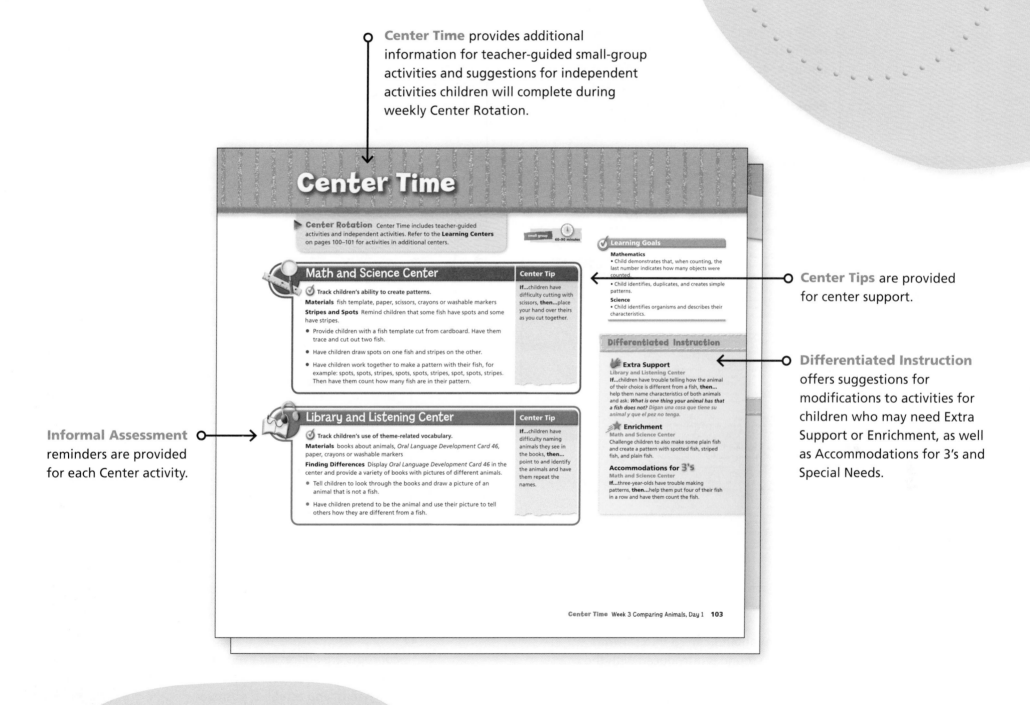

Center Time

▶ **Center Rotation** Center Time includes teacher-guided activities and independent activities. Refer to the **Learning Centers** on pages 100–101 for activities in additional centers.

small group
60–90 minutes

Math and Science Center

✓ Track children's ability to create patterns.

Materials fish template, paper, scissors, crayons or washable markers

Stripes and Spots Remind children that some fish have spots and some have stripes.

● Provide children with a fish template cut from cardboard. Have them trace and cut out two fish.

● Have children draw spots on one fish and stripes on the other.

● Have children work together to make a pattern with their fish, for example: spots, spots, stripes, spots, spots, stripes, spot, spots, stripes. Then have them count how many fish are in their pattern.

Center Tip

If...children have difficulty cutting with scissors, **then**...place your hand over theirs as you cut together.

Library and Listening Center

✓ Track children's use of theme-related vocabulary.

Materials books about animals, *Oral Language Development Card 46*, paper, crayons or washable markers

Finding Differences Display *Oral Language Development Card 46* in the center and provide a variety of books with pictures of different animals.

● Tell children to look through the books and draw a picture of an animal that is not a fish.

● Have children pretend to be the animal and use their picture to tell others how they are different from a fish.

Center Tip

If...children have difficulty naming animals they see in the books, **then**...point to and identify the animals and have them repeat the names.

✓ **Learning Goals**

Mathematics
• Child demonstrates that, when counting, the last number indicates how many objects were counted.

• Child identifies, duplicates, and creates simple patterns.

Science
• Child identifies organisms and describes their characteristics.

Differentiated Instruction

🐦 **Extra Support**
Library and Listening Center
If...children have trouble telling how the animal of their choice is different from a fish, **then**... help them name characteristics of both animals and ask: *What is one thing your animal has that a fish does not? Digan una cosa que tiene su animal y que el pez no tenga.*

⭐ **Enrichment**
Math and Science Center
Challenge children to also make some plain fish and create a pattern with spotted fish, striped fish, and plain fish.

Accommodations for 3's
Math and Science Center
If...three-year-olds have trouble making patterns, **then**...help them put four of their fish in a row and have them count the fish.

Center Time Week 3 Comparing Animals, Day 1 **103**

Center Tips are provided for center support.

Differentiated Instruction offers suggestions for modifications to activities for children who may need Extra Support or Enrichment, as well as Accommodations for 3's and Special Needs.

Informal Assessment reminders are provided for each Center activity.

Lesson Overview

Children have **Literacy Time** every day. During this time, children listen to and discuss a second Read Aloud from a nonfiction **Concept Big Book** or a **Big Book/Little Book** literature selection

Building Blocks online activities are provided each week during Math Time.

Children work in large groups on 15 minute math activities during daily **Math Time.**

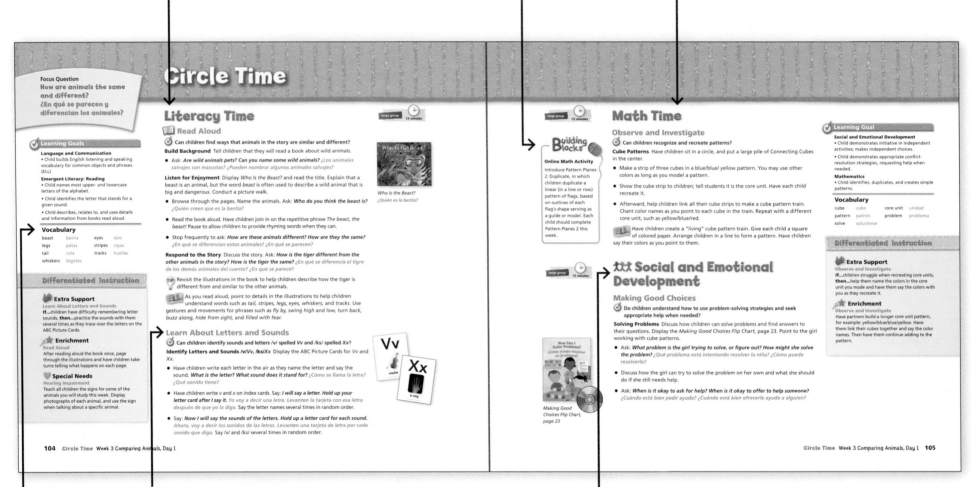

Circle Time

Focus Question
How are animals the same and different?
¿En qué se parecen y diferencian los animales?

Literacy Time

large group — *15 minutes*

Read Aloud

Can children find ways that animals in the story are similar and different?
Build Background Tell children that they will read a book about wild animals.

- Ask: *Are wild animals pets? Can you name some wild animals?* ¿Los animales salvajes son mascotas? ¿Pueden nombrar algunos animales salvajes? (ELL)

Listen for Enjoyment Display *Who Is the Beast?* and read the title. Explain that a beast is an animal, but the word *beast* is often used to describe a wild animal that is big and dangerous. Conduct a picture walk.

- Browse through the pages. Name the animals. Ask: *Who do you think the beast is?* ¿Quién creen que es la bestia?
- Read the book aloud. Have children join in on the repetitive phrase *The beast, the beast!* Pause to allow children to provide rhyming words when they can.
- Stop frequently to ask: *How are these animals different? How are they the same?* ¿En qué se diferencian estos animales? ¿En qué se parecen?

Respond to the Story Discuss the story. Ask: *How is the tiger different from the other animals in the story? How is the tiger the same?* ¿En qué se diferencia el tigre de los demás animales del cuento? ¿En qué se parece?

TIP Revisit the illustrations in the book to help children describe how the tiger is different from and similar to the other animals.

ELL As you read aloud, point to details in the illustrations to help children understand words such as *tail, stripes, legs, eyes, whiskers,* and *tracks.* Use gestures and movements for phrases such as *fly by, swing high and low, turn back, buzz along, hide from sight,* and *filled with fear.*

Who Is the Beast?
¿Quién es la bestia?

Learn About Letters and Sounds

Can children identify sounds and letters /v/ spelled *Vv* and /ks/ spelled *Xx*?
Identify Letters and Sounds /v/*Vv,* /ks/*Xx* Display the ABC Picture Cards for *Vv* and *Xx.*

- Have children write each letter in the air as they name the letter and say the sound. *What is the letter? What sound does it stand for?* ¿Cómo se llama la letra? ¿Qué sonido tiene?
- Have children write v and x on index cards. Say: *I will say a letter. Hold up your letter card after I say it.* Yo voy a decir una letra. Levanten la tarjeta con esa letra después de que yo la diga. Say the letter names several times in random order.
- Say: *Now I will say the sounds of the letters. Hold up a letter card for each sound.* Ahora, voy a decir los sonidos de las letras. Levanten una tarjeta de letra por cada sonido que diga. Say /v/ and /ks/ several times in random order.

Vv violin

Xx x-ray

Learning Goals

Language and Communication
- Child builds English listening and speaking vocabulary for common objects and phrases. (ELL)

Emergent Literacy: Reading
- Child names most upper- and lowercase letters of the alphabet.
- Child identifies the letter that stands for a given sound.
- Child describes, relates to, and uses details and information from books read aloud.

Vocabulary

beast	bestia
legs	patas
tail	cola
whiskers	bigotes
eyes	ojos
stripes	rayas
tracks	huellas

Differentiated Instruction

Extra Support
Learn About Letters and Sounds
If...children have difficulty remembering letter sounds, then...practice the sounds with them several times as they trace over the letters on the ABC Picture Cards.

Enrichment
Read Aloud
After reading aloud the book once, page through the illustrations and have children take turns telling what happens on each page.

Special Needs
Hearing Impairment
Teach all children the signs for some of the animals you will study this week. Display photographs of each animal, and use the sign when talking about a specific animal.

Math Time

large group — *15 minutes*

Observe and Investigate

Can children recognize and recreate patterns?
Cube Patterns Have children sit in a circle, and put a large pile of Connecting Cubes in the center.

- Make a strip of three cubes in a blue/blue/ yellow pattern. You may use other colors as long as you model a pattern.
- Show the cube strip to children; tell students it is the core unit. Have each child recreate it.
- Afterward, help children link all their cube strips to make a cube pattern train. Chant color names as you point to each cube in the train. Repeat with a different core unit, such as yellow/blue/red.

ELL Have children create a "living" cube pattern train. Give each child a square of colored paper. Arrange children in a line to form a pattern. Have children say their colors as you point to them.

Building Blocks

Online Math Activity
Introduce Pattern Planes 2: Duplicate, in which children duplicate a linear (in a line or row) pattern of flags, based on outlines of each flag's shape serving as a guide or model. Each child should complete Pattern Planes 2 this week.

👤👤👤 Social and Emotional Development

large group — *15 minutes*

Making Good Choices

Do children understand how to use problem-solving strategies and seek appropriate help when needed?
Solving Problems Discuss how children can solve problems and find answers to their questions. Display the *Making Good Choices Flip Chart,* page 23. Point to the girl working with cube patterns.

- Ask: *What problem is the girl trying to solve, or figure out? How might she solve the problem?* ¿Qué problema está intentando resolver la niña? ¿Cómo puede resolverlo?
- Discuss how the girl can try to solve the problem on her own and what she should do if she still needs help.
- Ask: *When is it okay to ask for help? When is it okay to offer to help someone?* ¿Cuándo está bien pedir ayuda? ¿Cuándo está bien ofrecerle ayuda a alguien?

How Can I Solve Problems?
¿Cómo puedo resolver un problema?

Making Good Choices Flip Chart, page 23

Learning Goal

Social and Emotional Development
- Child demonstrates initiative in independent activities; makes independent choices.
- Child demonstrates appropriate conflict-resolution strategies, requesting help when needed.

Mathematics
- Child identifies, duplicates, and creates simple patterns.

Vocabulary

cube	cubo	core unit	unidad
pattern	patrón	problem	problema
solve	solucionar		

Differentiated Instruction

Extra Support
Observe and Investigate
If...children struggle when recreating core units, then...help them name the colors in the core unit you made and have them say the colors with you as they recreate it.

Enrichment
Observe and Investigate
Have partners build a longer core unit pattern, for example: yellow/blue/blue/yellow. Have them link their cubes together and say the color names. Then have them continue adding to the pattern.

Vocabulary is provided in English and Spanish to help expand children's ability to use both languages.

Children learn about **Letters and Sounds** every day. The sound is introduced with the letter. Children also practice letter formation.

Social and Emotional Development concepts are addressed every day to help children better express their emotions and needs, and establish positive relationships.

Circle Time is devoted to longer activities focusing on different cross-curricular concepts each day. Day 1 is Science Time. Days 2 and 4 are Math Time. On Day 3, children have Social Studies Time. Fine arts are covered in Art Time or Music and Movement Time on Day 5.

An end-of-the-day **Writing** activity is provided each day.

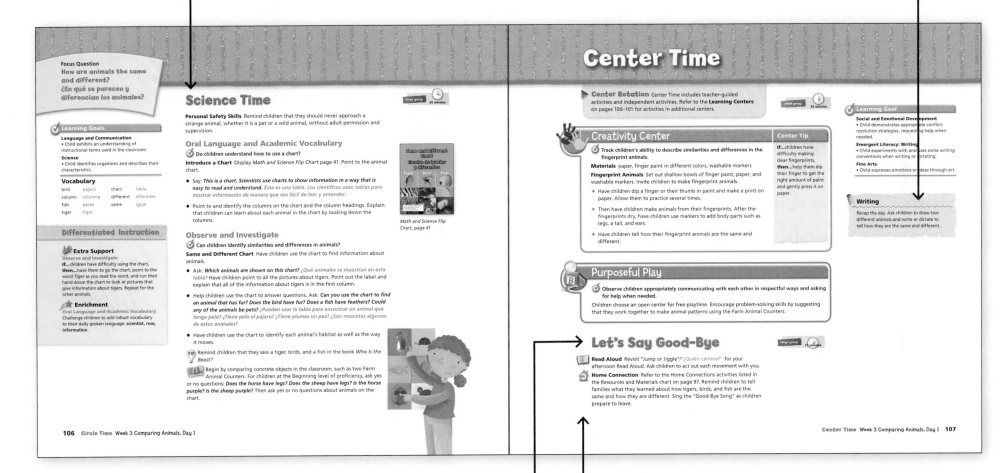

Focus Question
How are animals the same and different?
¿En qué se parecen y diferencian los animales?

Science Time

Personal Safety Skills Remind children that they should never approach a strange animal, whether it is a pet or a wild animal, without adult permission and supervision.

Oral Language and Academic Vocabulary

✓ Do children understand how to use a chart?

Introduce a Chart Display *Math and Science Flip Chart* page 41. Point to the animal chart.

- Say: *This is a chart. Scientists use charts to show information in a way that is easy to read and understand. Esta es una tabla. Los científicos usan tablas para mostrar información de manera que sea fácil de leer y entender.*
- Point to and identify the columns on the chart and the column headings. Explain that children can learn about each animal in the chart by looking down the columns.

Observe and Investigate

✓ Can children identify similarities and differences in animals?

Same and Different Chart Have children use the chart to find information about animals.

- Ask: *Which animals are shown on this chart? ¿Qué animales se muestran en esta tabla?* Have children point to all the pictures about tigers. Point out the label and explain that all of the information about tigers is in the first column.
- Help children use the chart to answer questions. Ask: *Can you use the chart to find an animal that has fur? Does the bird have fur? Does a fish have feathers? Could any of the animals be pets? ¿Pueden usar la tabla para encontrar un animal que tenga pelo? ¿Tiene pelo el pájaro? ¿Tiene plumas un pez? ¿Son mascotas algunos de estos animales?*
- Have children use the chart to identify each animal's habitat as well as the way it moves.

  Remind children that they saw a tiger, birds, and a fish in the book *Who Is the Beast?*

  Begin by comparing concrete objects in the classroom, such as two Farm Animal Counters. For children at the Beginning level of proficiency, ask yes or no questions: *Does the horse have legs? Does the sheep have legs? Is the horse purple? Is the sheep purple?* Then ask yes or no questions about animals on the chart.

Math and Science Flip Chart, page 41

Learning Goals

Language and Communication
• Child exhibits an understanding of instructional terms used in the classroom.
Science
• Child identifies organisms and describes their characteristics.

Vocabulary

bird	pájaro	chart	tabla
column	columna	different	diferente
fish	peces	same	igual
tiger	tigre		

Differentiated Instruction

Extra Support
Observe and Investigate
If...children have difficulty using the chart, **then**...have them go to the chart, point to the word *Tiger* as you read the word, and run their hand down the chart to look at pictures that give information about tigers. Repeat for the other animals.

Enrichment
Oral Language and Academic Vocabulary
Challenge children to add robust vocabulary to their daily spoken language: scientist, row, information.

Center Time

▶ **Center Rotation** Center Time includes teacher-guided activities and independent activities. Refer to the **Learning Centers** on pages 100–101 for activities in additional centers.

Creativity Center

✓ Track children's ability to describe similarities and differences in the fingerprint animals.

Materials paper, finger paint in different colors, washable markers
Fingerprint Animals Set out shallow bowls of finger paint, paper, and washable markers. Invite children to make fingerprint animals.

- Have children dip a finger or their thumb in paint and make a print on paper. Allow them to practice several times.
- Then have children make animals from their fingerprints. After the fingerprints dry, have children use markers to add body parts such as legs, a tail, and ears.
- Have children tell how their fingerprint animals are the same and different.

Center Tip
If...children have difficulty making clear fingerprints, **then**...help them dip their finger to get the right amount of paint and gently press it on paper.

Purposeful Play

✓ Observe children appropriately communicating with each other in respectful ways and asking for help when needed.

Children choose an open center for free playtime. Encourage problem-solving skills by suggesting that they work together to make animal patterns using the Farm Animal Counters.

Let's Say Good-Bye

Read Aloud Revisit "Jump or Jiggle"/"¿Quién camina?" for your afternoon Read Aloud. Ask children to act out each movement with you.

Home Connection Refer to the Home Connections activities listed in the Resources and Materials chart on page 97. Remind children to tell families what they learned about how tigers, birds, and fish are the same and how they are different. Sing the "Good-Bye Song" as children prepare to leave.

Learning Goal

Social and Emotional Development
• Child demonstrates appropriate conflict-resolution strategies, requesting help when needed.
Emergent Literacy: Writing
• Child experiments with and uses some writing conventions when writing or dictating.
Fine Arts
• Child expresses emotions or ideas through art.

Writing
Recap the day. Ask children to draw two different animals and write or dictate to tell how they are the same and different.

Let's Say Good-Bye includes the closing routines for each day. The Read Aloud from the beginning of the day is revisited with a focus on skills practiced during the day.

Each day provides a **Home Connection**. At the start of each week, a letter is provided to inform families of the weekly focus and offer additional literature suggestions to extend the weekly theme focus.

Focus Question

What are animals like?
¿Cómo son los animales?

This week children will identify traits, needs, and habitats of tame and wild animals. They will make animal masks, observe caterpillars, build animal homes, use shape sets and pattern blocks to depict animals, and write animal books.

Week 1 — Learning Goals

Social and Emotional Development	1	2	3	4	5
Child shows empathy and care for others.	✓	✓	✓	✓	✓

Language and Communication	1	2	3	4	5
Child demonstrates an understanding of oral language by responding appropriately.			✓	✓	
Child follows two- and three-step oral directions.				✓	
Child follows basic rules for conversations (taking turns, staying on topic, listening actively).				✓	✓
Child experiments with and produces a growing number of sounds in English words. (ELL).				✓	
Child names and describes actual or pictured people, places, things, actions, attributes, and events.	✓	✓	✓	✓	✓
Child exhibits an understanding of instructional terms used in the classroom.		✓			
Child understands or knows the meaning of many thousands of words, many more than he or she uses.	✓				✓
Child uses newly learned vocabulary daily in multiple contexts.	✓		✓	✓	
Child understands and uses regular and irregular plural nouns, regular past tense verbs, personal and possessive pronouns, and subject-verb agreement.				✓	

Emergent Literacy: Reading	1	2	3	4	5
Child enjoys and chooses reading-related activities.				✓	
Child generates words that rhyme.	✓	✓	✓	✓	✓
Child names most upper- and lowercase letters of the alphabet.	✓	✓	✓	✓	✓
Child identifies the letter that stands for a given sound.	✓	✓	✓	✓	✓
Child produces the most common sound for a given letter.		✓			✓
Child retells or reenacts poems and stories in sequence.				✓	
Child asks and answers questions about books read aloud (such as, "Who?" "What?" "Where?").	✓	✓			✓

Emergent Literacy: Writing	1	2	3	4	5
Child uses scribbles, shapes, pictures, symbols, and letters to represent language.			✓		✓

Mathematics	1	2	3	4	5
Child uses concrete objects or makes a verbal word problem to add up to 5 objects.			✓		✓
Child uses concrete objects or makes a verbal word problem to subtract up to 5 objects from a set.			✓		
Child recognizes, names, describes, matches, compares, and sorts common two-dimensional shapes (such as circle, square, rectangle, triangle, rhombus).	✓	✓		✓	✓
Child understands and uses words that describe position/location in space (such as under, over, beside, between, on, in, near, far away).		✓			
Child manipulates (flips, rotates) and combines shapes.				✓	
Child sorts objects and explains how the sorting was done.				✓	✓

Science	1	2	3	4	5
Child identifies organisms and describes their characteristics.	✓	✓			✓
Child observes, understands, and discusses the relationship of plants and animals to their environments.	✓		✓		✓
Child follows basic health and safety rules.	✓				

Social Studies	1	2	3	4	5
Child understands basic human needs for food, clothing, shelter			✓		
Child respects/appreciates the differing interests, skills, abilities, cultures, languages, and family structures of people.			✓		

Fine Arts	1	2	3	4	5
Child expresses emotions or ideas through art.			✓		✓
Child shares opinions about artwork and artistic experiences.				✓	✓

Physical Development	1	2	3	4	5
Child develops small-muscle strength and control.		✓			

Materials and Resources

DAY 1	DAY 2	DAY 3	DAY 4	DAY 5

Program Materials

• Teacher's Treasure Book • Oral Language Development Card 41 • Rhymes and Chants Flip Chart • Concept Big Book 3: *Amazing Animals* • ABC Big Book • Building Blocks Math Activities • Making Good Choices Flip Chart • Math and Science Flip Chart • Shape Set • Hand Lens • Sequence Cards: "Metamorphosis" • Home Connections Resource Guide	• Teacher's Treasure Book • Photo Library CD-ROM • Dog Puppets • Building Blocks Math Activities • Making Good Choices Flip Chart • Math and Science Flip Chart • Alphabet/Letter Tiles • Concept Big Book 3: *Amazing Animals* • ABC Big Book • Shape Set • Pattern Blocks	• Teacher's Treasure Book • Flannel Board Patterns for "My Very Own Pet" • Oral Language Development Card 42 • Rhymes and Chants Flip Chart • Two-Color Counters • Making Good Choices Flip Chart • ABC Big Book • Photo Library CD-ROM • Dog Puppets	• Teacher's Treasure Book • Flannel Board Patterns for "My Very Own Pet" • Photo Library CD-ROM • Dog Puppets • ABC Big Book • ABC Picture Cards • Shape Sets • Pattern Blocks	• Teacher's Treasure Book • Rhymes and Chants Flip Chart • Photo Library CD-ROM • Making Good Choices Flip Chart • Concept Big Book 3: *Amazing Animals* • ABC Picture Cards • Shape Sets • Alphabet/Letter Tiles • Pattern Blocks

Other Materials

• animal books • paper • crayons • scissors • markers • masking or colored tape • caterpillar and leaves • caterpillar books and pictures • index cards	• cup • construction paper • animal outlines • yarn • glue • crayons • paint • puppet (Mr. Mixup) • construction paper shapes	• animal pictures • construction paper • crayons • paper plates • glue, yarn, buttons • books about homes • blocks • toy furniture	• folk and fairy tale books • sock puppets (cat and dog) • blocks • paper • crayons	• magazines • glue • paper • crayons • glitter • finger paint, painting clothes • blocks • sticks • animal toys

Home Connection

Remind children to tell families what they have learned about caterpillars. Send home the following materials: Weekly Parent Letter, Home Connections Resource Guide, pp. 45–46. ABC Take-Home Book for *Cc*, (English) p. 9 or (Spanish) p. 37 .	Remind children to tell families about the pictures they made using shapes. Send home ABC Take-Home Book for *Uu* , (English) p. 27 or (Spanish) p. 58.	Remind children to tell families about different kinds of homes. Send home ABC Take-Home Book for *Xx*, (English) p. 30 or (Spanish) p. 61.	Remind children to tell families about what today's story said about why dogs chase cats. Send home ABC Take-Home Book for *Vv*, (English) p. 28 or (Spanish) p. 59.	Remind children to tell families what they learned this week about animals and describe their animal painting.

Assessment

As you observe children throughout the week, you may fill out an Anecdotal Observational Record Form to document an individual's progress toward a goal or signs indicating the need for developmental or medical evaluation. You may also choose to select work for each child's portfolio. The Anecdotal Observational Record Form and Weekly Assessment rubrics are available in the assessment section of DLMExpressOnline.com.

More Literature Suggestions

- **Please, Puppy, Please** by Spike Lee
- **Hidden Hippo** by Joan Gannij and Clare Beaton
- **Senses on the Farm** by Shelley Rotner
- **Ocean Babies** by Deborah Lee Rose
- **Bear in a Square** by Stella Blackstone

- **Insectos que trabajan en equipo** por Molly Aloian
- **Pinta ratones** por Ellen Stoll Walsh
- **Un pulpo en el mar** por Connie Roop y Peter Roop
- **El elefante** por José García Sánchez
- **El canto de las ballenas** por Dyan Sheldon

	DAY 1	DAY 2
Let's Start the Day **Language Time** `large group`	**Opening Routines** p. 26 **Morning Read Aloud** p. 26 **Oral Language and Vocabulary** p. 26 Animal Names and Body Parts **Phonological Awareness** p. 26 Recognize Rhyming Words	**Opening Routines** p. 32 **Morning Read Aloud** p. 32 **Oral Language and Vocabulary** p. 32 Animals All Around Us **Phonological Awareness** p. 32 Recognize Rhyming Words
Center Time `small group`	**Focus On:** **Library and Listening Center** p. 27 **Pretend and Learn Center** p. 27	**Focus On:** **ABC Center** p. 33 **Creativity Center** p. 33
Circle Time **Literacy Time** `large group`	**Read Aloud** *Amazing Animals/* *Animales asombrosos* p. 28 **Learn About Letters and Sounds:** *Cc* p. 28	**Read Aloud** *Amazing Animals/* *Animales asombrosos* p. 34 **Learn About Letters and Sounds:** *Uu* p. 34
Math Time `large group`	**Shape Step** p. 29	**Mr. Mixup (Shapes)** p. 35
Social and Emotional Development `large group`	**Being Helpful** p. 29	**Being Helpful** p. 35
Content Connection `large group`	**Science:** **Oral Language and Academic Vocabulary** p. 30 Talking About Caterpillars **Observe and Investigate** p. 30 Looking at Caterpillars	**Math:** **Talk About Shapes** p. 36 **Create Shape Pictures** p. 36
Center Time `small group`	**Focus On:** **Math and Science Center** p. 31 **Purposeful Play** p. 31	**Focus On:** **Math and Science Center** p. 37 **Purposeful Play** p. 37
Let's Say Good-Bye `large group`	**Read Aloud** p. 31 **Writing** p. 31 **Home Connection** p. 31	**Read Aloud** p. 37 **Writing** p. 37 **Home Connection** p. 37

DAY 3	**DAY 4**	**DAY 5**
Opening Routines p. 38 **Morning Read Aloud** p. 38 **Oral Language and Vocabulary** p. 38 Animal Names and Body Parts **Phonological Awareness** p. 38 Recognize Rhyming Words 	**Opening Routines** p. 44 **Morning Read Aloud** p. 44 **Oral Language and Vocabulary** p. 44 Animal Friends **Phonological Awareness** p. 44 Recognize Rhyming Words	**Opening Routines** p. 50 **Morning Read Aloud** p. 50 **Oral Language and Vocabulary** p. 50 Animal Characteristics **Phonological Awareness** p. 50 Recognize Rhyming Words 
Focus On: **Writer's Center** p. 39 **Creativity Center** p. 39	**Focus On:** **Library and Listening Center** p. 45 **Pretend and Learn Center** p. 45	**Focus On:** **Writer's Center** p. 51 **ABC Center** p. 51
Read Aloud "My Very Own Pet"/ "Mi propia mascota" p. 40 **Learn About Letters and Sounds:** *Xx* p. 40 	**Read Aloud** "Why Dogs Chase Cats"/ "Por qué los perros persiguen a los gatos" p. 46 **Learn About Letters and Sounds:** *Vv* p. 46  	**Read Aloud** *Amazing Animals/Animales asombrosos* p. 52 **Learn About Letters and Sounds: Review Letters** *Cc, Uu, Xx, Vv* p. 52 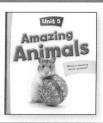
How Many Now? p. 41	Discuss Shape Pictures p. 47	Guess My Rule p. 53
Being Helpful p. 41 	Being Helpful p. 47 	Being Helpful p. 53 
Social Studies: **Oral Language and Academic Vocabulary** p. 42 Talking About People's Needs **Understand and Participate** p. 42 Looking at Home Books	**Math:** **Talk About Shapes** p. 48 **Guess My Rule** p. 48	**Art:** **Oral Language and Academic Vocabulary** p. 54 Animals in their Environment **Explore and Express** p. 54 Finger Paint Animals
Focus On: **Construction Center** p. 434 **Purposeful Play** p. 43	**Focus On:** **Math and Science Center** p.49 **Purposeful Play** p. 49	**Focus On:** **Construction Center** p. 55 **Purposeful Play** p. 55
Read Aloud p. 43 **Writing** p. 43 **Home Connection** p. 43	**Read Aloud** p. 49 **Writing** p. 49 **Home Connection** p. 49	**Read Aloud** p. 55 **Writing** p. 55 **Home Connection** p. 55

Week 1

I Know Animals

Learning Centers

Math and Science Center

Observing Caterpillars
Children work in pairs and, using hand lenses and pictures, observe and describe the characteristics of caterpillars. See p. 31.

Making Pets
Children create pets using construction-paper shapes in different sizes and colors and connect them with glue and yarn. See p. 37.

Copying Patterns
Children use a variety of shapes to create their own patterns and copy them onto paper. See p. 49.

Matching Shapes
Children match six different pairs of shapes that are randomly displayed (square, rectangle, triangle, rhombus, hexagon, and trapezoid).

ABC Center

Where's My Letter?
Children identify the letters *Cc* from among other letters they have learned and position the letters above, under, inside, and beside a cup as they say the sound /k/. See p. 33.

Matching Letters
Children match upper case and lower case forms of *Cc, Uu, Xx,* and *Vv* and talk about how they are alike and different. Children use glue to write each letter and then add glitter. See p. 51.

Under the Umbrella
Children draw a colorful umbrella on construction paper. Under the umbrella, they write upper case and lower case *Uu* several times.

Creativity Center

Animal Outlines
Children trace animal outlines with glue, place yarn on top of the glue, and then draw or paint animal details inside the outlines. See p. 33.

Animal Masks
Children make animal masks from paper plates and include details that show the animals' characteristics. See p. 39.

Animal Features
Children draw a picture of their favorite pet and describe three characteristics of that pet.

Awake or Asleep
Children draw or cut out pictures of animals that show them in active or restful states.

Library and Listening Center

Browsing Animal Books
Children choose a favorite animal from a book, name and describe it, and then draw a picture of it. See p. 27.

Browsing Make-Believe Stories
Children browse through folk tale and fairy tale books to distinguish things that are real from things that are make-believe. See p. 45.

Picture Walks
Children select a book about animals, a folk tale, or a fairy tale and use the pictures to tell a story to a partner.

Construction Center

Build a Shelter
Children work in pairs and use blocks to build a home they have seen in pictures or in real life. See p. 43.

Build an Animal Home
Children work in pairs, using blocks and art materials, to build an animal home they have seen, such as a doghouse or bird's nest. See p. 55.

Build an Animal
Children use blocks and art materials to build an animal that belongs in their animal home.

Writer's Center

Rhyme Time
Children match animal and object pictures whose names rhyme, and then choose a rhyming pair to draw. See p. 39.

Animal Books
Children create their own books about favorite animals, using animal pictures from magazines. See p.51.

How Pets Play
Children draw pictures that show how pets have fun, and then write or dictate words that describe what they are doing.

Pretend and Learn Center

Tracking a Friend
Children work in pairs to create their own animal tracks by tracing their footprints. See p. 27.

Retell and Act Out Stories
Children use flannel patterns or puppets to retell the stories they heard this week. See p. 45.

I'm an Iguana
Children pretend to be an iguana and describe how they move or find food.

Animal Sounds
Children make animal sounds and have their partners guess what animal they are imitating.

Let's Start the Day

Focus Question
What are animals like?
¿Cómo son los animales?

> **Opening Routines and Transition Tips**
For **Opening Routines** and **Transition Tips** turn to pages 178–181 and visit
DLMExpressOnline.com for more ideas.

 Read **"Party at Daisy's"/**"Fiesta en casa de Daisy" from the
Teacher's Treasure Book, page 180, for your morning Read Aloud.

 Learning Goals

Language and Communication
• Child understands or knows the meaning of many thousands of words, many more than he or she uses.

Emergent Literacy: Reading
• Child generates words that rhyme.

Vocabulary

body	cuerpo	claws	garras
climb	trepar	green	verde
iguana	iguana	limb	miembro

Differentiated Instruction

 Extra Support
Phonological Awareness
If...children have difficulty recognizing words that rhyme, **then...**segment the words to highlight the rhyming part. Say: *Listen carefully. /n/...est, nest. /r/...est, rest. Nest and rest rhyme because they both end in /est/.* Escuchen atentamente. /n/...est, nest. /r/...est, rest. Las palabras nest y rest riman porque las dos terminan en /est/.

⭐ **Enrichment**
Phonological Awareness
Challenge children to take turns choosing a word from the *Rhymes and Chants Flip Chart* and saying a word that rhymes with it.

Accommodations for 3's
Phonological Awareness
If...children have difficulty recognizing words that rhyme, **then...**show two photos or pictures of items that rhyme (e.g., bear/chair) and ask: *Do [bear] and [chair] rhyme? ¿Riman [bear] y [chair]?*

Language Time

large group 15 minutes

Social and Emotional Development Remind children to listen to each other's contributions rather than paying attention only when it's their turn.

Oral Language and Vocabulary

✓ **Can children use descriptive words to tell about an animal?**

Animal Names and Body Parts Talk about local animals, such as birds, farm animals, or pets. Ask: *What is one animal you see every day? What does that animal look like? ¿Qué animal ven todos los días? ¿Cómo es ese animal?*

● Display *Oral Language Development Card 41.* Name the animal (iguana) and its body parts, including tail and claws. Then follow the suggestions on the back of the card.

Oral Language Development Card 41

Phonological Awareness

✓ **Can children identify words that rhyme?**

Recognize Rhyming Words Display *Rhymes and Chants Flip Chart* page 21. Tell children that rhyming words end with the same sounds. For example, *sat* and *mat* both end in /at/. Read "Baby Birds." Guide children to find the rhyming words *nest/rest* and *munch/lunch.*

ELL Use the *Rhymes and Chants Flip Chart* to revisit the words *bird* and *nest.* Point to a bird in the picture. Say: *I see a bird.* Have children repeat as you touch the bird. Then point to the bird and ask: *What do you see?* Have children chorally respond. Continue with the word *nest.*

Baby Birds

See the baby birds curled up
Safe inside their nest?
It is such a comfy, cozy,
Homey place to rest!

Baby birds get hungry
And they want to munch!
FLAP! SQUAWK! Here's the mama!
Bringing worms for lunch!

Rhymes and Chants Flip Chart, page 21

Center Time

Center Rotation Center Time includes teacher-guided activities and independent activities. Refer to the **Learning Centers** on pages 24–25 for activities in additional centers.

 small group 60–90 minutes

Refer to the **Learning Centers** on pages 24–25

Learning Goals

Social and Emotional Development
• Child shows empathy and caring for others.

Language and Communication
• Child uses newly learned vocabulary daily in multiple contexts.

Library and Listening Center | Center Tip

✓ Track the use of animal names as children share favorite animal drawings.

Materials animal books, paper, crayons

Browsing Animal Books Have children browse through animal books and choose a favorite animal. Help them name and describe the animal.

• Have children draw their favorite animal and share their drawings.

• Ask: *What do you like about this animal?* ¿Qué les gusta de este animal?

Center Tip

If...children have difficulty recalling an animal name or a vocabulary word, **then...**give them a clue by offering a word that rhymes with it.

Differentiated Instruction

Extra Support
Library and Listening Center
If...children have difficulty drawing or coloring favorite animal pictures, **then...**have them review the animal's picture in the book and say specific words to describe its characteristics.

Enrichment
Library and Listening Center
Challenge children to take turns choosing a word and saying a word that rhymes with it.

Special Needs
Delayed Motor Development
Place animal books on the child's desk or wheelchair tray. As you talk about favorite animals, the child can point to the picture. If he or she is able, ask the child to try to tell you the sound the animal makes.

Pretend and Learn Center | Center Tip

✓ Look for examples of children helping one another, and point them out as examples of being helpful and caring.

Materials colored paper, scissors, markers

Tracking a Friend Explain that animal footprints are called tracks. Give each child sheets of colored paper. Have children work in pairs.

• Model making tracks by tracing around your shoes and then cutting out a print. Help children trace and cut out their own tracks.

• Have one child move like an animal and place tracks around the room. Once the first child is done, the partner should follow and collect the tracks.

Center Tip

If...children have difficulty cutting with scissors, **then...**hold the paper for them or place your hand near theirs as you cut together.

Focus Question
What are animals like?
¿Cómo son los animales?

Learning Goals

Emergent Literacy: Reading
• Child names most upper- and lowercase letters of the alphabet.
• Child identifies the letter that stands for a given sound.
• Child asks and answers questions about books read aloud (such as, "Who?" "What?" "Where?").

Science
• Child observes, understands, and discusses the relationship of plants and animals to their environments.

Vocabulary

alike	parecidos	amazing	asombrosos
different	diferentes	home	granja
pet	mascotas	wild	salvajes

Differentiated Instruction

Extra Support
Learn About Letters and Sounds
If...children have difficulty writing the letter *Cc*,
then...have them trace the letter using sand and shaving cream or make the letter out of clay to practice tracing.

Enrichment
Learn About Letters and Sounds
Challenge children to find words that begin with *Cc* in classroom books, then make the words using the Alphabet/Letter Tiles. Read the words children find and make.

Literacy Time

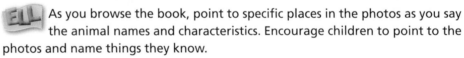

large group / 15 minutes

📖 Read Aloud

✓ **Can children describe and use pictures to construct meaning?**

Build Background Tell children that you will be reading a book about amazing animals—both wild animals and pets.

 Ask: *Which animals make good pets?* *¿Qué animales pueden ser buenas mascotas?*

Listen for Enjoyment Display *Concept Big Book 3: Amazing Animals* and read the title. Conduct a picture walk.

 Browse through the pages. Name and describe the physical characteristics of each animal.

● Ask: *What does this animal look like? Where does this animal live?* *¿Cómo es este animal? ¿Dónde vive este animal?*

Respond to the Story Have children name the animals you pointed out. Ask: *What does the giraffe look like? Which animals are pets? Where do pets live?* *¿Cómo es la jirafa? ¿Qué animales son mascotas? ¿Dónde viven las mascotas?*

TIP Be sure children can use picture details to describe the giraffe and goldfish. Point to a part of the giraffe, such as the neck. Ask: *Does a goldfish have a long neck, too?* *¿El pez también tiene un cuello largo?*

ELL As you browse the book, point to specific places in the photos as you say the animal names and characteristics. Encourage children to point to the photos and name things they know.

Learn About Letters and Sounds

✓ **Can children identify the letter Cc?**

Learn About the Letter *Cc* Page through the *ABC Big Book*, stopping when you get to the letter *Cc*. Point to the *cake* photo. Tell children that the word *cake* begins with the /k/ sound and with the letter *Cc*. Have them chant "/k/ /k/ /k/, cut the cake" as they pretend to cut a cake.

 Model how to write the upper case letter *C* using the ABC Picture Card. Have children trace the letter *C* with their fingers.

● While one child is tracing, the other children can be writing the letter in the air or on the floor using their finger. Have them say /k/ each time they write the letter.

● Repeat for the lower case *c*. Point out that upper case and lower case *Cc* are both curves, but uppercase *C* is larger.

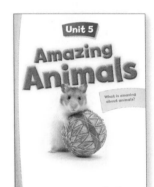

Amazing Animals
Animales
asombrosos

ABC Big Book

Math Time

Observe and Investigate

 Can children identify common shapes?

Shape Step Use masking or colored tape to make large shapes on the floor. Show children rhombuses from the Shape Set and tell them they will step only on rhombuses.

- Have a group of four or five children step on the rhombuses. Ask the rest of the class to watch carefully to make sure each group steps on all the rhombuses. Ask: *Why is that shape a rhombus? ¿Por qué esa figura es un rombo?* Repeat with other groups of children.

- Repeat with new shapes, such as hexagons, engaging different groups of children each time.

ELL Name a shape and have children repeat using the sentence frame *This shape is a [rhombus].* Then point to a shape and ask: *Is this a [rhombus]?*

⚞ Social and Emotional Development

Making Good Choices

 Do children show a desire to be helpful and caring?

Being Helpful Discuss how children have helped classmates. Display the *Making Good Choices Flip Chart* , page 21. Point to the boy and the blocks.

- Ask: *Do you think the boy would like to have a friend help him build a tower? If he asked you, how might you help him? ¿Creen que al niño le gustaría tener un amigo que lo ayudara a construir una torre? Si les pidiera ayuda a ustedes, ¿cómo lo ayudarían?*

- Then discuss whether the boy might want help putting the blocks away and how the other children could help. Ask: *What other jobs might the boy need help with? How would you feel if you were the boy and nobody offered to help you? ¿Para qué otros trabajos el niño podría necesitar ayuda? ¿Cómo se sentirían si fueran el niño y nadie les ofreciera ayuda?*

- Play the song "Everybody Needs Help Sometimes"/"Todos necesitan ayuda alguna vez" from the Making Good Choices Audio CD. Ask children to describe some of the ways they could help someone.

Making Good Choices Flip Chart, page 21

Building Blocks

Online Math Activity

Introduce Mystery Pictures 4: Name New Shapes, in which children have to identify each shape to create the mystery pictures. Each child should complete Mystery Pictures 4 during the week.

✔ Learning Goals

Social and Emotional Development
- Child shows empathy and care for others.

Mathematics
- Child recognizes, names, describes, matches, compares, and sorts common two-dimensional shapes (such as circle, square, rectangle, triangle, rhombus).

Vocabulary

help	ayuda
rhombus	rombo

hexagon   hexágono

Differentiated Instruction

👆 Extra Support

Observe and Investigate

If...children struggle identifying shapes, **then...**review the target shape's attributes while children feel and/or trace the shape with their fingers. You might also step on a target shape, and then ask children whether it is the correct shape.

⭐ Enrichment

Observe and Investigate

Have children find examples of target shapes in unusual places and/or teach them even less familiar shapes.

Accommodations for 3's

Observe and Investigate

If...children struggle identifying different shapes, **then...**focus on identifying only one shape, such as the rhombus. Remind children that a rhombus has four sides that are the same length.

Focus Question
What are animals like?
¿Cómo son los animales?

Science Time

large group 20 minutes

Personal Safety Skills Model how to properly hold the hand lens during the science activity and describe the safety and care of the caterpillar.

Oral Language and Academic Vocabulary

 Can children use words to describe animals and where they live?

Talking About Caterpillars Point to the caterpillar on the *Math and Science Flip Chart*. Say: *This animal is an insect. It is called a caterpillar. Say caterpillar. Este animal es un insecto. Se llama oruga. Digan oruga.*

- Point out that *caterpillar* begins with the /k/ sound and starts with *Cc*. Point to the word on the chart.

- Explain that a caterpillar is small and crawls on tree branches like an iguana. Say: *Small insects such as caterpillars live outside, or in the wild, just like bigger animals do. Los insectos pequeños como las orugas viven afuera, en la naturaleza, como muchos otros animales.* Discuss other insects that live outside.

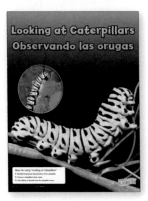

Math and Science Flip Chart, page 37

Observe and Investigate

 Can children use words to describe the characteristics of animals?

Looking at Caterpillars Place caterpillars and leaves in a clear container. Discuss how you can learn a lot about an animal by observing it, or watching it closely. Encourage children to describe the caterpillars before introducing the hand lens. Write down their observations on a class chart.

- Hold up a hand lens. Explain that this tool is called a *hand lens* and you will use it to watch the caterpillars. Model how to use the lens. Make comments as you observe, such as: *I see the caterpillar has stripes. Veo que la oruga tiene rayas.*

- Let children take turns using the lens. Ask: *Does the caterpillar look larger or smaller through the lens? ¿La oruga se ve más grande o más pequeña a través de la lupa?* Explain that the lens will magnify the caterpillar, or make it look larger. Have children describe what they see, and add their observations to the chart.

ELL Begin by asking children yes/no questions about caterpillars. *Is a caterpillar a small animal in the wild? Is a caterpillar larger than a giraffe?* To help children make comparisons, practice talking about "larger" and "smaller." Gather classroom objects and model: *The easel is larger than the book. Is the book smaller or larger than the blocks?* Hold up two objects and prompt a child to use a comparison.

For additional suggestions on how to meet the needs of children at the Beginning, Intermediate, Advanced, and Advanced-High levels of English proficiency, see pages 184–187.

Learning Goals

Language and Communication
- Child names and describes actual or pictured people, places, things, actions, attributes, and events.

Science
- Child identifies organisms and describes their characteristics.
- Child observes, understands, and discusses the relationship of plants and animals to their environments.
- Child follows basic health and safety rules.

Vocabulary

caterpillar   oruga   lens   lupa

magnify   aumentar   observe   observar

Differentiated Instruction

Extra Support

Observe and Investigate

If...children have difficulty focusing on the caterpillar's physical characteristics, **then...** suggest specific things for them to look at: *Look at the green caterpillar's legs. Look at the fuzzy caterpillar on the stem. Observen las patas de la oruga. Miren a la oruga en el tallo.*

Enrichment

Oral Language and Academic Vocabulary
Challenge children to add robust vocabulary to their spoken language repertoire: **insect, pattern, crawl.**

Center Time

▶ **Center Rotation** Center Time includes teacher-guided activities and independent activities. Refer to the **Learning Centers** on pages 24–25 for activities in additional centers.

 small group · 30 minutes

Learning Goals

Language and Communication
• Child names and describes actual or pictured people, places, things, actions, attributes, and events.

Science
• Child identifies organisms and describes their characteristics.

Math and Science Center

☑ **Encourage children to describe the characteristics that match their partner's caterpillar ticket.**

Materials caterpillar books, index cards, caterpillar images, hand lenses

Observing Caterpillars Prepare sets of "tickets" (cards with the same image). Tell children they will be observing pictures of caterpillars. Give each child a Look and Observe Ticket. Say: *Hold up your ticket and find your partners by matching your caterpillars. Sostengan su boleto y encuentren a los que tengan la misma oruga para saber quiénes son sus compañeros.*

• Give the first group hand lenses. Watch them observe.

• Have other children share caterpillar story books and the "Metamorphosis" set of Sequence Cards.

Center Tip

If... children need help focusing on one feature of their caterpillar ticket, **then...** say for example, *Look for a black stripe in the middle of the body.*

Writing

Recap the day. Have children name animals that they observed or learned about. Ask: *What did you learn about caterpillars? ¿Qué aprendieron sobre las orugas?* Record their answers. Read them back as you track the print, and emphasize the correspondence between speech and print.

Purposeful Play

☑ **Observe children appropriately handling classroom materials.**

Children choose an open center for free playtime. Encourage cooperation skills by suggesting they work together to create a caterpillar show or story.

Let's Say Good-Bye

 small group · 15 minutes

 Read Aloud Revisit the story "Party at Daisy's"/"Fiesta en casa de Daisy" for your afternoon Read Aloud. Ask children to listen for words with the /k/ sound.

 Home Connection Refer to the Home Connections activities listed in the Resources and Materials chart on page 21. Remind children to tell families what they have learned about caterpillars. Sing the "Good-Bye Song"/"Hora de ir a casa" as children prepare to leave.

Focus Question
What are animals like?
¿Cómo son los animales?

Language and Communication
• Child names and describes actual or pictured people, places, things, actions, attributes, and events.

Emergent Literacy: Reading
• Child generates words that rhyme.

Vocabulary

body	cuerpo	fur	pelaje
neighbor	vecino	pets	mascotas
spots	manchas		

Differentiated Instruction

Extra Support
Oral Language and Vocabulary
If...children have difficulty describing an animal, **then...**offer questions about specific animal details, such as: *Is the animal tall or short? Does the animal have two legs or four legs? ¿El animal es alto o bajito? ¿Tiene cuatro patas o tiene dos patas?*

⭐ Enrichment
Oral Language and Vocabulary
Expand children's vocabularies during the discussion by adding words such as *mammal, calf,* or *antenna.* Briefly define each word and reinforce during Center Time play.

Let's Start the Day

 Opening Routines and Transition Tips
For **Opening Routines** and **Transition Tips** turn to pages 178–181 and visit **DLMExpressOnline.com** for more ideas.

📖 Read **"Spiders"/"Araña"** from the *Teacher's Treasure Book,* page 88, for your morning Read Aloud.

Language Time

 large group 15 minutes

👫 **Social and Emotional Development** Remind children to listen carefully to each other's contributions and wait their turn before speaking.

Oral Language and Vocabulary
✓ **Can children identify animals kept as pets?**

Animals All Around Us Talk about animals people commonly keep as pets. Ask: *What kinds of pets do you or your neighbors have? ¿Qué tipos de mascotas tienen ustedes o sus vecinos?*

● Have children describe in detail what the pets look like. If two children name the same kind of pet, such as a dog, ask questions to help them compare the animals. For example: *What color is your dog? Does it have spots? Does your dog have spots, too? ¿De qué color son sus perros? ¿Tienen manchas? ¿Tu perro tiene manchas también?*

ELL Display animal photos from the *Photo Library CD-ROM.* Choose animals that are common in your area, such as pets. Ask children what animals they recognize. Then teach the names of the unfamiliar ones. Describe each animal's characteristics, such as color and body parts. Then ask simple questions about each one, such as: *Is this animal brown or green?*

For additional suggestions on how to meet the needs of children at the Beginning, Intermediate, Advanced, and Advanced-High levels of English proficiency, see pages 184–187.

Phonological Awareness
✓ **Can children identify words that rhyme?**

Recognize Rhyming Words Display the Dog Puppets. Tell children that each puppet will say a word. If the words rhyme, the children should stand up and cheer. Remind children that words rhyme when they have the same ending sounds, like *cat* and *sat.* Have the puppets say these and other word pairs: *nest/rest, lunch/happy, dog/log, pig/big, fish/finger, house/mouse.*

Center Time

▶ **Center Rotation** Center Time includes teacher-guided activities and independent activities. Refer to the **Learning Centers** on pages 24–25 for activities in additional centers.

small group   60–90 minutes

ABC Center

Center Tip

 Keep track of the letter-sounds children are beginning to master.

Materials Alphabet/Letter Tiles, cup

Where's My Letter? Place the letter Cc on the table beside a cup. Remind children that the letter Cc stands for /k/ as in /k/ /k/ cup.

- Place the letter Cc in a line with a few other letters previously taught. Say: *Pick up the letter Cc.* *Tomen la letra Cc.*

- Then provide simple directions, such as: *Place the letter Cc above the cup. Under the cup. Inside the cup. Beside the cup.* *Coloquen la letra Hh encima de la copa. Luego, debajo de la copa. Y luego, al lado de la copa.* After each direction is completed, ask: *What sound do we say for Cc? ¿Con qué letra empieza "copa"?*

If...children have difficulty remembering the sound for *Cc,* **then...**give them a clue by telling them to listen for the first sound in /k/ /k/ cup.

Creativity Center

Center Tip

 Listen for words children use to describe their animal's characteristics.

Materials construction paper, animal outlines, yarn, glue, art supplies (crayons, paint)

Animal Outlines Tell children that they will add special features to an animal.

- Distribute the animal outlines, such as dog, cat, fish, or giraffe. Have children trace the outline with glue, then place yarn on top of the glue. As they do, ask: *What part of the animal is this? ¿Qué parte del animal es ésta?*

- Then have children draw, color, or paint the animal details inside the outline. Say: *Tell me about your animal.* *Cuéntenme algo sobre su animal.*

If...children have difficulty gluing the yarn, **then...**give them small pieces of yarn to glue on one at a time. Hold the paper for them as they place the yarn on the glue.

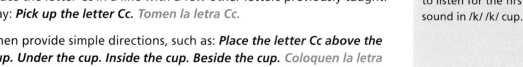

Learning Goals

Emergent Literacy: Reading
- Child names most upper- and lowercase letters of the alphabet.
- Child produces the most common sound for a given letter.

Mathematics
- Child understands and uses words that describe position/location in space (such as under, over, beside, between, on, in, near, far away).

Science
- Child identifies organisms and describes their characteristics.

Physical Development
- Child develops small-muscle strength and control.

Differentiated Instruction

✋ **Extra Support**

ABC Center

If...children have difficulty remembering the sound of a letter, **then...**have them trace or write the letter in sand or with shaving cream as they say the letter name and sound.

⭐ **Enrichment**

ABC Center

Challenge children to name words that begin with Cc.

Accommodations for 3's

ABC Center

If...children have difficulty finding the letter Cc among other letters, **then...**point to each letter, say its name and sound, and then ask: *Which letter is Cc? Listen again as I point to each letter and say its name and sound. ¿Cuál de estas letras es la Cc? Escuchen de nuevo cuando señalo cada letra y digan cómo se llama y qué sonido tiene.*

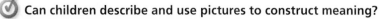

Focus Question
What are animals like?
¿Cómo son los animales?

Literacy Time

large group · 15 minutes

Read Aloud

☑ **Can children describe and use pictures to construct meaning?**

Build Background Tell children that you will read about amazing animals—both wild animals and pets.

- Ask: *Which animals make good pets? ¿Qué animales pueden ser buenas mascotas?*

Listen for Understanding Display *Concept Big Book 3: Amazing Animals* and read the title.

- Read pages 6–9. Point to the labels in the photographs and read them after reading the main text.

- Ask: *What do you learn about this animal from the photo? ¿Qué aprendieron sobre este animal a partir de la foto?*

Respond to the Story Have children name the animals read about. Ask: *How are the giraffe and the goldfish different? What did you learn from the photos about taking care of a pet? Can you find a word on the page? Touch it. ¿En qué se diferencian la jirafa y el pez de colores? ¿Qué aprendieron de las fotos acerca del cuidado de una mascota? ¿Pueden encontrar una palabra en la página? Tóquenla.*

TIP Be sure children can use picture details to describe each animal. Point to specific animal characteristics for children to talk about.

ELL As you read the book, point to specifics in the photos as you say the animal names and characteristics. Ask follow-up yes/no questions, such as: *Is the giraffe tall? Is a dog a good pet? Is the cat black?*

Learn About Letters and Sounds

☑ **Can children identify the letter *Uu*?**

Learn About the Letter *Uu* Sing the "ABC Song" with children as you page through the *ABC Big Book*, stopping when you get to the letter *Uu*. Point to the *umbrella* photo. Tell children that the word *umbrella* begins with the /u/ sound and the letter *Uu*. Have them chant "/u/ /u/ /u/ up goes the umbrella" as they pretend to open an umbrella.

- Model how to write the uppercase letter *U* using the ABC Picture Card. Have children trace the letter *U* with their fingers.

- While one child is tracing, the other children can be writing the letter in the air or on the floor using their finger. Have them say /u/ each time they write the letter.

- Repeat for the lowercase *u*. Point out the similarities in the uppercase and lowercase *Uu*: both have curves, but lowercase *u* also has a vertical line.

Amazing Animals
Animales asombrosos

ABC Big Book

Learning Goals

Emergent Literacy: Reading
- Child names most upper- and lowercase letters of the alphabet.
- Child produces the most common sound for a given letter.
- Child asks and answers questions about books read aloud (such as, "Who?" "What?" "Where?").

Science
- Child identifies organisms and describes their characteristics.

Vocabulary

care	cuidar	home	hogar
long	largo	pets	mascotas
tall	alto	wild	salvajes

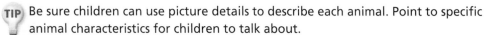

Differentiated Instruction

 Extra Support
Learn About Letters and Sounds
If...children have difficulty writing the letter Uu, **then...**help them form the letter using clay or yarn and then trace it with their fingers.

★ **Enrichment**
Learn About Letters and Sounds
Teach children how to read and write the word *up*. Sound out the two letter-sounds in the word *up*. Write the word for children to trace, then copy.

♥ **Special Needs**
Cognitive Challenges
Instead of asking the child to try to name all the animals mentioned in the book, open a page of the book and try to get him or her to tell you the name of one or two of the animals, as you point to them.

Building Blocks

Online Math Activity

Introduce Memory Geometry 4: Shapes of Things, in which children match shapes to common objects. Each child should complete Memory Geometry 4 during the week.

Math Time

Observe and Investigate

✓ **Can children identify common shapes?**

Mr. Mixup (Shapes) Ask children: *Do you remember Mr. Mixup? ¿Recuerdan al Sr. Confundido?* Explain that they are going to help Mr. Mixup name shapes. Remind them to stop Mr. Mixup as soon as he makes a mistake to correct him. Use a silly voice and have fun!

● Using Shape Set shapes, have Mr. Mixup start by confusing the names of a square and a rhombus. After children have identified the correct names, ask: *How are the angles different? ¿En qué se diferencian los ángulos?* (Squares must have all right angles; rhombuses may have different angles.) Review that all rhombuses and squares (which are actually a kind of rhombus) have four straight sides of equal length.

● Repeat with a trapezoid, a hexagon, and any other shapes you would like children to practice.

⅄⅄⅄ Social and Emotional Development

Making Good Choices

✓ **Do children show a desire to be helpful and caring?**

Being Helpful Revisit the *Making Good Choices Flip Chart* page 21, "How Can I Help Someone?"

● Display a Dog Puppet. Say: *Tell the puppet about what this boy is doing and how other children can help him. Digan al títere lo que este niño está haciendo y cómo sus amigos pueden ayudarlo.*

● Have a volunteers tell the puppet about the children being helpful and caring. Remind children to be helpful and caring when they work with blocks during Center Time.

ELL Provide sentence frames to help during the conversation with the dog puppet. Use these and others: *The boy is ____. His friends will ____.* Model the use of each frame. Have children repeat, then apply using their own words. Some children may feel more comfortable just repeating the completed frame you provided.

Making Good Choices Flip Chart, page 21

Focus Question

What are animals like?
¿Cómo son los animales?

Learning Goals

Language and Communication
• Child exhibits an understanding of instructional terms used in the classroom.

Mathematics
• Child recognizes, names, describes, matches, compares, and sorts common two-dimensional shapes (such as circle, square, rectangle, triangle, rhombus).

Vocabulary

design	diseño	hexagon	hexágono
pattern	patrón	rhombus	rombo
shape	figura	trapezoid	trapecio

Differentiated Instruction

 Extra Support

Math Time
If...children have difficulty making an animal shape, **then...**create one as a model for them to replicate.

⭐ **Enrichment**

Math Time
Challenge children to teach classmates how to make complicated patterns and designs by showing their design and helping a classmate replicate it.

Math Time

large group · 20 minutes

Language and Communication Skills Use instructional terms while discussing each design with children and check their understanding. Model as needed.

✓ **Can children name shapes?**

Talk About Shapes Display Shape Sets and Pattern Blocks. Ask children to name and discuss shapes, especially the trapezoids, rhombuses, and hexagons.

● Show several different rhombuses, including squares, and discuss their similarities and differences. Repeat for the other shapes.

● Ask: *What is the shape? How many sides does it have? How are the angles different in these two shapes? ¿Qué es esta figura? ¿Cuántos lados tiene? ¿En qué se diferencian los ángulos de estas dos figuras?*

● To simplify, have children feel a shape's sides and corners to help with their descriptions. For a challenge, have children tell how they know a shape is a trapezoid or a rhombus, for example, by describing their differences.

✓ **Can children use shapes to create pictures and designs?**

Create Shape Pictures Have children make designs and pictures with the Shape Sets and Pattern Blocks. Suggest they make animal shapes.

● Display *Math and Science Flip Chart* page 38, "Shape Pictures." Discuss the animals created and the shapes used to create them.

● Then distribute the design materials.

● Ask: *What animal are you making? What shapes are you using? Are you creating a pattern? ¿Qué animal están haciendo? ¿Qué figuras están usando? ¿Están creando un patrón?*

● In preparation for Day 4's small-group activity, sketch or photograph children's designs, especially those that show symmetry (mirror images) or patterns.

💡 TIP Tell children to keep their finished design until you have time to take a photo of it.

ELL Provide an animal photo for children to use as a model to create their animal design. Place shapes on top of the photo as you say, for example, *I can use a square for the dog's body.* Ask: *What shape can I use?* Continue providing language until the model is created.

Shape Pictures
Imágenes de formas

Math and Science Flip Chart, page 38

Center Time

▶ **Center Rotation** Center Time includes teacher-guided activities and independent activities. Refer to the **Learning Centers** on pages 24–25 for activities in additional centers.

 small group 30 minutes

Math and Science Center

	Center Tip
✓ **Observe children as they use shapes to create animal designs.** **Materials** construction-paper shapes, glue, yarn **Making Pets** Prepare construction-paper shapes of various sizes and colors, or have children cut shapes from paper on which you have traced shape outlines. Say: *Let's use these shapes to create our very own pet. Usemos estas figuras para crear nuestras propias mascotas.* ● Have children use the shapes to create their pet design. Ask: *What shapes will you use? What does your animal look like? ¿Qué figuras van a usar? ¿Qué forma tiene su animal?* ● Help children use glue and yarn to connect the shapes. ● Children can use the pet designs to role-play caring for a pet	**If...**children need help selecting a shape for their animal body parts, **then...** show a picture of the animal. Have children place shapes over the animal's body part to see which is most similar.

Purposeful Play

✓ **Observe children sharing classroom materials and working cooperatively.**

Children choose an open center for free playtime. Encourage cooperation skills by suggesting they work together to create a show or story with their pet creations or the Farm Animal Counters.

Let's Say Good-Bye

 small group 15 minutes

 Read Aloud Revisit the rhyme "Spiders"/"Araña" for your afternoon Read Aloud. Remind children to listen for words that describe what spiders look like and what they do.

 Home Connection Refer to the Home Connections activities listed in the Resources and Materials chart on page 21. Remind children to tell families about the pictures they made using shapes. Sing the "Good-Bye Song"/"Hora de ir a casa" as children prepare to leave.

✓ Learning Goals

Social and Emotional Development
• Child shows empathy and care for others.

Language and Communication
• Child names and describes actual or pictured people, places, things, actions, attributes, and events.

Mathematics
• Child recognizes, names, describes, matches, compares, and sorts common two-dimensional shapes (such as circle, square, rectangle, triangle, rhombus).

Writing

Recap the day. Have children name pets. Ask: *What did you learn about caring for pets? ¿Qué aprendieron sobre el cuidado de mascotas?* Ask them to draw a picture showing an example of pet care and help them label it.

Focus Question
What are animals like?
¿Cómo son los animales?

☑ Learning Goals

Language and Communication
• Child uses newly learned vocabulary daily in multiple contexts.

Emergent Literacy: Reading
• Child generates words that rhyme.

Vocabulary

cub	cachorro	paw	garra
roar	rugir	stripe	raya
tiger	tigre	tongue	lengua

Differentiated Instruction

🖐 Extra Support
Phonological Awareness
If...children have difficulty recognizing words that rhyme, **then...**segment the words to highlight the rhyming part. Say: *Listen carefully. /l/...unch, lunch. /m/...unch, munch. Lunch and munch rhyme because they both end in /unch/. Escuchen atentamente. /l/...unch, lunch. /m/... unch, munch. Las palabras* lunch y munch *riman porque las dos terminan con /unch/.*

⭐ Enrichment
Phonological Awareness
Challenge children to generate real and nonsense words that rhyme with *nest* and *lunch*.

💜 Special Needs
Speech/Language Delays
The phrase "E-I-E-I-O" can be used to help reinforce making the sounds correctly. Let the child practice saying each sound after you.

Let's Start the Day

▶ **Opening Routines and Transition Tips**
For **Opening Routines** and **Transition Tips** turn to pages 178–181 and visit DLMExpressOnline.com for more ideas.

📖 Read **"Old MacDonald"/**"El viejo MacDonald" from the *Teacher's Treasure Book,* page 248, for your morning Read Aloud.

Language Time

large group 15 minutes

👪 **Social and Emotional Development** Ask children who are ready to sit quietly and listen to raise one finger. Ask children who will treat others like they want to be treated to raise one elbow.

Oral Language and Vocabulary

☑ **Can children use descriptive words to tell about an animal?**

Animal Names and Body Parts Talk about pets, such as dogs or cats. Ask: *What does a dog look like? How many legs does it have? Can it have spots? Stripes? ¿Cómo es un perro? ¿Cuántas patas tiene? ¿Puede tener manchas? ¿Y rayas?*

● Display *Oral Language Development Card 42*. Name the animals (tigers) and their body parts. Point out the baby tiger, or cub. Then follow the suggestions on the back of the card.

Oral Language Development Card 42

Phonological Awareness

☑ **Can children identify words that rhyme?**

Recognize Rhyming Words Revisit *Rhymes and Chants Flip Chart*, p. 21. Remind children that rhyming words end with the same sounds. Have children join in as you recite "Baby Birds." Ask children to listen for the rhyming words. Say other words such as *best, test,* and *bunch.* Ask: *Does [best] rhyme with nest? Does [best] rhyme with lunch? Clap if the words rhyme. ¿Best rima con nest? ¿Best rima con lunch? Den una palmada si las palabras riman.*

🔤 Use the *Rhymes and Chants Flip Chart* to revisit the words *rest, hungry,* and *munch.* Use actions and gestures to teach the words, such as patting your belly to indicate hungry or pretend eating an apple to indicate munching.

Baby Birds
See the baby birds curled up
Safe inside their nest?
It is such a comfy, cozy,
Homey place to rest!

Baby birds get hungry
And they want to munch!
FLAP! SQUAWK! Here's the mama!
Bringing worms for lunch!

Rhymes and Chants Flip Chart, page 21

Center Time

> **Center Rotation** Center Time includes teacher-guided activities and independent activities. Refer to the **Learning Centers** on pages 24–25 for activities in additional centers.

small group 60–90 minutes

Refer to the **Learning Centers** on pages 24–25 for activities in additional centers.

Writer's Center

✓ Track children's ability to identify rhyming words.

Materials animal pictures, paper, crayons

Rhyme Time Have children match animal and object pictures whose names rhyme, then draw the rhyming pair.

- Display rhyming picture cards, such as cat, hat, fox, box, pig, and wig. Ask: **Which picture names rhyme?** *¿Qué palabras riman?*

- Help children fold a sheet of paper in half. On each half have them draw one of the rhyming pictures from a chosen rhyme pair. Ask children to label the pictures. Prompt them to write the letters they know, such as the letter *Cc* in *cat*.

Center Tip

If...children have difficulty finding a rhyming pair, **then...** state each animal or object name. Hold up one card, such as the cat card. Ask: **Do cat and pig rhyme? Do cat and hat rhyme?**

Creativity Center

✓ Track children's ability to describe the characteristics of animals.

Materials paper plates, glue, assorted art supplies (yarn, construction paper, buttons)

Animal Masks Tell children that they will make a mask of a favorite animal, including details about the animal's characteristics.

- Give each child a paper plate. Ask: **What animal face will you make?** *¿La cara de qué animal van a hacer?*

- Prompt children to use art supplies that mirror the animal's features, such as yarn for a lion mane or buttons for puppy eyes.

- Ask children to tell about their masks. Children can use the masks during Center Time.

Center Tip

If...children have difficulty remembering the animal's features, **then...**show photos or books containing pictures of the chosen animal for children to reference.

Learning Goals

Emergent Literacy: Writing
- Child uses scribbles, shapes, pictures, symbols, and letters to represent language.

Fine Arts
- Child expresses emotions or ideas through art.

Differentiated Instruction

✋ Extra Support
Creativity Center
If . . . children have difficulty deciding which art materials to use for the animal's features, **then** . . . model for them how to rip construction paper into small pieces for parts of the animal's face. Also suggest they use buttons for eyes and yarn for hair or fur.

⭐ Enrichment
Creativity Center
Challenge children to role play a conversation between their animal and a friend's using their completed masks. Suggest they tell each other about themselves (pretending to be their animals).

Accommodations for 3's
Writer's Center
If . . . children have difficulty writing letters in the rhyming words, **then** . . . lightly write the letters for children to trace and then copy.

Focus Question
What are animals like?
¿Cómo son los animales?

Literacy Time

large group | 15 minutes

 Read Aloud

✓ **Can children recall important story details about animals and their homes?**

Build Background Tell children that you will be reading a story about pets.

● Ask: *What pet would you like to have? Why? ¿Qué mascota les gustaría tener? ¿Por qué?*

Listen for Understanding Read aloud "My Very Own Pet"/ "Mi propia mascota" from the *Teacher's Treasure Book*, page 274. Display the flannel board patterns (page 402) as you read each reference in the story to help children connect the text to its meaning.

● Ask: *Would an elephant make a good pet? Why couldn't Austin keep the turtle at home? ¿Un elefante sería una buena mascota? ¿Por qué Austin no pudo quedarse con la tortuga en casa?*

Respond to the Story Have children name the animal Austin finally got as a pet. Ask: *How did Austin feel about getting a dog for his birthday? Is a dog a good pet? ¿Cómo se sintió Austin al recibir un perro en su cumpleaños? ¿Es un perro una buena mascota?*

TIP Help children use the flannel board patterns to recall story details. Tell children they can use the patterns during Center Time to retell the story to a friend.

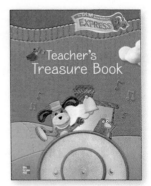

Teacher's Treasure Book, page 274

Learn About Letters and Sounds

✓ Can children identify the letter *Xx*?

Learn About the Letter *Xx* Sing the "ABC Song" with children as you page through the *ABC Big Book*, stopping when you get to the letter *Xx*. Point to the *X-ray* photo. Tell children that the word *X-ray* begins with the letter *Xx*. The letter *Xx* stands for the /ks/ sounds.

● Model how to write the upper case letter *X* using the ABC Picture Card. Have children trace the letter *X* with their fingers.

● While one child is tracing, the other children can be writing the letter in the air or on the floor using their fingers. Have them say /ks/ each time they write the letter.

● Repeat for the lower case *x*. Point out that upper case and lower case *Xx* are formed the same way, but that upper case *X* is taller.

ELL Show the *Xx* photos from the *ABC Big Book*: X-ray, exit, fox, and box. Read each word as you point to the picture. Help children find the EXIT sign in the school. Display a box and have them fill the box with items, naming each item they place in the box.

ABC Big Book

 Learning Goals

Language and Communication
● Child demonstrates an understanding of oral language by responding appropriately.

Emergent Literacy: Reading
● Child names most upper- and lowercase letters of the alphabet.
● Child identifies the letter that stands for a given sound.
● Child retells or reenacts poems and stories in sequence.

Science
● Child observes, understands, and discusses the relationship of plants and animals to their environments.

Vocabulary

birthday	cumpleaños	lake	lago
lizard	lagartija	pet	mascota
puppy	cachorro	zoo	zoológico

Differentiated Instruction

 Extra Support
Read Aloud
If...children have difficulty recalling why specific animals don't make good pets,
then...point to the flannel pattern for each animal. Name the animal and tell where it lives. Point out that these animals are wild; therefore they do not live in homes.

Enrichment
Read Aloud
Challenge children to draw pictures of the animals in the story in their natural habitats, such as the turtle in a lake or the lizard climbing a tree. Help children add details to their pictures.

Math Time

Observe and Investigate

 Can children add and subtract with sums and differences up to 5?

How Many Now? Show three counters to children, and, as a group, count and say how many counters there are.

- Add one counter, and ask: *How many counters are there now? ¿Cuántas fichas hay ahora?* Count together and check.

- Repeat by adding and removing one counter and, eventually, do the same with two counters.

- Once children are able, play this activity's hidden version by following the same steps, but hide the counters under a dark cloth (or paper plate). Keep counters hidden as you add or remove counters. For example, add two counters to the others under the cloth and, after children have answered, uncover the counters and count with the class to check.

ELL During the adding and subtracting activity, focus on the concepts of "more" and "fewer." For example, after adding a counter, say: *Now I have more counters.* Continue with other concrete objects, such as books. Ask: *How can I get more books?* Have children collect books to add to the pile.

✖✖✖ Social and Emotional Development

Making Good Choices

 Do children show a desire to be helpful and caring?

Being Helpful Display *Making Good Choices Flip Chart* page 21, "How Can I Help Someone?" Review with children the ways the other children helped him with the blocks.

- With a Dog Puppet, role play other situations to model people being helpful and caring. For example, explain that the puppet must clean up a large mess in the centers. Model what you would say and do to help the puppet with this task. Model how you would ask the puppet for help.

- After each role play, ask: *How did I help the puppet? What did I say? ¿Cómo ayudé al títere? ¿Qué dije?*

Online Math Activity

Children can complete Mystery Pictures 4 and Memory Geometry 4 during computer time or Center Time.

Making Good Choices Flip Chart, page 21

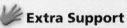

Learning Goal

Social and Emotional Development
- Child shows empathy and care for others.

Mathematics
- Child uses concrete objects or makes a verbal word problem to add up to 5 objects.
- Child uses concrete objects or makes a verbal word problem to subtract up to 5 objects from a set.

Vocabulary

caring	cuidar	count	contar
helpful	ayuda	how many	cuántos

Differentiated Instruction

✋ **Extra Support**

Observe and Investigate
If...children struggle adding and subtracting during the hidden activity, **then...**have children keep track of the counters using their fingers. When one is added, for example, they extend one more finger.

⭐ **Enrichment**

Observe and Investigate
Continue the activity, adding and subtracting to 10.

Accommodations for 3's

Observe and Investigate
If...children struggle adding and subtracting, **then...**focus on adding or subtracting only one counter. Chorally count the sum or number of counters remaining with children.

Focus Question
What are animals like?
¿Cómo son los animales?

Learning Goals

Language and Communication
• Child names and describes actual or pictured people, places, things, actions, attributes, and events.

Social Studies
• Child understands basic human needs for food, clothing, shelter.

• Child respects/appreciates the differing interests, skills, abilities, cultures, languages, and family structures of people.

Vocabulary

clothing	vestimenta	food	comida
needs	necesidades	people	personas
shelter	refugio	water	agua

Differentiated Instruction

 Extra Support
Understand and Participate
If...children have difficulty identifying items in a home, **then...**display the Home pictures from the *Photo Library*. Ask: **What is this? What room in a home does this belong in?** *¿Qué es esto? ¿A qué habitación de la casa corresponde?*

 Enrichment
Understand and Participate
Challenge children to create different kinds of shelters from play objects. These might include wooden or brick homes, tents, trailers, or igloos. Have children tell how these homes are the same as and different from their homes.

Social Studies Time

large group   20 minutes

Health Skills During the discussion of people's needs, explain which foods are most healthful to eat.

Oral Language and Academic Vocabulary

✓ **Can children identify their needs?**

Talking About People's Needs Ask children what they learned about pet care from *Staying Healthy*. Remind them that pets need food, water, and shelter. Explain that a shelter is a safe place to live.

• Ask: **Do you need food to live? Water? Shelter?** *¿Ustedes necesitan comida para vivir? ¿Agua? ¿Un refugio?*

• Point out that people need many of the same things that animals need.

Understand and Participate

✓ **Can children name the needs of all people (food, clothing, shelter)?**

Looking at Home Books Display books depicting homes around the world. Make sure some of the photos contain people.

• Page through the books with children, pointing out the types of homes people live in, including what the homes are made of.

• Ask: **Why do people need shelter? What is kept in a home? How does a home keep people safe? How are the people in these homes like you?** *¿Por qué las personas necesitan un refugio? ¿Qué se guarda adentro de una casa? ¿Por qué una casa mantiene a salvo a las personas?*

• Continue the discussion by pointing out that people also need food and clothing to live. Explain why. Then ask: **What kinds of food do you eat? Which foods are best to eat? What kinds of clothes do you wear?** *¿Qué tipos de comida comen? ¿Cuáles son los mejores alimentos? ¿Qué clase de vestimenta usan?*

• Have each child name an item, and list it on chart paper. Connect what the child says to what you write. Children can add a small picture beside their chart entry.

ELL Use the *Photo Library CD-ROM* pictures to teach children words associated with homes, such as *kitchen*, *bedroom*, *sofa*, *toilet*, and *stove*. Have children draw a room in their home, or use play objects to create a room. Help them identify the room and the items in it.

For additional suggestions on how to meet the needs of children at the Beginning, Intermediate, Advanced, and Advanced-High levels of English proficiency, see pages 184–187.

Center Time

▶ **Center Rotation** Center Time includes teacher-guided activities and independent activities. Refer to the **Learning Centers** on pages 24–25 for activities in additional centers.

 small group 30 minutes

Construction Center

	Center Tip

 Monitor children as they make and describe different types of shelters.

Materials blocks, miniature home toys (e.g., stove, bed, chair)

Build a Shelter Tell children that they will use blocks to build a shelter, such as one they saw in the books about homes. Children can build their home or a home they have seen in pictures.

- Have children work with a partner. Ask: *What will you build? How will you share the job?* ¿Qué van a construir? ¿Cómo se repartirán el trabajo?

- Have children describe their finished shelter. Encourage them to add details, such as interior furnishings. Ask: *What is inside your home?* ¿Qué hay adentro de sus casas?

Center Tip

If...children need help sharing the blocks and working together, **then**... suggest roles for each child in the building of the shelter. For example, one child can build the base while another builds the roof.

Learning Goals

Language and Communication
• Child names and describes actual or pictured people, places, things, actions, attributes, and events.

Social Studies
• Child understands basic human needs for food, clothing, shelter.

Writing

Recap the day. Have children name the things people need. Ask: *What do people need to stay alive?* ¿Qué necesitan las personas para vivir? Record their answers on chart paper. Share the pen by having children write letters and words they know. Ask children to draw a picture to illustrate each sentence.

Purposeful Play

✓ **Observe children as they work in pairs or small groups.**

Children choose an open center for free playtime. Encourage cooperation skills by suggesting they work together to create a play using their animal masks or a conversation between two people living in their home.

Let's Say Good-Bye

 small group 15 minutes

 Read Aloud Revisit "Old MacDonald"/"El viejo MacDonald" for your afternoon Read Aloud. Ask children to listen for the sounds that animals make.

 Home Connection Refer to the Home Connections activities listed in the Resources and Materials chart on page 21. Remind children to tell families about different kinds of homes. Sing the "Good-Bye Song"/"Hora de ir a casa" as children prepare to leave.

DAY 4

Focus Question
What are animals like?
¿Cómo son los animales?

Learning Goals

Language and Communication
• Child follows basic rules for conversations (taking turns, staying on topic, listening actively).

Emergent Literacy: Reading
• Child generates words that rhyme.

Vocabulary

chase	perseguir	climb	trepar
friends	amigos	hungry	hambriento
problem	problema	share	compartir

Differentiated Instruction

 Extra Support

Oral Language and Vocabulary
If...children have difficulty distinguishing real from make-believe, **then...**show pictures of animals from fiction and nonfiction books. Ask: *Does this animal look like a real animal you might see outside? Do animals in real-life wear clothes like these? ¿Este animal parece un animal real, de esos que suelen ver afuera? ¿Los animales de la vida real usan este tipo de ropa?*

 Enrichment

Oral Language and Vocabulary
Challenge children to create pretend dialogues between animals during Center Time. You might wish to provide a problem the animals have to solve together or ask them to think of a pretend problem the animals can solve.

Let's Start the Day

 Opening Routines and Transition Tips
For **Opening Routines** and **Transition Tips** turn to pages 178–181 and visit DLMExpressOnline.com for more ideas.

Read **"My Dog Rags"/**"Mi perrita Tita" from the *Teacher's Treasure Book*, page 118, for your morning Read Aloud.

Language Time

large group   15 minutes

Social and Emotional Development Remind children to listen carefully and wait until their classmate has finished speaking before they speak.

Oral Language and Vocabulary

Can children carry on an imaginary conversation?

Animal Friends Talk about animal stories previously read in which the animals acted like people. Ask: *What animals were in the story? Did they act like animals you have seen in real life? Did they talk like people? ¿Qué animales había en el cuento? ¿Actuaban como los animales que han visto en la vida real? ¿Hablaban como las personas?*

• Discuss how *real* animals, such as dogs and cats, act. Point out, for example, that they bark or meow rather than talk. Only *make-believe* animals can talk like people.

• Ask: *If dogs and cats could talk like people, what might they say to each other? Si los perros y los gatos pudieran hablar como las personas, ¿qué se dirían?* Model an animal conversation with a child. Then have partners conduct an "animal talk."

ELL Display *Photo Library CD-ROM* images for *dog, cow, duck, horse,* and *frog*. Imitate the sound that each animal makes, as children repeat. Then have children engage in pretend play using animals, such the Farm Animal Counters or stuffed animals. They can make the sound the animal makes or create simple, brief conversations with other animal friends. Provide language, such as question starters (What?, Where?, Why?).

Phonological Awareness

Can children identify words that rhyme?

Recognize Rhyming Words Display the Dog Puppets. Have pairs of children hold the puppets. Whisper a word in each child's ear. Have them say the word to their puppet. Ask the rest of the class: *Do these two words rhyme? ¿Estas dos palabras riman?* Remind children that rhyming words have the same ending sounds, such as *sat* and *mat*. Provide corrective feedback, as needed.

Center Time

▶ **Center Rotation** Center Time includes teacher-guided activities and independent activities. Refer to the **Learning Centers** on pages 24–25 for activities in additional centers.

small group   60–90 minutes

Learning Goals

Language and Communication
• Child uses newly learned vocabulary daily in multiple contexts.

Emergent Literacy: Reading
• Child enjoys and chooses reading-related activities.

Library and Listening Center

Center Tip

✓ **Track children's ability to distinguish real from make-believe.**

Materials traditional folk tale and fairy tale books

Browsing Make-Believe Stories Have children browse through folk and fairy tale books to distinguish things that are real from things that are make-believe.

● Say: *Look carefully at the illustrations. Which things could happen in real life? Which things could not happen in real life?* *Observen con atención las ilustraciones. ¿Qué cosas pueden suceder en la vida real? ¿Qué cosas no podrían suceder en la vida real?*

● Prompt children to use the terms *real* and *make-believe* in their responses.

If...children have difficulty using the terms real and make-believe in their discussions, **then...** provide the sentence frame: *The _____ is make-believe because _____. El ____ es inventado porque ___.* Model using the frame, then have children repeat.

Differentiated Instruction

✋ Extra Support
Pretend and Learn Center
If...children have difficulty retelling "My Very Own Pet", **then...**place the flannel patterns in the sequence in which they appear in the story. Prompt children to tell about each picture in order.

⭐ Enrichment
Pretend and Learn Center
Challenge children to make up additional dialogue between story characters. Ask: *What happens after the ending of the story? What might Austin say to his new puppy? ¿Qué sucede después de que termino ael cuento? ¿Que le puede haber dicho el niño a su nuevo cahorro?*

💜 Special Needs
Vision Loss
Take two shoeboxes, and work with the child to make a collection of things that are real and a collection of things that are make-believe. Later, ask him or her to tell you why each item is or is not real.

Pretend and Learn Center

Center Tip

✓ **Track how well children can retell stories read aloud to them.**

Materials flannel patterns, sock puppets (cat and dog)

Retell and Act Out Stories Explain to children that they will retell the stories you read aloud this week.

● Display the flannel patterns for "My Very Own Pet." Have children use the patterns as they retell or act out yesterday's story.

● Continue with today's story, "Why Dogs Chase Cats," after it is read. Have children use or make sock puppets for the retelling.

If...children have difficulty retelling one of the stories, **then...**remind them of specific story details, such as what the cat said to the dog. Or, ask questions and provide clues about story details, such as: *What pet did Austin get for his birthday? Remember, it says "ruff". ¿Qué mascota recibió el niño para su cumpleaños? Recuerden el sonido que hacía.*

Focus Question
What are animals like?
¿Cómo son los animales?

Literacy Time

 Read Aloud

 Can children answer questions about information read aloud?

Build Background Tell children that you will be reading a make-believe story about two common pets—cats and dogs.

- Ask: *Are cats and dogs usually friendly to each other?* *¿Se llevan bien en general los perros y los gatos?*

Listen for Enjoyment Read aloud "Why Dogs Chase Cats"/ "Por qué los perros persiguen a los gatos" in the *Teacher's Treasure Book*, page 321.

- Tell children to listen carefully to what the cat and dog say to each other.

- Ask: *What do both Cat and Dog want? Which animal doesn't want to share the ham?* *¿Qué quieren Gata y Perro? ¿Qué animal no quiere compartir el jamón?*

Respond to the Story Have children tell why Dog chased Cat. Ask: *Are Cat and Dog friends now?* *¿Son amigos ahora Gata y Perro?*

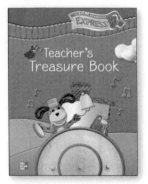

Teacher's Treasure Book, page 321

TIP Use voice inflection to emphasize the difference in what Cat and Dog say, especially when Cat says "*my* ham" instead of "a ham".

ELL Focus on the concepts of *my, your,* and *our.* Hold an object, such as a toy dog. Say: *This is my dog.* Give the dog to a child. Say: *This is your dog.* Then put the dog in the middle of everyone. Say: *This is our dog.* Point and use gestures after each sentence. Have children hold the dog and repeat the sequence, emphasizing the pronouns.

Learn About Letters and Sounds

 Can children identify the letter *Vv*?

Learn About the Letter *Vv* Sing the "ABC Song" with children as you page through the *ABC Big Book*, stopping when you get to the letter *Vv*. Point to the *violin* photo. Tell children that the word *violin* begins with the /v/ sound and the letter *Vv*. Have them chant "/v/ /v/ /v/ a very nice violin" as they pretend to play a violin.

- Model how to write the upper case letter *V* using the ABC Picture Card. Have children trace the letter *V* with their fingers.

- While one child is tracing, the other children can be writing the letter in the air or on the floor using their finger. Have them say /v/ each time they write the letter.

- Repeat for the lower case *v.* Point out that upper case and lower case *Vv* are written the same way, except that upper case *V* is taller.

ABC Big Book

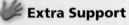
Learning Goals

Language and Communication
- Child demonstrates an understanding of oral language by responding appropriately.
- Child experiments with and produces a growing number of sounds in English words. (ELL)
- Child understands and uses regular and irregular plural nouns, regular past tense verbs, personal and possessive pronouns, and subject-verb agreement.

Emergent Literacy: Reading
- Child names most upper- and lowercase letters of the alphabet.
- Child identifies the letter that stands for a given sound.

Vocabulary

chase	perseguir	climb	trepar
friends	amigos	hungry	hambriento
my	mi	share	compartir

Differentiated Instruction

 Extra Support

Learn About Letters and Sounds
If...children have difficulty saying the /v/ sound, **then...**show them the correct mouth position (top teeth on bottom lip). Say these words slowly, emphasizing the beginning sound, and have children repeat: *vase, van, vote, volcano.*

 Enrichment

Learn About Letters and Sounds
Give children several thin sticks or pencils. Have them make the upper case letters you call out using the sticks: *X, V, T, A, E, F.* Ask them the sound that each letter stands for.

Math Time

Observe and Investigate

☑ **Can children recognize designs with symmetry?**

Discuss Shape Pictures Display children's designs you copied from Day 2's Math lesson.

- Discuss each design. Ask: *Does this design show an animal? If so, what animal?*
  ¿Este diseño muestra a un animal? Si es así, ¿a qué animal?

- Draw special attention to those designs with line or rotational symmetry. Talk about how designs with line (mirror) symmetry are the same on one side as the other, so that one side could be flipped over to look like the other. Demonstrate using symmetric pattern blocks such as rectangles and hexagons.

- Discuss designs with rotational symmetry as being the same when they are turned around. Demonstrate by turning the paper.

🏃🏃🏃 Social and Emotional Development

Making Good Choices

☑ **Do children show a desire to be helpful and caring?**

Being Helpful Display the Dog Puppets and a set of building blocks. Tell children that the puppets are disagreeing about who gets to use the blocks. Model a dialogue between the puppets that ends in them agreeing to divide and share the blocks.

- Ask: *What problem did the puppets have? How did they solve their problem?*
  ¿Qué problema enfrentan los títeres? ¿Cómo lo resolvieron?

- Remind children that being fair is a good way to show that you care for your classmates. Also, working together to use and clean-up center materials is a great way to be helpful to others.

- Play the song "Excuse Me"/"Permiso" from the Making Good Choices Audio CD. Ask children what the song says about sharing and being fair.

ELL Some children may have difficulties following the conversation between the Dog Puppets. While role playing, act out the dogs' actions, such as arguing and happily dividing up the blocks. Say simple phrases as you perform each action, such as: *We're fair.*

Building Blocks

Online Math Activity

Children can complete Mystery Pictures 4 and Memory Geometry 4 during computer time or Center Time.

Differentiated Instruction

✋ **Extra Support**

Observe and Investigate

If...children struggle identifying symmetry, **then...**use a stick or piece of yarn to draw a line down the middle of the design. Ask: *Are both sides of the line the same? ¿Son iguales los dos lados que divide la línea?*

⭐ **Enrichment**

Observe and Investigate

Give children a piece of yarn to use for a line. Have them create complex designs on either side of the yarn that show symmetry.

Accommodations for 3's

Observe and Investigate

If...children struggle identifying symmetry, **then...**place the same shape on either side of a yarn line. Ask: *Are the shapes on both sides of the line the same or different? ¿Son iguales o diferentes las figuras en ambos lados de la línea?* Continue with other shapes, some matching and some not matching.

Focus Question
What are animals like?
¿Cómo son los animales?

Math Time

large group 20 minutes

Learning Goals

Language and Communication
• Child follows two- and three-step oral directions.

Mathematics
• Child recognizes, names, describes, matches, compares, and sorts common two-dimensional shapes (such as circle, square, rectangle, triangle, rhombus).
• Child sorts objects and explains how the sorting was done.

Vocabulary

hexagon	hexágono	rhombus	rombo
rule	regla	shape	figura
sort	clasificar	trapezoid	trapecio

Differentiated Instruction

 Extra Support
Math Time
If...children have difficulty stating the sorting rule, **then...**provide sentence frames such as *All these shapes are _____. All these shapes are not _____. Todas estas figuras son ____. Todas estas figuas no son ____.*

 Enrichment
Math Time
Challenge children to make their own sorting rule for classmates to guess.

Language and Communication Skills After you model sorting, provide 2-step directions for children to follow. Say, for example: *Find the hexagons. Place them in a pile in front of you. Encuentren los hexágonos. Colóquenlos en una pila delante de ustedes.*

 Can children distinguish and describe shapes by their attributes?

Talk About Shapes Display Shape Sets. Ask children to name and discuss shapes. Focus on the trapezoids, rhombuses, and hexagons.

● Show several different rhombuses, including squares, and discuss their similarities and differences. Repeat for the other shapes.

● Ask: *What is the shape? How many sides does it have? How are the angles different in these two shapes? ¿Qué figura es ésta? ¿Cuántos lados tiene? ¿En qué se diferencian los ángulos de estas dos figuras?*

Can children figure out the sorting rule?

Guess My Rule Ask children to watch carefully as you sort Shape Set shapes into piles based on something that makes them alike. Tell children to silently guess your sorting rule, such as hexagons versus all other shapes.

● Sort shapes one at a time, continuing until there are at least two shapes in each pile. Signal "shhh," and pick up another shape. Looking uncertain, say: *Point to the pile in which the shape belongs. Señalen la pila en donde debe ir esta figura.* Place the shape in the proper pile.

● Ask children to explain to a classmate what the sorting rule is. As they talk, help them consider the following: *Why did you guess that rule? How did you know? Show me how the shapes match the rule. ¿Por qué adivinaron la regla? ¿Cómo lo supieron? Muéstrenme cómo las figuras se ajustan a esa regla.* Repeat with other shapes and new rules.

TIP Tell children that they can continue sorting shapes in the Math Center on their own or with a friend.

ELL Focus on the concepts "alike" and "different." Display two objects, such as two Farm Animal Counters. The counters should be the same animal. Say: *These two animals are alike.* Repeat by showing two counters that are not alike. Say: *These two animals are different.* Continue with other counters and classroom objects. Ask: *Are these animals alike? Are these animals different?*

For additional suggestions on how to meet the needs of children at the Beginning, Intermediate, Advanced, and Advanced-High levels of English proficiency, see pages 184–187.

Center Time

► **Center Rotation** Center Time includes teacher-guided activities and independent activities. Refer to the **Learning Centers** on pages 24–25 for activities in additional centers.

  small group 30 minutes

Math and Science Center

✓ Track children's ability to identify and use shapes to create and copy patterns.

Materials Shape Sets, Pattern Blocks, paper, crayons

Copying Patterns Tell children that they will continue to explore and create patterns using shapes.

● Give children shapes to create patterns of their choosing. Ask: *What are you making? What shapes are you using?* ¿Qué están haciendo? ¿Qué figuras están usando?

● Once children complete a design, have them copy it onto a sheet of paper. Prompt them to add their name to the paper. Display their shape-pattern art.

Center Tip

If...children need help creating new designs, **then...** show them pictures of other children's designs to copy or to generate ideas.

Purposeful Play

✓ Observe children appropriately handling classroom materials.

Children choose an open center for free playtime. Encourage cooperation skills by suggesting they work together to create a large shape design.

Let's Say Good-Bye

  small group 15 minutes

 Read Aloud Revisit the rhyme "My Dog Rags"/"Mi perrita Tita" for your afternoon Read Aloud. Tell children to listen for words that describe the dog Rags.

 Home Connection Refer to the Home Connections activities listed in the Resources and Materials chart on page 21. Remind children to tell families what today's story said about why dogs chase cats. Sing the "Good-Bye Song"/"Hora de ir a casa" as children prepare to leave.

✓ Learning Goals

Language and Communication
• Child names and describes actual or pictured people, places, things, actions, attributes, and events.

Mathematics
• Child recognizes, names, describes, matches, compares, and sorts common two-dimensional shapes (such as circle, square, rectangle, triangle, rhombus).

 Writing

Recap the day. Have children tell about a make-believe animal they have read about. Ask: *What did this make-believe animal do that real animals cannot?* ¿Qué hace este animal de fantasía que no pueden hacer los reales? Record their answers in a list. Read them back as you track the print, and emphasize the correspondence between speech and print.

DAY 5

Focus Question

What are animals like?
¿Cómo son los animales?

✓ Learning Goals

Language and Communication
• Child follows basic rules for conversations (taking turns, staying on topic, listening actively).

• Child understands or knows the meaning of many thousands of words, many more than he or she uses.

Emergent Literacy: Reading
• Child generates words that rhyme.

Vocabulary

bird	pájaro	eat	comer
feathers	plumas	feed	alimentar
nest	nido		

Differentiated Instruction

 Extra Support

Oral Language and Vocabulary

If...children have difficulty describing animals, **then...**use the animal *Photo Library CD-ROM* images. Point to animal body parts, name them, and have children repeat. Then ask questions such as: *Does this animal have a beak? Does this animal have brown fur? ¿Este animal tiene pico? ¿Este animal tiene pelaje de color café?*

 Enrichment

Oral Language and Vocabulary

Use the animal *Photo Library CD-ROM* images to teach the names and characteristics of other less familiar animals, such as the penguin, camel, octopus, and rhinoceros.

▶ **Opening Routines and Transition Tips**

For **Opening Routines** and **Transition Tips** turn to pages 178–181 and visit **DLMExpressOnline.com** for more ideas.

 Read **"Ms. Bumblebee Gathers Honey"/**"La abejorrita Zumbi lleva miel" from the *Teacher's Treasure Book*, page 207, for your morning Read Aloud.

Language Time

large group 15 minutes

👤👤👤 **Social and Emotional Development** Remind children to listen carefully as their classmates share their ideas. Remind them that they look at the person speaking to help them focus their attention.

Oral Language and Vocabulary

✓ **Can children share what they know about animals?**

Animal Characteristics Talk about what children have learned this week about animals. Ask: **What do you know about animals?** *¿Qué saben sobre los animales?*

• Display *Rhymes and Chants Flip Chart*, page 21. Recite "Baby Birds" with children. Ask: **What do the birds look like? Does the mommy bird look like the baby birds? Where do the birds live? What are the birds doing? What else do you know about birds?** *¿Cómo son los pájaros? ¿La mamá pájaro se parece a sus pajaritos? ¿Dónde viven los pájaros? ¿Qué están haciendo estos pájaros? ¿Qué más saben sobre pájaros?*

ELL Use the various bird pictures from the *Photo Library CD-ROM*. Name each type of bird. Ask yes/no questions about each picture, such as: **Does this bird have red feathers? Does this bird have a long beak?** Point to the specific characteristic of the bird as you ask the question.

Phonological Awareness

✓ **Can children identify words that rhyme?**

Recognize Rhyming Words Using *Rhymes and Chants Flip Chart,* page 21, recite "Baby Birds" once more with children. Remind children that rhyming words end with the same sounds. Point to the nest in the picture. Ask: **Which word in the song rhymes with nest? What are the baby birds munching on? Which word in the poem rhymes with munch?** *¿Qué palabra del poema rima con* nest*? ¿Qué palabra rima con* munch*?*

Baby Birds

See the baby birds curled up
Safe inside their nest?
It is such a comfy, cozy,
Homey place to rest!

Baby birds get hungry
And they want to munch!
FLAP! SQUAWK! Here's the mama!
Bringing worms for lunch!

Rhymes and Chants Flip Chart, page 21

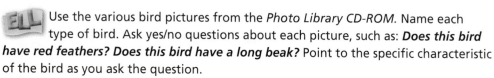

Center Time

► **Center Rotation** Center Time includes teacher-guided activities and independent activities. Refer to the **Learning Centers** on pages 24–25 for activities in additional centers.

 small group 60–90 minutes

Writer's Center

✓ **Track the use of descriptive words as children tell about their animal.**

Materials magazines, glue, paper, crayons

Animal Book Have children write a book about a favorite animal. Children will use animal pictures from magazines.

● Have children cut out and glue an animal picture to a sheet of paper.

● Ask: **What do you know about this animal?** *¿Qué saben sobre este animal?* Have children write on another sheet of paper what they know. Ask them to dictate their comments for you to record under their writings.

● Bind the two pages together to create an animal book.

Center Tip

If...children have difficulty recalling animal details, **then...**ask them questions about their animal, such as: *Does your animal have a tail? Is it a pet or does it live in the wild?* *¿Tiene cola? ¿Es una mascota o vive en la naturaleza?*

ABC Center

✓ **Track children's ability to match upper and lower case letters.**

Materials ABC Picture Cards, Alphabet/Letter Tiles, or magnetic letters; paper, glue, glitter

Matching Letters Explain to children that they will match the upper and lower case forms of this week's letters. Reinforce each letter's sound as children work.

● As children match the letter forms, ask: **How is the upper case C like the lower case c? How is it different?** *¿En qué se parecen la C mayúscula y la c minúscula? ¿En qué se diferencian?*

● Have children write each letter with glue on paper, then add glitter. They can add a drawing of a word whose name begins with that letter-sound.

Center Tip

If...children have difficulty recalling the letter's sound, **then...**have them trace the letter with their finger and repeat the sound you say before continuing with the activity.

✓ Learning Goals

Language and Communication
• Child names and describes actual or pictured people, places, things, actions, attributes, and events.

Emergent Literacy: Reading
• Child names most upper- and lowercase letters of the alphabet.

• Child produces the most common sound for a given letter.

Emergent Literacy: Writing
• Child uses scribbles, shapes, pictures, symbols, and letters to represent language.

Differentiated Instruction

🖐 Extra Support
Writer's Center
If...children have difficulty deciding what to write about their animal, **then...**help them focus on the animal's key characteristics, such as the giraffe's long neck or the rabbit's soft fur and floppy ears.

⭐ Enrichment
Writer's Center
Challenge children to make additional pages for their Animal Book. Each page can be about a different topic, such as what the animal eats, where it lives, and what its babies look like.

Accommodations for 3's
Writer's Center
If...children have difficulty cutting out small animal pictures, **then...**trace a large shape around the image and help children cut the larger area.

Circle Time

Learning Goals

Emergent Literacy: Reading
- Child names most upper- and lowercase letters of the alphabet.
- Child identifies the letter that stands for a given sound.
- Child asks and answers questions about books read aloud (such as, "Who?" "What?" "Where?").

Science
- Child identifies organisms and describes their characteristics.

Vocabulary

amazing	asombrosos	care	cuidar
describe	describir	home	hogar
pet	mascotas	wild	salvajes

Differentiated Instruction

 Extra Support

Learn About Letters and Sounds

If...children have difficulty writing this week's letters, **then**...focus on the letters with sticks (*Xx* and *Vv*), then move on to letters with curves (*Cc* and *Uu*). Use classroom materials such as sticks and clay to form the letters with children.

Enrichment

Learn About Letters and Sounds

Display a letter-card set of all the letters covered so far this year. Challenge children to name as many as they can.

Literacy Time

📖 Read Aloud

✓ **Can children describe and use pictures to construct meaning?**

Build Background Tell children that you will be rereading a book about amazing animals.

- Ask: *What did we learn about taking care of pets? ¿Qué aprendimos sobre el cuidado de las mascotas?*

Listen for Understanding Display *Concept Big Book 3: Amazing Animals* page 5, and read the title.

- Reread pages 6–9. Stop and have children name and describe the physical characteristics of each animal.

- Ask: *What does this animal look like? What can you learn about this animal by looking carefully at the photo? ¿Cómo es este animal? ¿Qué cosa pueden saber de este animal con sólo mirar atentamente su foto?*

Respond and Connect Have children connect their new learning to their daily lives. Ask: *What pet would you like to have? What would it look like? What would you do to take care of that pet? ¿Qué tipo de mascota les gustaría tener? ¿Qué aspecto tendría? ¿Qué harían para cuidar a esa mascota?*

TIP Be sure children can use picture details to describe the animals. Model as needed.

Learn About Letters and Sounds

✓ **Can children identify letters and sounds?**

Review Letters Cc, Uu, Xx, Vv Place ABC Picture Cards *C, U, X,* and *V* on the floor in a path. Have children hop the path as they say the name of each letter.

- Then display photo cards of words beginning with *Cc, Uu,* and *Vv,* and ending with *Xx.* These include *cat, camel, cow, vest, van,* and *fox* from the *Photo Library CD-ROM.* Add *x-ray* and *umbrella* picture cards, if available.

- Say a picture name. Have children match the beginning sound of the picture name to a ABC Picture Card. (For *fox,* children will focus on the ending sound.) Ask: *Does cat begin with the letter Cc? Listen, /k/ /k/ cat. ¿La palabra cat empieza con la letra Cc? Escuchen, /k/ /k/ cat.*

ELL Provide sentence frames to help children talk about the photos. Use frames such as *I see a ___* and *The [animal name] has ___.* Model using each frame, then have children repeat and apply the sentence frame to other details in the photo.

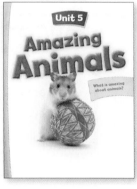

Amazing Animals
Animales asombrosos

small group 15 minutes

Math Time

Observe and Investigate

✓ **Can children identify rules used for sorting?**

Guess My Rule This is a small-group version of the activity done in a whole group on Day 4. Ask children to watch carefully as you sort Shape Set shapes into piles based on something that makes them alike. Tell children to silently guess your sorting rule, such as trapezoids versus all other shapes.

● Sort shapes one at a time, continuing until there are at least two shapes in each pile. Signal "shhh," and pick up a shape. Say: ***Point to the pile in which the shape belongs.*** *Señalen la pila en que debe ir esta figura.* Place the shape in the pile.

● Ask children to explain to a classmate what the sorting rule is. As they talk, help them consider the following: ***Why did you guess that rule? How did you know? Show me how the shapes match the rule.*** *¿Por qué adivinaron esa regla? ¿Cómo lo supieron? Muéstrenme cómo las figuras se ajustan a esa regla.*

● Have children work in pairs with one child sorting shapes and the other child guessing the rule. Then have children switch roles.

ELL Continue to focus on the concepts "alike" and "different." Display three objects, such as three Farm Animal Counters. Two counters should be the same animal. Ask: ***Which two animals are alike? Which animal is different?*** Slowly increase the number in the set. Hold up one counter. Ask: ***Which animals are like this one? Place them in a pile in front of you.***

large group 15 minutes

ᠵᠵᠵ Social and Emotional Development

Making Good Choices

✓ **Do children show a desire to be helpful and caring?**

Being Helpful Display *Making Good Choices Flip Chart,* page 21.

● Point to the flip chart illustration. Ask: ***What did we learn about helping and caring for other people?*** *¿Qué aprendimos sobre ayudar y cuidar a otras personas?*

● Place a pile of pattern blocks and the container they belong in on the table. Say: ***Let's work together to put these blocks in the jar. We can all be helpful by taking turns picking up one shape at a time. I'll start by picking up all the rhombuses. What will you pick up?*** *Vamos a trabajar juntos para colocar estos bloques en el tarro. Todos podemos ayudar si nos turnamos para elegir una figura por vez. Yo comenzaré tomando todos los rombos. ¿Qué tomarán ustedes?.* Have children name the shape they choose to pick up.

Building Blocks

Online Math Activity

Children can complete Mystery Pictures 4 and Memory Geometry 4 during computer time or Center Time.

Making Good Choices Flip Chart, page 21

✓ **Learning Goals**

Social and Emotional Development
● Child shows empathy and care for others.

Mathematics
● Child recognizes, names, describes, matches, compares, and sorts common two-dimensional shapes (such as circle, square, rectangle, triangle, rhombus).

● Child sorts objects and explains how the sorting was done.

Vocabulary

alike	parecido	different	diferente
rule	regla	shape	figura
sort	clasificar		

Differentiated Instruction

👆 **Extra Support**

Observe and Investigate

If...children have difficulty stating the sorting rule, **then...**provide sentence frames such as *All these shapes are _____. All these shapes are not _____. Todas estas figuras son _____. Todas estas figuras no son _____.*

⭐ **Enrichment**

Observe and Investigate

Challenge children to make their own sorting rule for classmates to guess

Accommodations for 3's

Observe and Investigate

If...children struggle sorting shapes, **then...**work on the concept of sorting by including only two different shapes in the pile. The shapes should also be the same color (e.g., red squares and blue hexagons). Have children sort the shapes, using the color clues to help them.

Focus Question
What are animals like?
¿Cómo son los animales?

Learning Goals

Science
• Child observes, understands, and discusses the relationship of plants and animals to their environments.

Fine Arts
• Child expresses emotions or ideas through art.
• Child shares opinions about artwork and artistic experiences.

Vocabulary

animal	animal	home	casa
pet	mascota	shape	granja
wild	salvajes		

Differentiated Instruction

 Extra Support

Oral Language and Academic Vocabulary
If...children have difficulty remembering details about pet homes or pet care,
then...display *Amazing Animals* pages 7–9 for children to refer to while painting.

 Enrichment

Explore and Express
Have children add labels to their paintings. Encourage them to write the letters they know.

 Special Needs

Vision Loss
This unit will provide a great opportunity to introduce how animals can be used to help. Even if the child in your class does not have an assistance dog, he or she may eventually use one. Invite someone into your class to show how dogs can be used as service animals.

Art Time

 large group | 20 minutes

Personal Safety Skills Model how to properly use, clean, and store art tools and supplies.

Oral Language and Academic Vocabulary

✓ **Can children describe where pets live and how to care for them?**

Animals in their Environment Remind children that they learned about animals that live with people. These animals are called pets.

● Ask: *Which animals make good pets? Where do these animals live?* *¿Qué animales pueden ser buenas mascotas? ¿Dónde viven?*

● Ask: *Which animal do not make good pets? Where do these animals live?* *¿Qué animales no podrían ser buenas mascotas? ¿Dónde viven?*

● Have children discuss specific details of pet homes and pet care. This can include animals found near people's homes, such as birds and farm animals.

Explore and Express

✓ **Can children paint an animal in its natural environment?**

Finger Paint Animals Tell children that they will paint a scene with a favorite pet or familiar animal, such as a dog being fed at home or a bird in its nest. To start, have them choose an animal.

● Distribute finger paints and proper painting clothes, if needed.

● Prompt children to include details in their paintings.

● When completed, say: *Tell me about your painting. What shapes did you use? What colors did you use? What do you think about your painting?* *Háblenme sobre sus pinturas. ¿Qué figuras usaron? ¿Qué colores usaron? ¿Qué piensan de sus pinturas?*

TIP Display children's paintings for all to see. Ask children to tell what they like about each painting.

ELL Display the Unit 5 *Oral Language Development Card* photos (or other available pictures) to provide children with details of animal environments. When asking children to consider adding a detail (such as adding a tree for a bird's nest), point to the detail in one of the displayed photos.

For additional suggestions on how to meet the needs of children at the Beginning, Intermediate, Advanced, and Advanced-High levels of English proficiency, see pages 184–187.

Center Time

▶ **Center Rotation** Center Time includes teacher-guided activities and independent activities. Refer to the **Learning Centers** on pages 24–25 for activities in additional centers.

  small group · 30 minutes

Construction Center

| | Center Tip |

☑ **Monitor children as they make and describe familiar animal homes.**

Materials blocks, sticks, construction paper, animal toys

Build an Animal Home Tell children that they will use blocks and other art materials to build an animal home they have seen. It can be anything from a doghouse to a bird's nest.

- Have children work with a partner. Ask: *What will you build? How will you share the job?* *¿Qué van a construir? ¿Cómo se repartirán el trabajo?*

- Have children describe their finished animal home. Ask: *What animal lives in this home? What does the animal do there? What does the animal look like?* *¿Qué animal vive en esta casa? ¿Qué hace ahí? ¿Cómo es el animal?*

Center Tip

If...children need help sharing the materials and working together, **then...**suggest roles for each child in the building of the animal home.

Learning Goals

Social and Emotional Development
- Child shows empathy and care for others.

Language and Communication
- Child names and describes actual or pictured people, places, things, actions, attributes, and events.

Science
- Child observes, understands, and discusses the relationship of plants and animals to their environments.

Writing

Recap the day and week. Say: *Tell me one thing you learned about animals this week*. *Digan una cosa sobre los animales que hayan aprendido esta semana*. Record children's answers on chart paper. Share the pen with children as you write. Have all children write their names beside their entries.

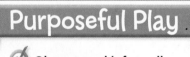

Purposeful Play

☑ **Observe and informally assess children sharing classroom materials and working cooperatively.**

Children choose an open center for free playtime. Encourage cooperation skills by suggesting they work together to create an animal home, such as a home for a pet.

Let's Say Good-Bye

  small group · 15 minutes

 Read Aloud Revisit the story "Ms. Bumblebee Gathers Honey"/"La abejorrita Zumbi lleva miel" for your afternoon Read Aloud. Ask children to listen for words that describe what Ms. Bumblebee does.

 Home Connection Refer to the Home Connections activities listed in the Resources and Materials chart on page 21. Remind children to tell families what they learned this week about animals and describe their animal painting. Sing the "Good-Bye Song"/"Hora de ir a casa" as children prepare to leave.

Focus Question

Where do animals live and what do they eat?

¿Dónde viven los animales y qué comen?

This week children will learn about animal needs. They will observe local animals in their habitats, record observations, sing about farm animals, mimic animal movements, group animals by habitat, and pretend play taking care of animals.

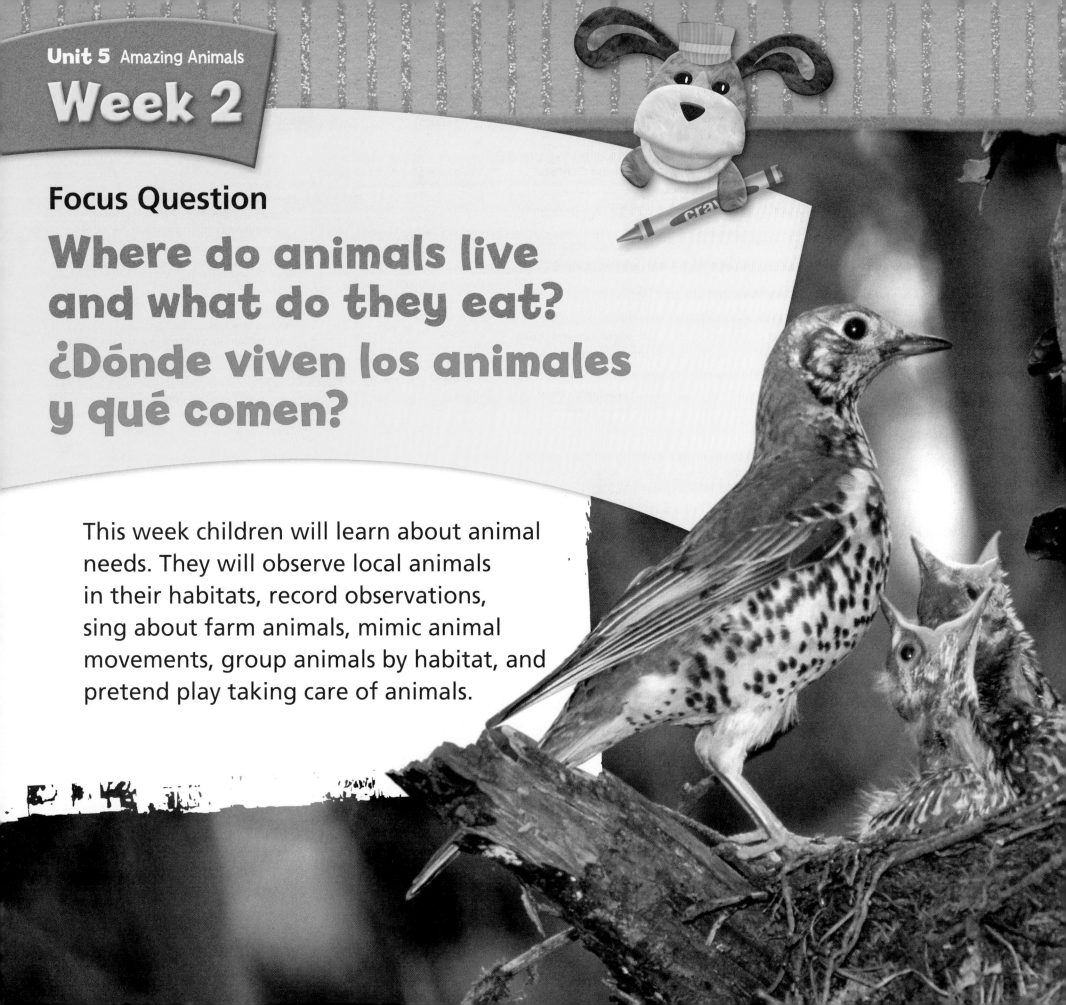

Unit 5 Amazing Animals
Week 2

✓ Learning Goals

Social and Emotional Development	1	2	3	4	5
Child follows simple classroom rules and routines.			✓		
Child uses classroom materials carefully.		✓		✓	
Child initiates interactions with others in work and play situations.	✓	✓	✓	✓	✓
Child accepts responsibility for and regulates own behavior.				✓	✓
Child initiates play scenarios with peers that share a common plan and goal.				✓	✓

Language and Communication	1	2	3	4	5
Child demonstrates an understanding of oral language by responding appropriately.	✓				
Child follows two- and three-step oral directions.	✓				
Child uses oral language for a variety of purposes.		✓			
Child experiments with and produces a growing number of sounds in English words. (ELL)	✓				
Child names and describes actual or pictured people, places, things, actions, attributes, and events.	✓	✓		✓	
Child exhibits an understanding of instructional terms used in the classroom.		✓	✓	✓	
Child understands or knows the meaning of many thousands of words, many more than he or she uses.					✓
Child uses newly learned vocabulary daily in multiple contexts.	✓		✓	✓	
Child uses words to identify and understand categories.	✓	✓			
Child builds English listening and speaking vocabulary for common objects and phrases. (ELL)	✓				
Child uses individual words and short phrases to communicate. (ELL)		✓			

Emergent Literacy: Reading	1	2	3	4	5
Child independently engages in pre-reading behaviors and activities (such as, pretending to read, turning one page at a time).	✓				
Child generates words that rhyme.	✓	✓	✓	✓	✓
Child names most upper- and lowercase letters of the alphabet.	✓	✓	✓		✓
Child identifies the letter that stands for a given sound.	✓	✓	✓	✓	✓
Child asks and answers questions about books read aloud (such as, "Who?" "What?" "Where?").	✓		✓		✓

Emergent Literacy: Writing	1	2	3	4	5
Child participates in free drawing and writing activities to deliver information.		✓			
Child uses scribbles, shapes, pictures, symbols, and letters to represent language.		✓	✓	✓	
Child writes own name or a reasonable approximation of it. not necessarily with full correct spelling or well-formed letters.					✓

Mathematics	1	2	3	4	5
Child measures passage of time using standard or non-standard tools.			✓		
Child identifies, duplicates, and creates simple patterns.	✓	✓	✓	✓	✓

Science	1	2	3	4	5
Child identifies organisms and describes their characteristics.	✓		✓		✓
Child observes, understands, and discusses the relationship of plants and animals to their environments.	✓	✓	✓	✓	✓

Social Studies	1	2	3	4	5
Child identifies common events and routines.			✓		

Fine Arts	1	2	3	4	5
Child uses and experiments with a variety of art materials and tools in various art activities.	✓			✓	
Child expresses emotions or ideas through art.	✓			✓	✓
Child shares opinions about artwork and artistic experiences.	✓				
Child participates in a variety of music activities (such as listening, singing, finger plays, musical games, performances).					✓
Child expresses thoughts, feelings, and energy through music and creative movement.		✓			

Physical Development	1	2	3	4	5
Child engages in a sequence of movements to perform a task.		✓			
Child completes tasks that require eye-hand coordination and control.				✓	

Technology Applications	1	2	3	4	5
Child opens and correctly uses age-appropriate software programs.		✓		✓	
Child names and uses various computer parts (such as mouse, keyboard, CD-ROM, microphone, touch screen).		✓			

Materials and Resources

DAY 1	DAY 2	DAY 3	DAY 4	DAY 5

Program Materials

DAY 1	DAY 2	DAY 3	DAY 4	DAY 5
• Teacher's Treasure Book • Oral Language Development Cards 43, 44 • Rhymes and Chants Flip Chart • *Castles, Caves and Honeycombs* Big Book • Sequence Cards: "Three Little Pigs" • ABC Picture Cards • Building Blocks Math Activities • Math and Science Flip Chart • Pattern Blocks • Making Good Choices Flip Chart • Hand Lenses • Home Connections Resource Guide	• Teacher's Treasure Book • *Castles, Caves, and Honeycombs* Big Book • Photo Library CD-ROM • Dog Puppets • Sequence Cards: Building a Home • ABC Picture Cards • Building Blocks Math Activities • Making Good Choices Flip Chart • Math and Science Flip Chart	• Teacher's Treasure Book • Oral Language Development Card 45 • Rhymes and Chants Flip Chart • Vehicle counters • Concept Big Book 3 • ABC Letter Tiles • ABC Big Book • Making Good Choices Flip Chart • Dog Puppets	• Teacher's Treasure Book • Farm Animal counters • Flannel Board Patterns for "Animal Homes" • Dog Puppets • Math and Science Flip Chart • Pattern Blocks • Home Connections Resource Guide	• Teacher's Treasure Book • Rhymes and Chants Flip Chart • ABC Picture Cards • ABC Letter Tiles • *Castles, Caves and Honeycombs* Big Book • Pattern Blocks • Farm Animal Counters • Making Good Choices Flip Chart

Other Materials

DAY 1	DAY 2	DAY 3	DAY 4	DAY 5
• Animal books • Finger paint • Newspaper • White paper • Leaves • Crayons • Pencils	• Stuffed animals • Boxes • Blocks • Construction materials • Objects with rhyming names (see page 71) • Paper • Crayons and pencils • Music about animals • Books with patterns	• Bowls • Small stuffed toys • Pictures of cane, star, coat, and duck • Paper, crayons and markers • Beads • Daily picture schedule • Large cup with arrow on front • Newspaper or magazine headlines • Scissors	• Small and big items • Box • Bag • Paper • Crayons • Paint , easel, and paintbrushes of different sizes • Classroom games • Flat plastic stirrers • Patterns on strips of paper	• Butcher paper • Paint and paintbrush • Crayons and markers • Scissors • Glue • Various art materials • Chalkboard • Water • Stuffed farm animals • Farm dress-up clothes

Home Connection

DAY 1	DAY 2	DAY 3	DAY 4	DAY 5
Remind children to describe to their family any animals they see outside. Send home Weekly Parent Letter, Home Connections Resource Guide, pp. 47-48.	Remind children to show families how they can dance in a pattern.	Remind children to tell families about their daily schedule.	Remind children to point out patterns they see at home (in their clothing or elsewhere). Send home Story Book 13, Home Connections Resource Guide, pp. 129–132.	Remind children to sing "Old MacDonald Had a Farm" for their families.

Assessment

As you observe children throughout the week, you may fill out an Anecdotal Observational Record Form to document an individual's progress toward a goal or signs indicating the need for developmental or medical evaluation. You may also choose to select work for each child's portfolio. The Anecdotal Observational Record Form and Weekly Assessment rubrics are available in the assessment section of DLMExpressOnline.com.

More Literature Suggestions

- **Posy** by Linda Newbery
- **Snuggle Up Sleepy Ones** by Claire Freedman
- **On the Farm** by David Elliot
- **And Tango Makes Three** by Justin Richardson and Peter Parnell
- **Spotted Yellow Frogs** by Matthew Van Fleet

- **Conejito y el mar** por Gavin Bishop
- **El gato tragón** por Phyllis King
- **El chivo en la huerta** por Lada J. Kratky
- **Turquesita** por Silvia Dubovoy
- **El árbol de los pájaros** por Jesús Ballaz

Daily Planner

		DAY 1	DAY 2
Let's Start the Day Language Time	large group	**Opening Routines** p. 64 **Morning Read Aloud** p. 64 **Oral Language and Vocabulary** p. 64 What Animals Eat **Phonological Awareness** p. 64 Recognize Rhyming Words	**Opening Routines** p. 70 **Morning Read Aloud** p. 70 **Oral Language and Vocabulary** p. 70 Animal Homes **Phonological Awareness** p. 70 Recognize Rhyming Words
Center Time	small group	**Focus On:** Library and Listening Center p. 65 Creativity Center p. 65	**Focus On:** Construction Center p. 71 Writer's Center p. 71
Circle Time Literacy Time	large group	**Read Aloud** *Castles, Caves, and Honeycombs* /*Castillos, cuevas y panales* p. 66 **Learn About Letters and Sounds:** *Cc* and *Uu* p. 66	**Read Aloud** *Castles, Caves, and Honeycombs*/*Castillos, cuevas y panales* p. 72 **Learn About Letters and Sounds:** *Cc* and *Uu* p. 72
Math Time	large group	**Pattern Strips** p. 67	**Count and Move in Patterns** p. 73
Social and Emotional Development	large group	**Starts Play Activities** p. 67	**Starts Play Activities** p. 73
Content Connection	large group	**Science:** **Oral Language and Academic Vocabulary** p. 68 Talking About Animal Homes **Observe and Investigate** p. 68 Looking at Animals Outdoors	**Math:** **Dancing Patterns** p. 74 **Pattern Strips** p. 74
Center Time	small group	**Focus On:** Math and Science Center p. 69 Purposeful Play p. 69	**Focus On:** Library and Listening Center p. 75 Purposeful Play p. 75
Let's Say Good-Bye	large group	**Read Aloud** p. 69 **Writing** p. 69 **Home Connection** p. 69	**Read Aloud** p. 75 **Writing** p. 75 **Home Connection** p. 75

Focus Question
Where do animals live and what do they eat?
¿Dónde viven los animales y qué comen?

DAY 3

Opening Routines p. 76
Morning Read Aloud p. 76
Oral Language and Vocabulary
p. 76 Animal Homes
Phonological Awareness
p. 76 Recognize Rhyming Words

Focus On:
Pretend and Learn Center p. 77
Writer's Center p. 77

Read Aloud
Amazing Animals/
Animales asombrosos
p. 78
Learn About Letters and Sounds: *Cc* and *Uu*
p. 78

Stringing Beads p. 79

Starts Play Activities p. 79

Social Studies:
Oral Language and Academic Vocabulary
p. 80 Daily Schedule
Understand and Participate
p. 80 Daily Routine

Focus On:
ABC Center p. 81
Purposeful Play p. 81

Read Aloud p. 81
Writing p. 81
Home Connection p. 81

DAY 4

Opening Routines p. 82
Morning Read Aloud p. 82
Oral Language and Vocabulary
p. 82 Animal Sizes
Phonological Awareness
p. 82 Rhyming Box

Focus On:
Writer's Center p. 83
Creativity Center p. 83

Read Aloud "Animal Homes"/*"Hogares de animales"* p. 84
Learn About Letters and Sounds:
Cc and *Uu* p. 84

Computer Show p. 85

Starts Play Activities p. 85

Math:
Pattern Strips p. 86

Focus On:
Math and Science Center p. 87
Purposeful Play p. 87

Read Aloud p. 87
Writing p. 87
Home Connection p. 87

DAY 5

Opening Routines p. 88
Morning Read Aloud p. 88
Oral Language and Vocabulary
p. 88 Animal Characteristics
Phonological Awareness
p. 88 Recognize Rhyming Words

Focus On:
Construction Center p. 89
ABC Center p. 89

Read Aloud *Castles, Caves, and Honeycombs/Castillos, cuevas y panales*
p. 90
Learn About Letters and Sounds:
Review Letters *Cc, Uu* p. 90

Pattern Strips p. 91

Being Helpful p. 91

Music and Movement:
Oral Language and Academic Vocabulary
p. 92 Farm Animals
Explore and Express p. 92 Old MacDonald Had a Farm

Focus On:
Pretend and Learn Center p. 93
Purposeful Play p. 93

Read Aloud p. 93
Writing p. 93
Home Connection p. 93

Learning Centers

Math and Science Center

Record Observations
Children draw a picture of an animal they observed outdoors. They include the animal's habitat and what they saw the animal do. See p. 69.

Pattern Strips
Children copy pattern strip models using Pattern Blocks and extend the pattern. Then they make up their own patterns. See p. 87.

Sorting Animals
Children sort pictures of animals into two groups: pets and wild animals.

Search for Patterns
Children look through magazines to find examples of patterns, such as stripes on a shirt. They cut out the pictures and paste them on construction paper.

ABC Center

Fill the Up Cup
Children search through newspaper and magazine headlines for the letters Cc and Uu, cut them out, and place them inside a large cup called the "Up Cup." See p. 81.

Matching Letters
Children match uppercase and lowercase forms of Cc and Uu, describe how the letters are alike and different, and "paint" Cc and Uu with water on the chalkboard. See p. 89.

A Cave for Cc
Children draw a cave on a large piece of construction paper. Inside the cave, they write the letters Cc and draw pictures of objects whose names begin with /k/, such as cub, cap, and cow.

Creativity Center

Make Leaf Prints
Children collect leaves, spread finger paint on them, and press the leaves on paper to create leaf prints. See p. 65.

Big and Small
Children use big and small paintbrushes to paint pictures of big and small objects and then describe the objects. See p. 83.

Pet Portraits
Children paint a portrait of a pet they have or would like to have, and label it with a favorite pet's name.

What Pets Need
Children draw three or more things that pets need in order to live and write or dictate labels for each.

Library and Listening Center

Look at Animal Books
Children look through books about wild animals and pets and select one animal to tell a friend about. See p. 65.

Browsing Pattern Books
Children browse through books about patterns, describe the patterns they see, and tell what comes next in the patterns. See p. 75.

New Endings
Partners revisit one of the stories they heard this week and make up a new ending for it.

Construction Center

Building a Home
Children choose a stuffed animal in the classroom and use boxes, blocks, and other materials to build a home for it. See p. 71.

Animal Home Mural
Children paint a mural that includes a lake, a tree, and a farm. Then they construct animals and place them in the appropriate homes in the mural. See p. 89.

Animals Inside and Outside
Children build a house with a backyard from blocks and boxes. Then they make pets out of clay to live inside the house and wild animals to live outside in the backyard.

Writer's Center

Do They Rhyme?
Children select objects from a box until they find two objects whose names rhyme. Then they draw and label pictures of the two rhyming objects. See p. 71.

Mini Motor Match
Children match transportation-themed counters to pictures of objects whose names rhyme with them. Children draw and label one rhyming pair. See p. 77.

Flap Books
Children create rhyming Flap Books by folding a piece of paper in half and drawing a farm animal on the front cover. Inside the book, they draw a picture of an object whose name rhymes with the farm animal. See p. 140.

Hibernating Bears
Children draw a picture of a family of bears nestled in their cave for a long winter's sleep. They write or dictate a label for their drawing, such as *Goodnight bears!*

Pretend and Learn Center

Pretend Puppies
Children use the "Playful Puppies" Oral Language Development Card to role-play how the girl takes care of her puppies. Children take turns playing the girl and the puppies. See p. 77.

On a Farm
Children pretend to be farmers and show how they take care of their farm animals. See p. 93.

Yum Yum!
Children pretend to be a pet or a wild animal and describe what they like to eat.

Make Up a New Song
Children change the song "Mary Had a Little Lamb" to make up a song about themselves and a different animal that follows them to school.

Let's Start the Day

Focus Question

Where do animals live and what do they eat?
¿Dónde viven los animales y qué comen?

Opening Routines and Transition Tips
For **Opening Routines** and **Transition Tips** turn to pages 178–181 and visit DLMExpressOnline.com for more ideas.

Read **"The Baby Chicks"/"Los pollitos"** from the *Teacher's Treasure Book*, page 181, for your morning Read Aloud.

Learning Goals

Language and Communication
- Child demonstrates an understanding of oral language by responding appropriately.
- Child uses newly learned vocabulary daily in multiple contexts.

Emergent Literacy: Reading
- Child generates words that rhyme.

Vocabulary

calf	ternero	giraffe	jirafa
horns	cuernos	neck	cuello
tail	cola	tall	alto

Differentiated Instruction

✋ Extra Support
Phonological Awareness
If...children have difficulty recognizing words that rhyme, **then...**segment the words to emphasize the rhyme. Say: **Me and free *rhyme*. Listen. /m/ /eee/, me. /fr/ /eee/, free. Me and free end with /eee/.** *Las palabras* me *y* free *riman. Escuchen. /m/ /eee/, me. /fr/ /eee/, free. Me y free terminan con /eee/.* Repeat with *own/grown*.

⭐ Enrichment
Phonological Awareness
Challenge children to name additional words that rhyme with *me/free* and *own/grown*.

Accommodations for 3's
Phonological Awareness
If...children have difficulty recognizing words that rhyme, **then...**say nursery rhymes like "Jack and Jill" or "Twinkle, Twinkle, Little Star" and point out the rhyming words in each. Then leave off rhyming words for children to provide.

Language Time

large group — 15 minutes

👥 **Social and Emotional Development** Encourage children to try singing along with the song "Where Do Animals Live?"

Oral Language and Vocabulary

✓ **Can children tell facts about giraffes?**

What Animals Eat Talk about animals that eat plants. Ask: **Where do leaves grow?** *¿Dónde crecen las hojas?* Explain that some animals eat leaves. The leaves are high on a tree where these animals live. (point up high) The animal must be tall to reach the leaves. (Stand and reach up high.) **What tall animals do you know?** *¿Qué animales altos conocen?*

- Display *Oral Language Development Card 43*. Name the giraffe. Use the tips on the back.

Oral Language Development Card 43

Phonological Awareness

✓ **Can children identify words that rhyme?**

Recognize Rhyming Words Display *Rhymes and Chants Flip Chart,* page 22. Remind children that words that rhyme end with the same sounds. Sing "Where Do Animals Live?" to the tune of "My Bonnie Lies Over the Ocean." Say the rhyming pairs *me/tree* and *nest/rest*. Repeat the song, leaving out the last word in each stanza, having children complete the rhyme.

ELL Use the *Rhymes and Chants Flip Chart* to revisit each stanza. Sing the song and have children act out the last line in each stanza: point to themselves for *me*, look around for *where*, and put their head in their hands for *rest*.

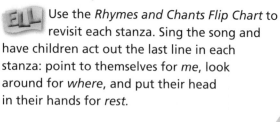

Rhymes and Chants Flip Chart, page 22

Center Time

► **Center Rotation** Center Time includes teacher-guided activities and independent activities. Refer to the **Learning Centers** on pages 62–63 for activities in additional centers.

small group 60–90 minutes

Library and Listening Center

 Listen for the use of new vocabulary words and other animal-related words.

Materials animal books

Look at Animal Books Have children look through books about wild and pet animals and choose one animal to tell a friend about.

- Have children show the animal picture to a friend and tell one thing about the animal.

- Ask: **Does this animal live in a house like you or is this animal free?** *¿Ese animal vive en una casa como la de ustedes o vive en libertad?*

Center Tip

If...children have difficulty telling something about an animal, **then...**ask detail questions such as, *What color is it? Does it have horns? a tail? Is it tall or small? ¿De qué color es el animal? ¿Tiene cuernos? ¿Cola? ¿Es alto o bajo?*

Creativity Center

 Monitor children's ability to arrange leaves creatively.

Materials finger paint, newspaper, white paper, leaves

Make Leaf Prints If possible, take children on a walk outside to collect fallen leaves. Point out how high on trees leaves grow. Otherwise, bring in a selection of real or artificial leaves. Encourage children to use leaves with prominent vein patterns.

- Have children spread a thin layer of finger paint on the veined side of their leaves.

- Have them place the leaves, paint-side down, on white paper, set newspaper on top, and press down on the newspaper.

- With clean hands, have them peel off the newspaper and leaves. Let children compare their leaf prints.

Center Tip

If...children have difficulty identifying the veins on the leaves, **then...**have them close their eyes and run their fingers on each side of the leaf to find the bumpy side.

Learning Goals

Language and Communication
- Child follows two- and three-step oral directions.
- Child uses words to identify and understand categories.

Emergent Literacy: Reading
- Child independently engages in pre-reading behaviors and activities (such as, pretending to read, turning one page at a time).

Fine Arts
- Child uses and experiments with a variety of art materials and tools in various art activities.
- Child shares opinions about artwork and artistic experiences.

Differentiated Instruction

✋ Extra Support
Library and Listening Center
If...children have trouble identifying an animal's home, **then...**point out background clues in the picture and talk about whether the animal is indoors or outside.

⭐ Enrichment
Creativity Center
Challenge children to compare and contrast two leaf prints by asking, **How are the leaves the same?** *¿En qué se parecen las hojas?* and **How are the two leaves different?** *¿En qué se diferencian las dos hojas?*

Accommodations for 3's
Creativity Center
If...three-year-olds have difficulty finger painting on the veins, **then...**hold their hands and guide them on the leaf.

Focus Question

Where do animals live and what do they eat? ¿Dónde viven los animales y qué comen?

Learning Goals

Language and Communication
• Child experiments with and produces a growing number of sounds in English words. (ELL)

Emergent Literacy: Reading
• Child names most upper- and lowercase letters of the alphabet.
• Child identifies the letter that stands for a given sound.
• Child asks and answers questions about books read aloud (such as, "Who?" "What?" "Where?").

Vocabulary

den	guarida	home	casa
nest	nido	place	lugar
rest	descanso		

Differentiated Instruction

Extra Support
Read Aloud
If...children have difficulty with vocabulary in the book, **then...**display clear photographs of animal homes from the Internet or nonfiction resources.

Enrichment
Read Aloud
Have children chime in on the rhyming words.

Special Needs
Cognitive Challenges
Learning the difference between real and make-believe is an important life-long skill for children with cognitive challenges. Play a game with the child where you make a sentence, and he or she says "yes" or holds up a "yes" card if the statement is real and a "no" if it is not.

Literacy Time

📖 Read Aloud

✓ Can children tell whether the animals in a book are real or make-believe?

Build Background Tell children you will be reading a book about different kinds of homes for different kinds of animals.

● Ask: *What kinds of homes do people live in? What animal homes can you name?* *¿En qué tipo de casas viven las personas? ¿Qué casas para animales pueden nombrar?*

Listen for Enjoyment Display *Castles, Caves, and Honeycombs* and read the title. Conduct a picture walk.

● Point to each animal, name it, and have children repeat the name.

● Read the story aloud. Emphasize the rhyming words.

Respond to the Story Discuss the book. Help children recall the animals and some of their homes. Ask: *Do animals talk in real life? Do the animals in this story talk?* *¿Hablan los animales en la vida real? ¿Hablan los animales de este cuento?* Explain that this story is real. *Do the animals in "Three Little Pigs"* (or other familiar fantasy) *talk? ¿Hablan los animales de "Los tres chanchitos"* (o de cualquier otro cuento fantástico)? Have children use the Sequence Card set "Three Little Pigs" as you discuss the story. Explain that in a make-believe story, animals talk, wear clothes, and act like people.

Learn About Letters and Sounds

✓ Can children make *Cc* and *Uu* and recognize the letter sounds?

Learn About Letters Cc and Uu Review the /k/ sound for *Cc* and the /u/ sound for *Uu*. Point to the cover of *Castles, Caves, and Honeycombs*. Say: **Castle and cave both begin with the letter C. Trace C on your desk with your finger. Say the sound and the word: /k/, cave.** *Castle y cave comienzan con la letra C. Dibujen una C con el dedo en su escritorio. Digan el sonido y la palabra: /k/, cave.* Point to ABC Picture Card *Uu*. Say: **Umbrella *starts with the letter* Uu. Trace Uu on your desk. Say /u/, umbrella.** *Umbrella empieza con la letra Uu. Dibujen con el dedo Uu en su escritorio. Digan /u/, umbrella.*

● Have children make *C* and *U* with their left hand. Model making a *C* by curving your thumb and fingers of your left hand into a *C*. Have children copy you. Then have them move their hands so the curve makes a *U*. Discuss with children how the two letters are alike.

ELL Act out three or four words that begin with /u/, such as *under, up,* and *upside-down.* Say each word, stretching out the /u/ sound. Have children repeat the action and word. Use each word in a sentence and have children repeat the word making sure they can pronounce the /u/ sound.

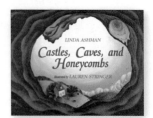

Castles, Caves, and Honeycombs
Castillos, cuevas y panales

Sequence Cards: "Three LIttle Pigs"

Uu
unicornio

ABC Picture Card

large group 15 minutes

Math Time

Observe and investigate

Can children recognize, duplicate, and extend repeating patterns?

Pattern Strips Sing with children the lyrics below to the tune of "Oh Dear, What Can the Matter Be?"

> **O dear, what can the pattern be?** Este patrón me desvive.
> ***(Repeat two more times.)***
> **Let's look at the pattern and see.** Pero yo soy detective.

- Display *Math and Science Flip Chart* page 40, "Patterns."
- Show children the first pattern (red rhombus/blue square and so on) and have them describe the pattern.
- Copy the pattern using Pattern Blocks. Have children chant the pattern as you point to each shape. Repeat using one or two more patterns.

Math and Science Flip Chart, page 40

Building Blocks

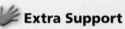

Online Math Activity

Introduce Pattern Planes 1: Duplicate AB, in which children duplicate a linear (in a line or row) AB pattern of flags based on outlines of each flag's shape, serving as a guide or model. Each child should complete Pattern Planes 1 this week.

Social and Emotional Development

Making Good Choices

Do children initiate play activities?

Starts Play Activities Discuss what children do when they want to play with others. Display the *Making Good Choices Flip Chart,* page 22. Point to the children on the playground.

- Ask: ***What do you think the children would like to do? What could the boy who is standing say to help things get started?*** *¿Qué creen que les gustaría hacer a los niños? ¿Qué podría decir el niño que está de pie para que comience el juego?*
- Then discuss what activities the children could play together.

ELL Point to and name the objects on the playground in the *Making Good Choices Flip Chart.* Have children repeat using the sentence frame ***This is a [tricycle].*** Reinforce the vocabulary by asking ***What is this?*** about the same equipment in your classroom and on your playground.

For additional suggestions on how to meet the needs of children at the Beginning, Intermediate, Advanced, and Advanced-High levels of English proficiency, see pages 184–187.

Making Good Choices Flip Chart, page 22

Learning Goals

Social and Emotional Development
- Child initiates interactions with others in work and play situations.

Mathematics
- Child identifies, duplicates, and creates simple patterns.

Vocabulary

pattern patrón

Differentiated Instruction

Extra Support

Observe and Investigate

If...children need help during Pattern Strips, **then...**help them start and verbalize an AB pattern, such as red/blue, red/blue, red/blue, and encourage them to extend the pattern. Review how a pattern's core unit repeats.

Enrichment

Observe and Investigate

Have children make up their own patterns, or provide more difficult pattern strips.

Accommodations for 3's

Observe and Investigate

If...children struggle making patterns, **then...** have them use string (or ribbon) and beads of two different colors to string the AB pattern.

Learning Goals

Language and Communication
• Child names and describes actual or pictured people, places, things, actions, attributes, and events.

Science
• Child identifies organisms and describes their characteristics.

• Child observes, understands, and discusses the relationship of plants and animals to their environments.

• Child follows basic health and safety rules.

Vocabulary

bird	pájaro	butterfly	mariposa
different	diferente	food	comida
home	casa	same	igual

Differentiated Instruction

 Extra Support
Oral Language and Academic Vocabulary
If...children have trouble distinguishing a bird from a butterfly, **then...**discuss the characteristics of each (bird has feathers and beak; butterfly has antenna and delicate wings) showing more photos to illustrate.

 Enrichment
Oral Language and Academic Vocabulary
Discuss with students where birds go to find the foods they like, such as worms, seeds, insects, fish, and fruit. Have children draw pictures of birds finding food.

Science Time

  large group · 20 minutes

Personal Safety Skills Review and model any outdoor safety procedures before taking children outside for the science activity.

Oral Language and Academic Vocabulary

 Can children describe where animals live and what they eat?

Talking About Animal Homes Point to the mother bird on the *Math and Science Flip Chart,* page 39. Ask: *What animal do you see? What is it doing?* *¿Qué animal ven? ¿Qué está haciendo?*

● Explain that the bird's home is called a nest and have them describe the materials used to build the nest. Ask children to name some things that birds eat. Ask: *Where do you think the mother bird found the food to feed her babies?* *¿Dónde piensan que la mamá pájaro encontró la comida para alimentar a sus polluelos?* Discuss other details they notice in the picture.

Display Oral Language Development Card 44. Name the insect. Have children repeat it. Say: *Butterflies don't make their own homes. They sleep under leaves, in grass, or between rocks. During the day, they fly around to find food. They get their food from flowers. Las mariposas no hacen sus propias casas. Duermen debajo de las hojas, en el pasto o entre las rocas. Durante el día, vuelan y buscan comida, que obtienen de las flores.* Use the suggestions on the back of the card to talk more about butterflies.

Ask: *How are a bird and a butterfly the same? How are they different? ¿En qué se parecen un pájaro y una mariposa? ¿En qué se diferencian?*

ELL Begin by asking children yes/no questions about birds and butterflies. *Can a butterfly fly? Can a bird fly? Does a bird have feathers? Does a butterfly have feathers?* To help children compare and contrast, practice talking about how two things are "alike" and "different." Gather two objects and model: *How are the golf ball and tennis ball alike? They are both round; they both bounce; they both are used in sports. How are they different? One is big and feels fuzzy; one is small and feels bumpy.*

Observe and Investigate

 Can children observe and discuss animals in their natural habitat?

Looking at Animals Outdoors Take children outside to use Jumbo Hand Lenses to observe animals in their habitats (birds or squirrels in trees, spiders on webs, or insects on plants or the ground). Instruct children to be very quiet and not disturb the animals.

● Make comments as you observe, such as: *Those ants are going in and out of their home. It is called an anthill. Esas hormigas entran y salen de su casa. Su casa se llama hormiguero.*

● Ask questions to stimulate discussion and curiosity, such as: *How many ants might live in this anthill? How do you think they get food home? ¿Cuántas hormigas creen que viven en este hormiguero? ¿Cómo llevan la comida a su casa?*

Math and Science Flip Chart, page 39

Oral Language Development Card 44

Center Time

> **Center Rotation** Center Time includes teacher-guided activities and independent activities. Refer to the **Learning Centers** on pages 62–63 for activities in additional centers.

small group · 30 minutes

Refer to the **Learning Centers** on pages 62–63 for activities in additional centers.

Math and Science Center

✓ **Encourage children to describe their picture to a friend.**

Materials drawing paper, crayons, pencils

Record Observations After discussing what children observed outdoors in the Science Time activity, have them draw a picture of one creature they observed.

- Instruct children to draw a picture of one of the animals they watched. Encourage them to include the place where they observed the animal and anything they saw the animal do. Add dictated writing to each child's drawing.

- Compile their pictures into a class book. Display it in the Library Center for children to look at independently.

Center Tip

If...children have trouble remembering what they observed, **then...**provide additional pictures or illustrations displayed in the center.

Purposeful Play

✓ **Observe children appropriately handling classroom materials.**

Children choose an open center for free playtime. Encourage cooperation skills by suggesting they play together pretending to be birds, butterflies, or the animal they observed.

Let's Say Good-Bye

large group · 15 minutes

Read Aloud Revisit "The Baby Chicks"/"Los pollitos" for your afternoon Read Aloud. Discuss with children whether the story is real or make-believe.

Home Connection Refer to the Home Connections activities listed in the Resources and Materials chart on page 59. Remind children to describe to their family any birds, butterflies, or other animals they see outside. Sing the "Good-Bye Song" as children prepare to leave.

✓ Learning Goals

Social and Emotional Development
- Child initiates play scenarios with peers that share a common plan and goal.

Emergent LIteracy: Writing
- Child experiments with and uses some writing conventions when writing or dictating.

Science
- Child observes, understands, and discusses the relationship of plants and animals to their environments.

Fine Arts
- Child expresses emotions or ideas through art.

Writing

Have each child dictate a sentence or story to go with the picture drawn in the Science Center. As you print, point out concepts of print such as capitalization of first word in sentence, spacing between words, and ending punctuation. As you read it back, track the print.

DAY 2

Focus Question

Where do animals live and what do they eat?

¿Dónde viven los animales y qué comen?

Learning Goals

Emergent Literacy: Reading
• Child names and describes actual or pictured people, places, things, actions, attributes, and events.

Technology Applications
• Child opens and correctly uses age-appropriate software programs.

• Child names and uses various computer parts (such as mouse, keyboard, CD-ROM, microphone, touch screen).

Vocabulary

back	lomo	house	casa
shell	caparazón	water	agua

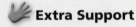

Differentiated Instruction

✋ Extra Support

Oral Language and Vocabulary
If...children have difficulty finding animal homes in the art, **then...**point out details in the art, such as: *See the beaver in the blue area. It is swimming. What is blue that you swim in? Yes, beavers live by water. Observen al castor que está en la parte azul de la imagen. Está nadando. ¿Qué es de color azul y se nada en ella? Si, los castores viven junto al agua.*

⭐ Enrichment

Phonological Awareness
When a puppet says two rhyming words, have children name other rhyming words. Accept both real and nonsense words as responses.

Let's Start the Day

Opening Routines and Transition Tips
For **Opening Routines** and **Transition Tips** turn to pages 178–181 and visit **DLMExpressOnline.com** for more ideas.

📖 Read **"The Squirrel"**/**"La ardilla"** from the *Teacher's Treasure Book*, page 102, for your morning Read Aloud.

Language Time

 large group 15 minutes

👪 Social and Emotional Development Encourage children to tell which is their favorite picture in *Castles, Caves, and Honeycombs.* Have them tell which animal that they talked about in today's activity is their favorite. Make a simple graph to show children's preferences.

Oral Language and Vocabulary

✓ **Can children identify places where animals live?**

Animal Homes Display *Castles, Caves, and Honeycombs.* Slowly turn the pages and ask: **Which animals have homes in or by water?** *¿Qué animales tienen su casa en el agua o cerca del agua?* Point out that the beaver, crab, seagull, and starfish live in or by water.

● Turn to the last page in the book. Have children tell who lives in a house.

● Show and read the pages for the turtle and the snail. Ask children to tell about these animals' homes. Explain that the animals carry their homes on their back. Their home is called a *shell.*

ELL Set up the flash card activity in the *Photo Library CD-ROM.* Choose *ant, beaver , cat, crab, dog, turtle,* and *starfish.* Instruct children how to click the *yes* and *no* buttons to answer the questions. Let children practice the animal names independently.

For additional suggestions on how to meet the needs of children at the Beginning, Intermediate, Advanced, and Advanced-High levels of English proficiency, see pages 184–187.

Phonological Awareness

✓ **Can children identify words that rhyme?**

Recognize Rhyming Words Display the Dog Puppets. Tell children that each puppet will say a word. If the words rhyme, children should give a thumbs up. If the words do not rhyme, they should give a thumbs down. Remind children that words rhyme when they have the same ending sounds, like *me* and *free.* Have the puppets say these and other word pairs: *cat/hat, crab/catch, hog/dog, ant/apple, shell/bell, house/mouse.* Have children echo the rhyming pairs.

Castles, Caves, and Honeycombs
Castillos, cuevas y panales

Center Time

▶ **Center Rotation** Center Time includes teacher-guided activities and independent activities. Refer to the **Learning Centers** on pages 62–63 for activities in additional centers.

 small group 60–90 minutes

Construction Center

Center Tip

✓ **Listen for the use of oral vocabulary from previous activities.**

Materials stuffed animals, boxes, blocks, construction materials

Building a Home Children identify stuffed animals in the classroom and the kinds of homes the animals would live in.

- Instruct small groups to work together to build a home for one stuffed animal. Ask: *What does the animal need? How will you work together to build it? ¿Qué necesita el animal? ¿Cómo van a trabajar juntos para construirlo?*

- Have children describe their finished home and how the animal will live there.

If…children have difficulty staying with their own group, **then**…provide designated working space for each group with tape on the floor.

Writer's Center

Center Tip

✓ **Have children find objects whose names rhyme.**

Materials small toys or objects whose names rhyme, such as *duck/truck, shell/bell, cat/hat, mouse/house, jar/car*; box to hold objects; drawing paper; crayons

Do They Rhyme? Tell children that they will name objects until they find two whose names rhyme.

- Instruct the child to reach into the box, pull out two objects, and name them. If the names do not rhyme, child puts them back and pulls out two more. Tell them to continue pulling out objects until two have rhyming names.

- Then have the child draw a picture of the rhyming objects. Help children label the pictures. Prompt them to write the letters they know, such as *c* in *car*.

If…children have difficulty naming each object, **then**… name the object and have the child repeat after you *This is a _____*

Learning Goals

Language and Communication
- Child uses oral language for a variety of purposes.

Emergent Literacy: Reading
- Child generates words that rhyme.

Emergent Literacy: Writing
- Child uses scribbles, shapes, pictures, symbols, and letters to represent language.

Differentiated Instruction

✋ **Extra Support**
Writer's Center
If…children have difficulty finding a rhyming pair, **then**…have them segment the two words to see if they end with the same sound. Model: */j/ /ar/, /d/ /uk/. No, they do not end with the same sound. /j/ /ar/, /k/ /ar/. Yes, they end with the same sound. Jar and car rhyme.* */j/ /ar/, /d/ /uk/. No, no terminan con el mismo sonido. /j/ /ar/, /k/ /ar/. Sí, terminan con el mismo sonido. Jar y car riman.*

⭐ **Enrichment**
Construction Center
Challenge children to tell where the animal's home would be located (near water, in a tree, etc.) and where the animal would go to find food.

Accommodations for 3's
Writer's Center
If…children have difficulty finding rhyming names, **then**…put only four objects in the box and have child pull one object, name it, and then pull each object to see which one rhymes with the first one.

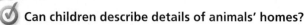

Circle Time

 Learning Goals

Language and Communication
• Child uses complex sentences that include many details, tell about one topic, and communicate meaning clearly.

Emergent Literacy: Reading
• Child names most upper- and lowercase letters of the alphabet.
• Child identifies the letter that stands for a given sound.

Science
• Child observes, understands, and discusses the relationship of plants and animals to their environment.

Vocabulary

beaver   castor   eagle   águila

Differentiated Instruction

 Extra Support

Learn About Letters and Sounds
If...children have difficulty finding a letter card, **then...**remove three cards so they choose from three. As they get to know letters, add more back in.

 Enrichment

Learn About Letters and Sounds
When children find a card, have them say the letter, name the picture, and say an additional word that begins with the same sound.

Literacy Time

large group   15 minutes

📖 Read Aloud

☑ **Can children describe details of animals' homes?**

Build Background Tell children that you will reread the story about all kinds of animal homes.

● Ask: *What do you remember about this story? ¿Qué recuerdan de este cuento?*

Listen for Understanding Display *Castles, Caves, and Honeycombs*, and point out the homes on the cover.

● Turn to the title page and track the print as you reread the title. Read the author's name and explain that she wrote the words in the story. Explain that the illustrator drew the pictures.

● Tell children to think about a question as you read: *How did the animal make its home? ¿Cómo hizo el animal su casa?*

Respond to the Story Have children use complete sentences to tell what animal homes are made of. Ask: *How did the beavers make their home? How did the eagle make its home? Are these homes made from the same thing? ¿Cómo hicieron los castores su casa? ¿Cómo hizo el águila su casa? ¿Estas casas están hechas del mismo material?*

TIP Build on the concept of animal homes by using the Sequence Card set "Building a Home."

Learn About Letters and Sounds

☑ **Can children identify *Cc* and *Uu*?**

Learn About Letters *Cc* and *Uu* Mix up the ABC Picture Cards for *B, I, N, K, C,* and *U* and spread them letter-side up in the center of a group of children.

● Call on a child to find the card for *Cc*. When the card is found, have the child say the letter, say its sound, and name the picture. All of the children repeat.

● Put the cards back on the floor and mix them up again. Call on a child to find the card for *Uu* and repeat the game.

● Continue until each child has found both *Cc* and *Uu*.

● Have children find and name the appropriate letter for the beginning sound in *cake, up, us,* and *cat*. Be sure to stretch out each word to make it easier for children to distinguish the sounds.

ELL Some English language learners may substitute /g/ for /k/. Provide fun alliterative sentences for children to practice the /k/ sound such as, *Calico Cat and Carmen Cow eat crunchy carrots.*

Castles, Caves, and Honeycombs
Castillos, cuevas y panales

ABC Picture Cards

large group 15 minutes

Math Time

Observe and Investigate

☑ **Can children count and move in a pattern?**

- Count aloud with children to 20 (or more as appropriate) in patterns of 4, such as 1 *(clap)* 2 *(clap)*, 3 *(clap)*, 4 *(hop)*, 5 *(clap)* 6 *(clap)*, 7 *(clap)*, 8 *(hop)*, and so on.

- Clap in patterns a certain amount of times. For example: clap, clap, pause, clap, long pause, clap, clap, pause, clap, long pause, and so on. Keep the pauses distinct. Ask children to repeat what you did and to identify the pattern (two claps then one or AAB).

- Increase the number of claps, and do rhythmic patterns, such as two medium-paced claps, a pause, three fast claps, and so on.

✗✗✗ Social and Emotional Development

Making Good Choices

☑ **Do children recognize how to initiate play?**

Starts Play Activities Revisit the *Making Good Choices Flip Chart,* page 22, "How Can I Get Others to Play with Me?"

- Display the Dog Puppet. Say: *Tell the puppet about this boy and what he is going to say to get the children to play.* *Hablen con el títere sobre este niño y lo que va a decir para que los demás niños jueguen con él.*

- Provide each child a turn to tell the puppet what the boy might say.

 Provide sentence frames to help during the conversation with the dog puppet. Use these and others: *Would you like to _____ with me? We can _____.* Model the use of each frame. Have children repeat, then apply using their own words. Some children may feel more comfortable just repeating the completed frame you provided.

For additional suggestions on how to meet the needs of children at the Beginning, Intermediate, Advanced, and Advanced-High levels of English proficiency, see pages 184–187.

Building Blocks

Online Math Activity

Introduce Marching Patterns 1: Extend AB, in which children extend a linear (in a line or row) AB pattern by one full repetition of an entire core unit of marching band members. Each child should complete Marching Patterns 1 this week.

large group 15 minutes

Making Good Choices Flip Chart, page 22

 Learning Goals

Social and Emotional Development
- Child initiates interactions with others in work and play situations.

Language and Communication
- Child uses individual words and short phrases to communicate. (ELL)

Mathematics
- Child identifies, duplicates, and creates simple patterns.

Vocabulary

clap   palmada   patterns   patrones

Differentiated Instruction

✋ **Extra Support**

Observe and Investigate

If...children have trouble following the pattern, **then...**simplify it to an AB pattern such as 1 (clap), 2 (hop), 3 (clap), 4 (hop). As children feel more comfortable, add on to the pattern.

⭐ **Enrichment**

Observe and Investigate

Encourage children to try more advanced patterning such as AAB, ABC, and so on.

💜 **Special Needs**

Hearing Impairment

Making whole sentences is very difficult for a child with a hearing loss. Encourage him or her to make a sentence. Write it down correctly. Then ask the child to repeat each word as you point to it.

Focus Question
Where do animals live and what do they eat?
¿Dónde viven los animales y qué comen?

Learning Goals

Language and Communication
• Child exhibits an understanding of instructional terms used in the classroom.

Mathematics
• Child identifies, duplicates, and creates simple patterns.

Fine Arts
• Child expresses thoughts, feelings, and energy through music and creative movement.

Physical Development
• Child engages in a sequence of movements to perform a task.

Vocabulary

color	color	pattern	patrón
repeat	repetición	shape	figura

Differentiated Instruction

 Extra Support

Math Time

If...children need help duplicating visual patterns, **then...**place more than one copy of the pattern end-to-end to allow them to see more repeats of the pattern.

Enrichment

Math Time

Challenge children to create a pattern and help a classmate replicate it.

Math Time

large group   20 minutes

 Can children follow a pattern?

Dancing Patterns Tell children they will follow a pattern while dancing. The first AB pattern's core unit is toe/heel. When modeling a pattern, always repeat its core three times so, for example, show toe/heel, toe/heel, toe/heel to children.

● Play age-appropriate music you can dance to while doing the pattern, and, if applicable, sing together as you dance. Once finished, ask children to describe the pattern.

● More advanced patterns to try are clap/kick/kick (an ABB pattern) and swing left arm/swing right arm/twirl/twirl (an ABCC pattern). Be sure to clarify left and right, if needed, as you model such patterns.

● Ask children to mimic how animals might dance such as flapping wings, swinging a trunk, and so on. Play the classical music piece "The Carnival of the Animals" by Camille Saint-Saëns or other music about animals to stimulate responses.

 Can children identify and replicate a pattern?

Pattern Strips Have children describe and copy different patterns.

● Display *Math and Science Flip Chart* page 40, "Patterns." Cover the pattern strips so only the first one is showing.

● Have children describe the pattern.

● Have children use Pattern Blocks or shapes cut from construction paper to copy the pattern. Have children chant the pattern as you point to each shape.

● Continue with each pattern in the upper portion of the chart.

TIP First, refer to patterns just by color. Then refer to them by shape. Finally, use both color and shape.

ELL Explain to Spanish-speaking children that some English words are like Spanish words they already know, such as *pattern* and *patrón* or *to repeat* and *repetir*.

Math and Science Flip Chart, page 40

Center Time

▶ **Center Rotation** Center Time includes teacher-guided activities and independent activities. Refer to the **Learning Centers** on pages 62–63 for activities in additional centers.

✓ Learning Goals

Social and Emotional Development
• Child uses classroom materials carefully.

Emergent Literacy: Writing
• Child participates in free drawing and writing activities to deliver information.

Mathematics
• Child identifies, duplicates, and creates simple patterns.

Library and Listening Center

Center Tip

✓ Observe children as they identify patterns in engaging books.

Materials books with patterns, such as *I See Patterns* by Linda Benton; *Lots and Lots of Zebra Stripes: Patterns in Nature* by Stephen Swinburne; *Busy Bugs: A Book About Patterns* by Jayne Harvey

Browsing Pattern Books Have children browse through the books to identify patterns.

- Say: *Look at the pictures. Turn the pages slowly. What patterns do you see?* *Vean las imágenes. Pasen las páginas lentamente. ¿Qué patrones pueden ver?*

- Prompt children to tell what comes next in a pattern.

If...children need help recognizing a pattern, **then**...point to each picture and have the child name it. Repeat what child says until child notices the repeating pattern.

✏ Writing

Recap the day. Have children name animal homes. Ask them to draw a picture showing an animal and its home and label it. Allow children to use scribbles or letters to convey ideas.

Purposeful Play

✓ Observe children taking care of classroom materials.

Children choose an open center for free playtime. Encourage children to make patterns using Farm Animal Counters or Vehicle Counters. Remind children to clean up and put away all materials at the end of free playtime.

Let's Say Good-Bye

 Read Aloud Revisit "The Squirrel"/"La ardilla" for your afternoon Read Aloud. Ask children to listen for rhyming words.

 Home Connection Refer to the Home Connections activities listed in the Resources and Materials chart on page 59. Remind children to show families how they can dance in a pattern. Sing the "Good-Bye Song" as children prepare to leave.

Let's Start the Day

Focus Question
Where do animals live and what do they eat?
¿Dónde viven los animales y qué comen?

Learning Goals

Social and Emotional Development
• Child follows simple classroom rules and routines.

Language and Communication
• Child uses newly learned vocabulary daily in multiple contexts.

Emergent Literacy: Reading
• Child generates words that rhyme.

Vocabulary

black	negro	girl	nina
puppy	cachorro	spots	manchas
white	blanco		

Differentiated Instruction

 Extra Support
Oral Language and Vocabulary
If...children have difficulty with vocabulary words that describe puppies, **then...**have children act like puppies and wag their tails, use their hands to make puppy ears, and move their bodies like puppies by crawling on the floor.

Enrichment
Oral Language and Vocabulary
Challenge children to share their experiences with puppies and dogs.

 Special Needs
Speech/Language Delays
If...children have difficulty singing the song, **then...**sing one line and have children sing it back. Point to pictures of animals named in the lyrics to help trigger the words.

▶ **Opening Routines and Transition Tips**
For **Opening Routines** and **Transition Tips** turn to pages 178–181 and visit DLMExpressOnline.com for more ideas.

Read **"Fish Games"/"Juego de peces"** from the *Teacher's Treasure Book*, page 275, for your morning Read Aloud.

Language Time

large group   15 minutes

Social and Emotional Development As children sit quietly during the animal homes discussion, use positive cues to remind children what to do with their bodies. Ask: *What do you do with your hands and your feet when listening? ¿Qué hacen con sus manos y sus pies cuando están escuchando algo?*

Oral Language and Vocabulary

☑ **Can children tell about puppies' homes?**

Animal Homes Review animal homes children read about earlier in the week. Ask whether puppies live in nests, caves, or water. Explain that puppies live in houses with people.

● Display *Oral Language Development Card 45*. Name and count the puppies. Then follow the suggestions on the back of the card.

Oral Language Development Card 45

Phonological Awareness

☑ **Can children identify words that rhyme?**

Recognize Rhyming Words Revisit *Rhymes and Chants Flip Chart*, page 22. Remind children that rhyming words end with the same sounds. Have children join in as you sing "Where Do Animals Live?" to the tune of "My Bonnie Lies Over the Ocean." Repeat the first stanza and ask: *What word rhymes with tree, jungle or me? ¿Qué palabra rima con tree: jungle o me?* Repeat for the last stanza having children identify the rhyming word for *nest*.

ELL Use the *Rhymes and Chants Flip Chart* to revisit the words *me, where,* and *rest.* Use actions and gestures to teach the words, such as pointing to yourself for *me*, looking around for *where*, and putting your head in your hands for *rest.* Have children repeat the word and make the motion after you.

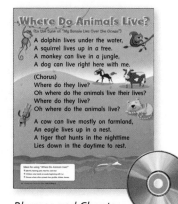
Rhymes and Chants Flip Chart, page 22

Center Time

▶ **Center Rotation** Center Time includes teacher-guided activities and independent activities. Refer to the **Learning Centers** on pages 62–63 for activities in additional centers.

 small group

 60–90 minutes

 Learning Goals

Emergent Literacy: Writing
• Child uses scribbles, shapes, pictures, symbols, and letters to represent language.

Science
• Child identifies organisms and describes their characteristics.

Pretend and Learn Center

| | **Center Tip** |

✓ **Track what children know about puppy and dog behavior.**

Materials *Oral Language Development Card 45*, bowls, small stuffed toys

Pretend Puppies Have children take the role of puppy and little girl.

• Display the "Playful Puppies" Oral Language Development Card and have one child volunteer to be the little girl and one or two to be puppies.

• Let children pretend the roles and make sure the girl pretends to feed the puppies and plays with them. Halfway through Center Time, have children switch roles.

• When play has ended, discuss with children what needs the puppies had that the girl had to provide, such as food and water.

Center Tip

If...children get too rambunctious when portraying puppies, **then...**return to the picture on the card and remind them that puppies are small and stay near the ground and that puppies like to take naps. Encourage them to use small movements and use small voices.

 Differentiated Instruction

👋 **Extra Support**
Pretend and Learn Center
If...children have difficulty knowing how the girl should act with the puppy, **then...**remind them what they learned about pet care last week. Use the flannel board story "My Very Own Pet" to aid in the discussion.

🌠 **Enrichment**
Pretend and Learn Center
Challenge children by having them pretend that dogs can talk. Have them act out a conversation between a puppy and the little girl.

Accommodations for 3's
Writer's Center
If...children have difficulty writing letters in the rhyming words, **then...**lightly write the letters for children to trace and then copy.

Writer's Center

✓ **Track children's ability to match rhyming words.**

Materials Vehicle Counters: plane, car, boat, truck; pictures of cane, star, coat, and duck; paper and crayons

Mini Motor Match Tell children that they will match Vehicle Counters to pictures of things whose names rhyme.

• Review the names of the vehicles and the pictured items.

• Instruct children to hold up one vehicle, say its name, and then find a picture whose name rhymes with it. When they find a match they should park the vehicle on top of the picture.

• After all vehicles are parked, have children pick one pair and draw it on the paper and label the pictures. Prompt them to write the letters they know, such as the letter *c* in *coat* or *car*.

Center Tip

If...children have difficulty finding the rhyming pair, **then...**state each vehicle or picture name. Hold up a vehicle, such as the plane. Ask: *Do plane and star rhyme? Do plane and cane rhyme?* ¿Riman plane y star? ¿Riman plane y cane?

Focus Question

Where do animals live and what do they eat?
¿Dónde viven los animales y qué comen?

Emergent Literacy: Reading
• Child names most upper- and lowercase letters of the alphabet.
• Child identifies the letter that stands for a given sound.
• Child asks and answers questions about books read aloud (such as, "Who?" "What?" "Where?").

Science
• Child observes, understands, and discusses the relationship of plants and animals to their environment

Vocabulary

farm	granja	forests	bosques
grass	pastizales	jungles	selvas
pastures	pasto	roam	vagar
wild	salvajes		

Differentiated Instruction

 Extra Support

Learn About Letters and Sounds
If...children have difficulty differentiating between the two sounds, **then...**use only the /k/ sound spelled *Cc*.

Enrichment
Read Aloud
Challenge children to draw a farm scene and include farm animals in the picture. Have children share and describe their pictures.

Literacy Time

 Read Aloud

 Can children recall important book details about animals and their homes?

Build Background Tell children that you will be reading a book about what animals are like and where they live.

● Ask: *What animal do you think is amazing? Where would you see this animal?*
¿Qué animal les parece asombroso? ¿Dónde podrían ver este animal?

Listen for Understanding Display *Concept Big Book 3: Amazing Animals* and read the title. Conduct a picture walk.

● Point to each animal, name it, and have children repeat the name.

● Read the story aloud.

Respond to the Story Help children recall the animals and some of their homes. Display page 10. Ask: *Where do sheep and cows live? Why do they live on farms?* *¿Dónde viven las ovejas y las vacas? ¿Por qué viven en granjas?* Display page 11. Ask: *Where do bears and elephants live? Why do they live in forests and jungles? ¿Dónde viven los osos y los elefantes? ¿Por qué viven en bosques y selvas?*

TIP Discuss with children what a farm is for and the kinds of animals that live on a farm.

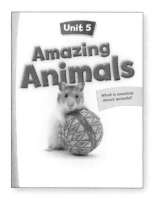

Amazing Animals
Animales asombrosos

Learn About Letters and Sounds

Can children identify the /k/ sound spelled *Cc* and the /u/ sound spelled *Uu*?

Learn About the Letters *Cc* and *Uu* Give each child Letter Tiles for *Cc* and *Uu*. Review the name of each letter and its sound.

● Display the *ABC Big Book* photo for *cat*. Say: *Listen to the word* cat. Does *cat* **begin with the sound /k/ or /u/?** *Escuchen la palabra* cat. *¿Empieza con /k/ o con /u/?* Have children hold up the letter that matches the beginning sound. Continue using the pictures for *crayons, under,* and *up.*

ELL Show the photos from the *ABC Big Book* for *cat, crayons, under, up.* Read each word as you point to the picture. Have children repeat the word. Then ask: *What is this?* Have children complete the sentence stem *This is _____* for each picture. For Spanish-speaking children, point out that the Spanish word *creyón* is a cognate *crayon.*

ABC Big Book

Math Time

Observe and Investigate

✓ **Can children recognize, duplicate, and extend repeating patterns?**

Stringing Beads Show a string with an AB pattern. Model creating the AB pattern using beads of two different colors, such as red and blue. After three complete repetitions of the pattern's core unit, for example, red/blue, red/blue, red/blue, ask children what comes next. Encourage them to answer red/blue, not just red. Use two fingers to simultaneously point to each red/blue core unit, and repeat the pattern as necessary. Chant the entire pattern with children.

- If possible, repeat with an ABB pattern such as red, blue, blue, red, blue, blue. If not, repeat the AB pattern but with differently colored or shaped beads. It is important children know there are more than just AB patterns.

Online Math Activity

Children can complete Pattern Planes 1 and Marching Patterns 1 during computer time or Center Time.

✖✖✖ Social and Emotional Development

Making Good Choices

✓ **Do children initiate play activities?**

Starts Play Activities Display *Making Good Choices Flip Chart* page 22, "How Can I Get Others to Play with Me?"

- Tell children to imagine the dog puppet walked out onto this playground. Have them describe what the dog puppet sees.

- Ask each child to role play being the dog puppet and how the puppet will get children to play. Ask: *What will you say to the children? What do you want them to do? ¿Qué les dirían a los niños? ¿Qué quieren que hagan?*

ELL Give children a chance to assume the role of the dog puppet. Prompt children by having children repeat the question *Will you play with me?*

For additional suggestions on how to meet the needs of children at the Beginning, Intermediate, Advanced, and Advanced-High levels of English proficiency, see pages 184–187.

Making Good Choices Flip Chart, page 22

✓ Learning Goals

Social and Emotional Development
- Child initiates interactions with others in work and play situations.

Mathematics
- Child identifies, duplicates, and creates simple patterns.

Vocabulary

next	siguiente
pattern	patrón
repeat	repetición

Differentiated Instruction

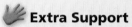

✋ Extra Support
Observe and Investigate
If...children struggle during Stringing Beads, **then...**help them verbalize the pattern, for example, red/blue, red/blue, red/blue, and ask what comes next. Emphasize that the core unit (red/blue) comes next.

⭐ Enrichment
Observe and Investigate
Have children make up their own patterns, or provide more difficult pattern strips.

Accommodations for 3's
Observe and Investigate
If...children struggle during Stringing Beads, **then...**make a construction paper pattern on the floor of red/blue, red/blue, red/blue. As children step from color to color, have them name them, chanting the pattern. Repeat, and then hold up red and blue construction paper and have the child place the next two on the ground in order.

Focus Question
Where do animals live and what do they eat?
¿Dónde viven los animales y qué comen?

Learning Goals

Language and Communication
• Child exhibits an understanding of instructional terms used in the classroom.

Mathematics
• Child measures passage of time using standard or non-standard tools.

Social Studies
• Child identifies common events and routines.

Vocabulary

next	siguiente	time	hora
today	hoy	tomorrow	mañana
yesterday	ayer		

Differentiated Instruction

 Extra Support

Oral Language and Academic Vocabulary
If...children have difficulty remembering the events of the day, **then...**pause periodically throughout the day and review what they have done so far. Build on this little by little, until you review a whole day's events.

Enrichment

Oral Language and Academic Vocabulary
Challenge children to create a picture journal. At the end of each day, allow time for children to draw a picture about their day at school. At the end of a week, review the pictures with children discussing the order of events.

Social Studies Time

 large group · 20 minutes

Language and Communication Skills At the beginning of the day, have a volunteer use the daily picture schedule to tell the class what they will do that day. The child begins by saying **Today, we will...** *Hoy, vamos a...*

Oral Language and Academic Vocabulary

✓ **Can children describe the events of the day?**

Daily Schedule Post a daily picture schedule. At the beginning of each day, point to the schedule and review what activities will be going on in the classroom.

● Throughout the day, refer back to the chart, asking a different child each time to check and give everyone a reminder of what they will do next.

● At the end of the day, ask children to describe their day. Encourage them to refer back to the daily picture schedule for clues.

Understand and Participate

✓ **Can children name daily events and routines?**

Daily Routines Display a daily picture schedule for a whole week.

● Point to a common event on the schedule. Explain what the picture represents (for example, snack time).

● Have children find and point to "snack time" on each day. Ask: **What did we do after recess today? What will we do after recess tomorrow? When do we have snack time?** *¿Qué hicimos después del receso hoy? ¿Qué haremos después del receso mañana? ¿Cuándo tenemos la hora del refrigerio?*

● Continue the discussion by pointing out other common events on the schedule and having children identify that the event is something they do at school every day.

TIP During a time of common routines, stop and ask children what they will do next before transitioning to the next activity. For example, when the children come in from recess, ask: **What are we going to do next?** *¿Qué vamos a hacer a continuación?*

ELL Begin to teach the concepts of *yesterday, today,* and *tomorrow,* by drawing pictures of the weather on a calendar. Each day, review yesterday's weather and record today's. Let children predict what tomorrow's will be. Continue each day so children begin to see a physical change with time.

Center Time

> **Center Rotation** Center Time includes teacher-guided activities and independent activities. Refer to the **Learning Centers** on pages 62–63 for activities in additional centers.

 small group 30 minutes

ABC Center

 Are children identifying *Cc* and *Uu*?

Materials large cup with an up arrow taped to front, large print from newspaper and magazines (i.e., headlines), scissors, marker

Fill the Up Cup Tell children that the large cup is called the "Up Cup." Point out the up arrow. Tell children that they will be filling the cup with letters that stand for /u/ as in *up* and /k/ as in *cup*.

● Have children work with a partner. Have them look through the headlines to find and circle a letter *Cc* for the first sound in *cup* and a *Uu* for the first sound in *up*.

● Then have children cut out the two letters and place them inside the Up Cup.

Center Tip

If...children have trouble cutting around just one letter, **then...**trace a cutting line for them to use. Or, if necessary, do the cutting for them.

Learning Goals

Social and Emotional Development
● Child initiates play scenarios with peers that share a common plan and goal.

Emergent Literacy: Reading
● Child names most upper- and lowercase letters of the alphabet.

● Child identifies the letter that stands for a given sound.

Writing

Recap the day. Have children name one activity they did today. Record their answers on chart paper. Share the pen by having children write letters and words they know. Ask children to pick one activity and draw a picture to show what happened.

Purposeful Play

Observe children as they transition from one activity to another.

Children choose an open center for free playtime. Encourage cooperation skills by suggesting they play and work together as people and animals on a farm.

Let's Say Good-Bye

 small group 15 minutes

 Read Aloud Revisit the story, "Fish Games"/"Juego de peces" for your afternoon Read Aloud. Ask children to listen for descriptions of where the fish live.

 Home Connection Refer to the Home Connections activities listed in the Resources and Materials chart on page 59. Remind children to tell families about their daily schedule. Sing the "Good-Bye Song" as children prepare to leave.

Let's Start the Day

Focus Question
Where do animals live and what do they eat?
¿Dónde viven los animales y qué comen?

Learning Goals

Social and Emotional Development
• Child accepts responsibility for and regulates own behavior.

Language and Communication
• Child exhibits an understanding of instructional terms used in the classroom.

Emergent Literacy: Reading
• Child generates words that rhyme.

Vocabulary

big   grande   small   pequeño

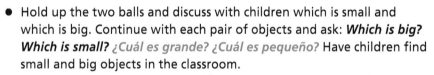
Differentiated Instruction

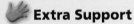 **Extra Support**
Oral Language and Vocabulary
If...children have difficulty distinguishing big from small, **then...**have the child hold each small object and say *This is small;* then hold the big object and say *This is big.*

 **Enrichment**
Oral Language and Vocabulary
Challenge children to sort the ABC Picture Cards for *ant, horse, iguana, turtle,* and *worm* into piles of small and big animals. (There will only be one big animal.)

▶ **Opening Routines and Transition Tips**
For **Opening Routines** and **Transition Tips** turn to pages 178–181 and visit DLMExpressOnline.com for more ideas.

📖 Read **"Going on a Bear Hunt"/**"Vamos a cazar un oso" from the *Teacher's Treasure Book*, page 201, for your morning Read Aloud.

Language Time

large group   15 minutes

 Social and Emotional Development Ask children to remember where their bodies are and not bump into other children.

Oral Language and Vocabulary

✓ **Can children compare size?**

Animal Sizes. Review with children some of the animals they have learned about this week. Explain that some animals are big and some animals are small.

● Display sets of small and big items such as a golf ball and a basketball, the Vehicle Counters truck and a big toy truck, and two pieces of precut construction paper–one small and one big. Ask: *What do you notice about these objects?* ¿Qué notan de estos objetos?

● Hold up the two balls and discuss with children which is small and which is big. Continue with each pair of objects and ask: *Which is big? Which is small?* ¿Cuál es grande? ¿Cuál es pequeño? Have children find small and big objects in the classroom.

● Have children make their bodies big and then small, open their mouths big and then small, and show how they would hold a small puppy and then a big dog.

Phonological Awareness

✓ **Can children identify words that rhyme?**

Rhyming Box Fill a box with five familiar classroom objects. Identify the objects before playing the game.

● Pass the box around. As each child gets the box say a word that rhymes with one of the objects. For example, say *shoe.* Ask the child to pull out an object whose name rhymes with that word (glue). Use both real and nonsense words as rhyming cues.

ELL Teach children familiar nursery rhymes such as, "Twinkle, Twinkle Little Star" using motions to illustrate words. Once children are familiar, leave off the last word in each rhyming couplet and have the child supply the word.

Center Time

▶ **Center Rotation** Center Time includes teacher-guided activities and independent activities. Refer to the **Learning Centers** on pages 62–63 for activities in additional centers.

 small group 60–90 minutes

on pages 62–63 for activities in additional centers.

Writer's Center

 Track children's ability to produce rhyming words.

Materials bag with Farm Animal Counters *pig, sheep, duck, cow*; drawing paper, crayons

Flap Books Have children pull one animal from the bag. Invite children to think of words that rhyme with the name of the animal.

- Have children make a flap book by folding the paper in half to form a book. Ask children to draw the farm animal on the front of the book.

- Then have them draw a picture whose name rhymes with the animal on the inside of the book. Ask children to label their pictures. Prompt them to write letters they know.

Center Tip

If...children have difficulty thinking of a rhyming word, **then...**state the animal name and make suggestions. Ask: *Do pig and boat rhyme? Do pig and dig rhyme? ¿Riman pig y boat? ¿Riman pig y dig?*

Creativity Center

 Track how well children can differentiate big and small.

Materials paint, easel, paintbrushes of different sizes, paper

Big and Small Explain to children that they will paint pictures of two things: one big and one small.

- Have children identify one big and one small paintbrush. Prompt them to paint a picture of a small thing with the small brush and a big thing with the big brush.

- Display children's paintings and have them tell the class about the two objects they painted.

Center Tip

If...children have difficulty painting two objects on one sheet of paper, **then...**divide paper in two with a line down the middle or let them paint on two separate sheets of paper. Remind them to paint one small and one big picture.

Learning Goals

Language and Communication
• Child exhibits an understanding of instructional terms used in the classroom.

Emergent Literacy: Reading
• Child identifies the letter that stands for a given sound.

Science
• Child observes, understands, and discusses the relationship of plants and animals to their environments.

Vocabulary

barn	establo	bees	abejas
beehive	colmena	fishbowl	pecera
hollow	hoyo	spider	araña
web	telaraña		

Differentiated Instruction

 Extra Support

Read Aloud

If...children have difficulty identifying flannel board animals, **then...**use photographs of animals in the *Photo Library CD-ROM* to help them recognize *bee, cow, robin (bird), trout (fish), raccoon, bear,* and *turtle.*

 Enrichment

Learn About Letters and Sounds
Have children use play dough to make an upper and lower case *Cc* and upper and lower case *Uu.*

Literacy Time

  large group 15 minutes

Read Aloud

☑ **Can children compare and contrast based on size?**

Build Background Tell children that you will be reading a story that tells more about animal homes.

• Ask: ***Do you think a small animal has a small home? Do you think a big animal has a big home? Do you think they always have homes that size?*** *¿Creen que un animal pequeño tiene una casa pequeña? ¿Creen que un animal grande tiene una casa grande? ¿Creen que siempre tienen casas de ese tamaño?*

Listen for Enjoyment Read aloud the story "Animal Homes"/"Hogares de animales" from the *Teacher's Treasure Book*, page 238. Display the flannel board patterns (page 353).

• Tell children to listen carefully for anything new they haven't learned before.

Respond to the Story One at a time, display an animal and its home on the flannel board. Have children identify each animal. Show a picture of a nest. Say: ***This is a nest. A cow lives here.*** *Este es un nido. Aquí vive una vaca.* When children say that's not true have them describe how they know that. Then ask children to identify the animal whose home this really is. Say: ***Yes. This is the bird's nest. The bird is small enough to fit into the nest.*** *Sí. Este es el nido de un pájaro. El pájaro es lo suficientemente pequeño como para entrar en un nido.*

TIP Set aside each animal and its home before introducing the next so children focus on comparing the size of the animal to its home, not to other animals.

ELL Focus on the concepts of *small* and *big*. Hold up two objects, one *small* and one *big*, such as the Vehicle Counters plane and a toy plane. Have the child echo you as you hold one and say ***This is small,*** then hold the other and say ***This is big.*** Continue with a variety of objects.

Learn About Letters and Sounds

☑ **Can children identify the /k/ sound spelled *Cc*?**

Learn About the Letters *Cc* and *Uu* Review the /k/ sound for *c* and the /u/ sound for *u*.

• Put the cow from the "Animal Homes" flannel board story on the flannel board. Tell children that the word *cow* begins with the /k/ sound and the letter *Cc*. Have them chant "/k/ /k/ /k/, cute cow" as they make a C by curving the thumb and fingers of their left hand.

• Put the bird in the tree from the "Animal Homes" flannel board story on the flannel board. Tell children that the word *up* begins with the /u/ sound and the letter *Uu*. Have them chant "/u/ /u/ /u/, up high in the tree" as they make a U with their thumb and fingers.

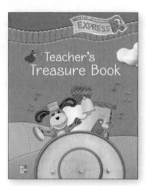

Teacher's Treasure Book, page 238

Math Time

 large group 15 minutes

Observe and Investigate

 Can children recognize, duplicate, and extend repeating patterns?

Computer Show Have the class gather around the computer at the Computer Center. Ask a volunteer for each of this week's computer patterning activities to complete a pattern, and then talk about it (what the pattern consists of, its core unit, what type pattern it is, and so on).

- Summarize by asking the rest of the class what they learned about patterns this week on the computer.

Building Blocks

Online Math Activity

Children can complete Pattern Planes 1 and Marching Patterns 1 during computer time or Center Time.

large group 15 minutes

✗✗✗ Social and Emotional Development

Making Good Choices

 Do children initiate play activities?

Starts Play Activities Display several popular classroom games and then act out a scenario with the Dog Puppets. One puppet is sitting near the games. The other puppet walks up. Explain to children that the second puppet would like to play but he doesn't know what to do.

- Ask: *What can the dog who wants to play say or do?* *¿Qué puede decir o hacer el perro que quiere jugar?*

- Discuss with children how to ask nicely and smile and be friendly. Remind children that if they want to be treated fairly, they should invite other children to join them. Let children take turns inviting a puppet to play.

- Play the song "I'm Going to Play, Too"/"Yo, tambien, jugare" from the Making Good Choices Audio CD. Ask children what the song says about polite ways to start to play.

ELL Some children may have difficulties following the conversation between the Dog Puppets. While role playing, act out the dog's words, pointing to the game the dog suggests. Repeat key words and phrases as you perform each action, such as: *Will you play with me? Let's play with blocks.*

For additional suggestions on how to meet the needs of children at the Beginning, Intermediate, Advanced, and Advanced-High levels of English proficiency, see pages 184–187.

 **Learning Goals**

Social and Emotional Development
- Child initiates interactions with others in work and play situations.

Mathematics
- Child identifies, duplicates, and creates simple patterns.

Technology Applications
- Child opens and correctly uses age-appropriate software programs.

Vocabulary

pattern patrón repeat repetición

Differentiated Instruction

✋ Extra Support

Observe and Investigate

If...children struggle with naming the core unit, **then...**help them verbalize the pattern, for example, pear, orange, orange, pear, orange, orange, pear, orange, orange (say the pattern at least three times), and ask what comes next. Emphasize that the core unit (pear/orange/orange) comes next.

⭐ Enrichment

Observe and Investigate

Show children something that does not have a pattern. Ask: *Is there a pattern? How do you know? ¿Hay un patrón? ¿Cómo lo saben?*

Accommodations for 3's

Observe and Investigate

If...children struggle with patterns on the computer, **then...**use the Pattern Blocks to make AB and ABB patterns for children to describe.

Learning Goals

Language and Communication
• Child uses newly learned vocabulary daily in multiple contexts.

Mathematics
• Child identifies, duplicates, and creates simple patterns.

Physical Development
• Child completes tasks that require eye-hand coordination and control.

Vocabulary

diagonal	diagonal
horizontal	horizontal
vertical	vertical

Differentiated Instruction

👋 Extra Support
Math Time

If...children need help during Pattern Strips, **then...**make copies of the patterns on strips of paper. Allow children to use the pattern strips to copy a strip's pattern, placing more than one copy of the same pattern strip end-to-end if necessary. Color in the pattern strips for those children who need extra support.

⭐ Enrichment
Math Time

Challenge children by providing a material other than stirrers and challenge them to use it to make the same pattern, thus translating the pattern from one material to another.

Math Time

large group — 20 minutes

✓ Can children understand and demonstrate positional words?

Introduce the terms *vertical, horizontal,* and *diagonal*. Have children stand up straight with their arms straight overhead and say *vertical*. Draw a line on the board and have children repeat "vertical." Repeat with *horizontal* (holding arms straight out to the sides) and *diagonal* (leaning to one side).

✓ Can children observe, copy, and create a pattern?

Pattern Strips Have children describe and copy different patterns.

● Display *Math and Science Flip Chart* page 40, "Patterns." Cover the pattern strips so only the first one in the lower section is showing (row 4).

● Have children describe the pattern.

● Have children use flat plastic stirrers to copy the pattern. Have children chant the pattern as you point to each line.

● Continue with the next pattern in the lower portion of chart.

● Then have children create their own pattern and have a partner copy it.

TIP Tell children that they can continue making patterns in the Math Center on their own or with a friend.

Math and Science Flip Chart, page 40

Center Time

▶ **Center Rotation** Center Time includes teacher-guided activities and independent activities. Refer to the **Learning Centers** on pages 62–63 for activities in additional centers.

Math and Science Center

 Track children's ability to copy and create patterns.

Materials Patterns drawn on strips of paper, Pattern Blocks, stirrers

Pattern Strips Tell children that they will continue to explore and create patterns on their own.

- Have children copy pattern strip models using Pattern Blocks or stirrers.

- Observe whether children truly understand the pattern (and its core unit) or are merely matching it shape by shape.

- Encourage children to copy and extend the pattern without having to place Pattern Blocks or stirrers directly on or below a pattern strip.

- Have children make up their own patterns.

Center Tip

If...children struggle with the patterns, **then...**encourage them to use only the AB patterns.

Purposeful Play

 Observe children taking care of classroom materials.

Children choose an open center for free playtime. Encourage cooperation skills by suggesting they work together to create patterns of classroom toys or using art supplies. Remind children to clean up and put away all materials at the end of free playtime.

Let's Say Good-Bye

 Read Aloud Revisit "Going on a Bear Hunt"/"Vamos a cazar un oso" for your afternoon Read Aloud. Ask children to listen for patterns in the chant.

 Home Connection Refer to the Home Connections activities listed in the Resources and Materials chart on page 59. Remind children to point out patterns they see at home (in their clothing or elsewhere). Sing the "Good-Bye Song" as children prepare to leave.

✓ Learning Goals

Social and Emotional Development
- Child uses classroom materials carefully.

Language and Communication
- Child names and describes actual or pictured people, places, things, actions, attributes, and events.

Mathematics
- Child identifies, duplicates, and creates simple patterns.

Writing

Recap the day. Have children tell about an animal they read about. Ask: *Is the animal big or small? What kind of home does it have?* ¿Este animal es grande o pequeño? ¿Qué tipo de casa tiene? Record their answers in a two-column chart labeled *big* and *small*. Read them back as you track the print, and emphasize the correspondence between speech and print.

DAY 5

Focus Question

Where do animals live and what do they eat?

¿Dónde viven los animales y qué comen?

Learning Goals

Language and Communication
• Child understands or knows the meaning of many thousands of words, many more than he or she uses.

Emergent Literacy: Reading
• Child generates words that rhyme.

Science
• Child identifies organisms and describes their characteristics.

Vocabulary

farm	granja	fly	volar
free	libre	house	casa

Differentiated Instruction

 Extra Support

Oral Language and Vocabulary
If...children have difficulty answering questions about song lyrics, **then...**read one stanza like a poem and ask questions on it before moving on to the next.

Enrichment

Oral Language and Vocabulary
Have children tell which animals in the song fly, have four feet, are pets, and are wild.

Let's Start the Day

▶ **Opening Routines and Transition Tips**
For **Opening Routines** and **Transition Tips** turn to pages 178–181 and visit **DLMExpressOnline.com** for more ideas.

📖 Read **"Crocodile"/"El cocodrilo"** from the *Teacher's Treasure Book*, page 99, for your morning Read Aloud.

Language Time

large group · 15 minutes

👫👫 **Social and Emotional Development** Encourage children to all participate in singing together as a group.

Oral Language and Vocabulary

✓ **Can children share what they know about animal homes?**

Animal Characteristics Talk about what children have learned this week about animal homes. Ask: *What can you tell me about animal homes? ¿Qué pueden decirme sobre las casas de los animales?*

● Display *Rhymes and Chants Flip Chart* page 22. Sing "Where Do Animals Live?" with children. Ask: *Which animal in the song is a pet and lives in a house? Which animal has a nest for a home? Which animal lives on a farm? Which animals are wild and live free? Which animal in the song do you think is most amazing? Why? ¿Qué animal de la canción es una mascota y vive en una casa? ¿Qué animal tiene un nido como casa? ¿Qué animal vive en una granja? ¿Qué animales son salvajes y viven libres? ¿Qué animal de la canción creen que es el más asombroso? ¿Por qué?*

ELL Using the illustration on the *Rhymes and Chants Flip Chart*, point to an animal and have the child name it by using the sentence stem *This is a/an _____.* When the child correctly names an animal that appears in the song, sing the line from the song that mentions it and have the child sing it back.

For additional suggestions on how to meet the needs of children at the Beginning, Intermediate, Advanced, and Advanced-High levels of English proficiency, see pages 184–187.

Phonological Awareness

✓ **Can children identify words that rhyme?**

Recognize Rhyming Words Using *Rhymes and Chants Flip Chart* page 22, sing "Where Do Animals Live?" once more with children. Remind children that rhyming words end with the same sounds. Read the words of the first stanza Ask: *Which word in the song rhymes with* **me**? *¿Qué palabra de la canción rima con* me? Read the words of the second stanza. Ask: *Which word in the song rhymes with* **rest**? *¿Qué palabra de la canción rima con* rest?

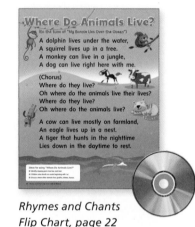

Rhymes and Chants Flip Chart, page 22

Center Time

▶ **Center Rotation** Center Time includes teacher-guided activities and independent activities. Refer to the **Learning Centers** on pages 62–63 for activities in additional centers.

Construction Center

Center Tip

☑ **Monitor children as they categorize animals by their homes.**

Materials butcher paper, paint, crayons, markers, scissors, glue, various art materials such as paper plates, small boxes, construction paper, yarn, fabric scraps

Animal Home Mural Attach sheets of butcher paper to a wall. Together with children, paint a background scene of a lake, a large tree, and farmland. Tell children that they are going to construct animals and place them on the wall in their homes. Assign animals discussed this week to pairs of children.

- Have children work with a partner. Ask: **What animal will you build? How are you going to make it?** *¿Qué animal van a hacer? ¿Cómo van a hacerlo?*

- When the mural is complete, discuss which animals live in water, in a tree, or on a farm.

If...children need help sharing the materials and working together, **then...**suggest roles for each child.

ABC Center

Center Tip

☑ **Track children's ability to match upper and lower case letters and write C and U.**

Materials letter cards, letter tiles, or magnetic letters; chalkboard, paintbrush, water

Matching Letters Explain to children that they will match the upper and lower case forms of this week's letters. Reinforce each letter's sound as children work.

- As children match the letterforms, ask: **How is the uppercase C like the lowercase c? How is it different? How is the uppercase U like the lowercase u? How is it different?** *¿En qué se parecen la C mayúscula y la c minúscula? ¿En qué se diferencian? ¿En qué se parecen la U mayúscula y la u minúscula? ¿En qué se diferencian?*

- Have children practice making C and U by painting with water on the chalkboard.

If...children have making C and U independently, **then...**have them trace the letters with their finger. Provide letters cut from sandpaper for a tactile experience.

Learning Goals

Emergent Literacy: Reading
- Child names most upper- and lowercase letters of the alphabet.

Science
- Child observes, understands, and discusses the relationship of plants and animals to their environments.

Fine Arts
- Child expresses emotions or ideas through art.

Differentiated Instruction

 Extra Support

Construction Center

If...children have difficulty constructing an animal, **then...**help them focus on the animal's key characteristics, such as a sheep's fur or a fish's tail.

Enrichment

Construction Center

Challenge children to make a home for their animal and add it to the mural such as a nest in the tree along with their bird.

Accommodations to 3's

Writer's Center

If...children have difficulty building an animal, **then...**have them draw the animal, cut it out, and glue one detail onto it.

Focus Question

Where do animals live and what do they eat?

¿Dónde viven los animales y qué comen?

 Learning Goals

Emergent Literacy: Reading

• Child names most upper- and lowercase letters of the alphabet.

• Child identifies the letter that stands for a given sound.

• Child asks and answers questions about books read aloud (such as, "Who?" "What?" "Where?").

Science

• Child identifies organisms and describes their characteristics.

Vocabulary

amazing	asombroso	best	mejor
home	casa		

Differentiated Instruction

 Extra Support

Learn About Letters and Sounds

If...children have difficulty differentiating letters *C* and *U*, **then...**provide multi-sensory experiences with the letters including writing them in sand, painting them with a large paintbrush, forming them with their bodies on the floor, and using flashcards.

 Enrichment

Learn About Letters and Sounds

Display a letter-card set of all the letters covered so far this year. Challenge children to name as many as they can.

Literacy Time

large group   15 minutes

📖 Read Aloud

✓ **Can children tell the difference between real and make-believe animals in books?**

Build Background Tell children that you will be rereading *Castles, Caves, and Honeycombs* about animal homes.

• Ask: *What do you remember about the animal homes in this story?* *¿Qué recuerdan sobre las casas de animales de este libro?*

Listen for Understanding Display the Big Book *Castles, Caves, and Honeycombs*.

• Reread the first four pages. Ask: *Is this story about real animals or make-believe animals?* *¿Esta lectura es sobre animales reales o de fantasía?*

Respond and Connect Have children connect what they learned about animals and their homes to why animals are amazing. Ask: *What animal's home do you like the best? What is its home like? Would you say that home is amazing or just okay?* *¿Qué casa de animal es la que les gusta más? ¿Cómo es esa casa? ¿Dirían que esa casa es asombrosa o es normal?*

TIP If children think the story is about make-believe animals, display a familiar book about fictional animals and help children contrast the illustrations with those in *Castles, Caves, and Honeycombs.*

ELL Provide pictures of cartoon animals such as a duck, a mouse, and a rabbit. Display the pictures next to the *ABC Big Book* photos of the real animals. Point to one and say: *This (duck) is make-believe.* Point to the other and say: *This (duck) is real.* Have children point and repeat the sentences.

Learn About Letters and Sounds

✓ **Can children identify letters and sounds?**

Review Letters *Cc, Uu* Display ABC Picture Card *Cc.* Have children trace a *C* in the air. Then have children hold their arms in a *C* shape.

• Say: *Cake, /k/, /k/, /k/ ake. Cake begins with* **C!** *¡Cake, /k/, /k/, /k/ ake. Cake comienza con C!* Have children echo the chant, still making a *C* with their arms. Repeat the chant using *cut, cat, cone, cook,* and *cave.*

• Display ABC Picture Card *Uu.* Point out the umbrella. Have children trace a *U* in the air. Then have children hold their arms in a *U* shape.

• Say: *Umbrella, /u/, /u/, /u/ mbrella. Umbrella begins with* **U!** *¡Umbrella, /u/, /u/, /u/ mbrella. Umbrella comienza con U!* Have children echo the chant, making a *U* with their arms. Repeat the chant using *up, under,* and *upside-down.*

Castles, Caves, and Honeycombs

Castillos, cuevas y panales

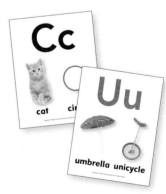

ABC Picture Cards

Building Blocks

Online Math Activity

Children can complete Pattern Planes 1 and Marching Patterns 1 during computer time or Center Time.

Math Time

Observe and Investigate

 Can children form and describe a pattern?

Pattern Strips Children work in pairs or individually to copy pattern models using Pattern Blocks.

- Observe whether children truly understand the pattern (and its core unit) or are merely matching it shape by shape. Encourage them to copy and extend the pattern without having to place Pattern Blocks directly on or below a pattern strip.

- Have children describe the pattern. Use fingers to simultaneously point to each element of the core unit, such as pointing with three fingers to ABC, and then moving the same fingers to the next ABC, and so on. During discussion, put the word *and* between the core units. For example, say: *yellow/green, and yellow/green, and yellow/green. amarillo/verde y amarillo/verde y amarillo/verde.*

ELL Continue to focus on the concepts "alike" and "different." Display three objects, such as three Farm Animal Counters. Two counters should be the same animal. Ask: *Which two animals are alike? Which animal is different?* Slowly increase the number in the set. Hold up one counter. Ask: *Which animals are like this one? Place them in a pile in front of you.*

Social and Emotional Development

Making Good Choices

 How can I get others to play with me?

Being Helpful Display *Making Good Choices Flip Chart* page 22, "How Can I Get Others to Play with Me?"

- Point to the flip chart illustration. Ask: *What did you learn about joining other children's games? ¿Qué aprendieron sobre participar en juegos con otros niños?*

- Have two children sit in front of the Block Center. Have a third child walk up and invite the two children to play blocks. Let different children assume the roles and act out the scenario several times. Review with children what worked best.

Making Good Choices Flip Chart, page 22

Learning Goals

Social and Emotional Development
- Child initiates interactions with others in work and play situations.

Mathematics
- Child identifies, duplicates, and creates simple patterns.

Vocabulary

pattern   patrón   repeat   repetición

Differentiated Instruction

Extra Support

Making Good Choices

If...children have difficulty in the role-playing scenario, **then**...provide sentence frames such as *Would you like to play _____ with me? ¿Les gustaría jagar a _____ conmigo?*

Enrichment

Observe and Investigate

Challenge children to use the Pattern Blocks to make ABB, AAB, and ABC repeating patterns. For each response, have the child describe the core unit of the pattern.

Focus Question
Where do animals live and what do they eat?
¿Dónde viven los animales y qué comen?

Learning Goals

Social and Emotional Development
• Child accepts responsibility for and regulates own behavior.

Science
• Child observes, understands, and discusses the relationship of plants and animals to their environments.

Fine Arts
• Child participates in a variety of music activities (such as listening, singing, finger plays, musical games, performances).

Vocabulary

cow	vaca	duck	pato
farm	granja	horse	caballo
pig	cerdo	rabbit	conejo
sheep	oveja		

Differentiated Instruction

 Extra Support
Explore and Express
If...children have difficulty remembering the song lyrics, **then...**encourage them to just name the animal and make the sounds until they become more familiar with the song through repetition.

Enrichment
Explore and Express
Let one child be "Old MacDonald." Have the child place the Farm Animal Counters in order from left to right. Then let "Old MacDonald" lead the song, following the order displayed.

 Special Needs
Hearing Impairment
Making the sound "E-I-E-I-O" may seem strange for the child. Place his or her hands on your lips so that the child can feel the sounds as you make them.

Music and Movement Time

large group — 20 minutes

Social and Emotional Development Before beginning the singing activity, remind children to wait and each take one turn at a time choosing the animal to sing about. Ask why that's a good rule. Observe and mentally assess to see if children wait patiently rather than grabbing the bag. Remind children of the rules as needed.

Oral Language and Academic Vocabulary

☑ **Can children name animals that live on a farm?**

Farm Animals Remind children that a farm is a home to some animals.

● Ask: *What animals live on a farm? ¿Qué animales viven en granjas?*

● Have children use their mural from the Construction Center and page 10 of *Amazing Animals* to remind them of animals that live on a farm.

Explore and Express

☑ **Can children recognize and use a pattern to sing new verses of a song?**

Old MacDonald Had a Farm Hold up one of each of the Farm Animal Counters and ask children identify the animal and the noise the animal makes. Ask where all these animals live.

● Teach children a verse of "Old MacDonald Had a Farm" using "pig" as a first example.

● Practice it line by line until children are comfortable singing it.

● Place one set of Farm Animal Counters in a bag. For each verse of "Old MacDonald" have a child pick a counter from the bag and name the animal. Then sing the verse about that animal.

TIP Make up a movement for each animal and have children use it when they make the animal noise. For example, they can put their hands up for rabbit ears.

ELL Provide a variety of pictures of farms to help children understand the concept of farm. Have children match Farm Animal Counters to animals they see in the farm pictures. For each match, ask: *Is this a rabbit? Is this a pig?* Have children respond *Yes, it is* or *No, it is not.*

Center Time

► **Center Rotation** Center Time includes teacher-guided activities and independent activities. Refer to the **Learning Centers** on pages 62–63 for activities in additional centers.

small group · 30 minutes

Pretend and Learn Center

Center Tip
If…many children want to play on the farm, **then…** have some children pretend to be animals instead of using stuffed animals.

✓ Observe that children cooperate, share in play scenarios, and problem solve.

Materials stuffed animals that represent farm animals, farm dress-up clothes such as straw hats and bandanas

On a Farm Discuss with children how animals are cared for on a farm. Explain that a farmer must feed, brush, and take care of the animals.

● Instruct children to pretend to be farmers. Before play begins, have children name each animal they have on their farm.

● Remind children that a good farmer takes care of the animals.

Purposeful Play

✓ Observe children initiating play with others.

Children choose an open center for free playtime. Encourage cooperation skills by suggesting they work together to create an animal home, such as a home for a farm animal.

Let's Say Good-Bye

large group · 15 minutes

 Read Aloud Revisit "Crocodile"/ "El cocodrilo" for your afternoon Read Aloud. Ask children to listen for rhyming words.

Home Connection Refer to the Home Connections activities listed in the Resources and Materials chart on page 59. Remind children to sing "Old Macdonald Had a Farm" for their families. Sing the "Good-Bye Song" as children prepare to leave.

✓ **Learning Goals**

Social and Emotional Development
• Child initiates play scenarios with peers that share a common plan and goal.

Emergent Literacy: Writing
• Child writes own name or a reasonable approximation of it.

Science
• Child observes, understands, and discusses the relationship of plants and animals to their environments.

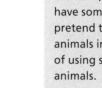

Writing

Recap the day and week. Say: *Tell us one thing you learned about animal homes this week. Díganos algo que hayan aprendido esta semana sobre las casas de los animales.* Record children's answers on chart paper. Share the pen with children as you write. Have each child write his/her name (all or part of it) beside their entry.

Week 3

Focus Question

How are animals the same and different?

¿En qué se parecen y diferencian los animales?

This week children will compare animals. They will interpret an animal traits chart, draw animal habitats, write pet care books, build farms, retell stories on a flannel board, make animal mobiles, and describe animal coverings and movements.

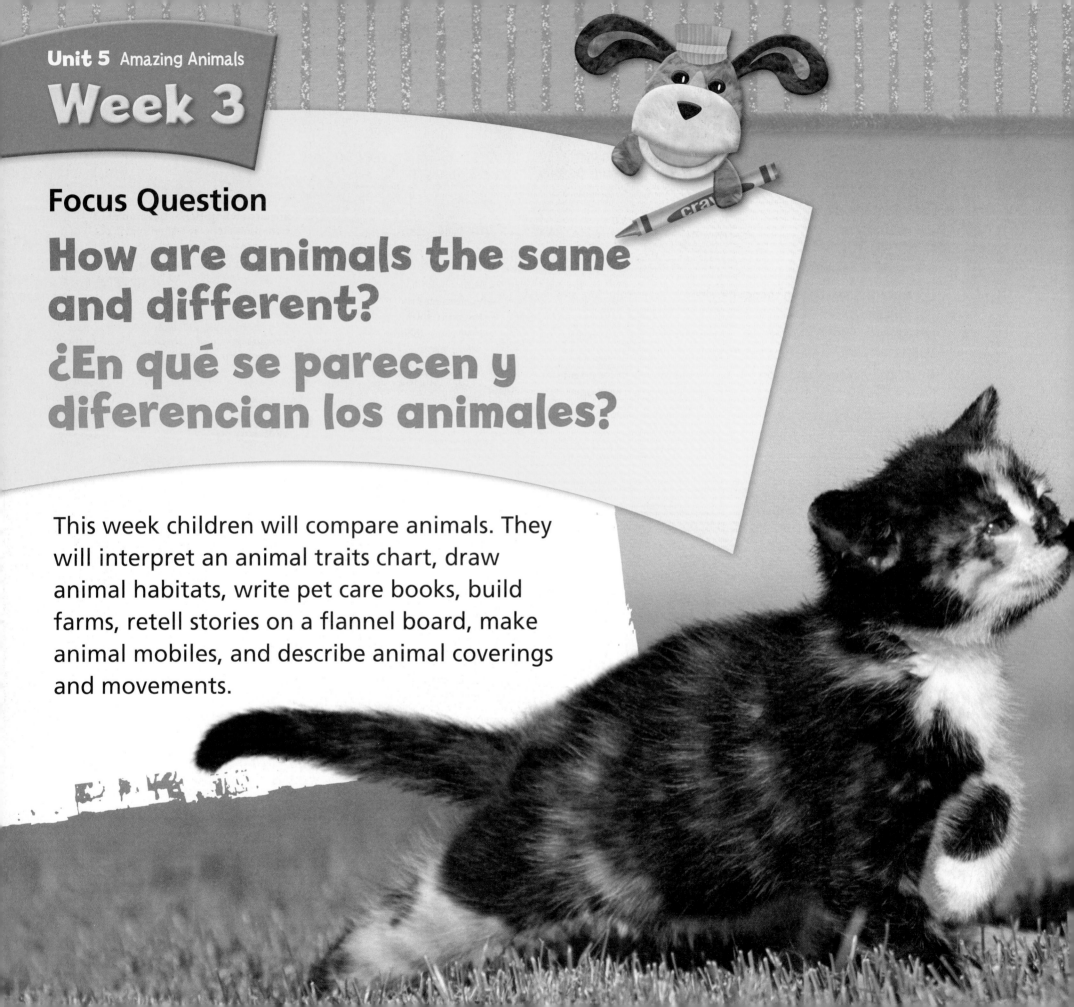

Social and Emotional Development

	1	2	3	4	5
Child demonstrates initiative in independent activities; makes independent choices.	✓	✓	✓	✓	✓
Child initiates play scenarios with peers that share a common plan and goal.					✓
Child demonstrates appropriate conflict-resolution strategies, requesting help when needed.	✓	✓	✓	✓	✓

Language and Communication

	1	2	3	4	5
Child demonstrates an understanding of oral language by responding appropriately.				✓	
Child uses oral language for a variety of purposes.				✓	
Child begins and ends conversations appropriately.				✓	
Child matches language to social setting.					✓
Child names and describes actual or pictured people, places, things, actions, attributes, and events.	✓	✓	✓		
Child exhibits an understanding of instructional terms used in the classroom.	✓	✓			
Child uses newly learned vocabulary daily in multiple contexts.			✓		✓
Child builds English listening and speaking vocabulary for common objects and phrases. (ELL)	✓				
Child speaks in complete sentences of four or more words including a subject, verb, and object.			✓	✓	
Child understands and uses sentences of increasing length and complexity.					✓

Emergent Literacy: Reading

	1	2	3	4	5
Child enjoys and chooses reading-related activities.				✓	
Child generates words that rhyme.	✓	✓	✓	✓	✓
Child names most upper- and lowercase letters of the alphabet.	✓	✓	✓	✓	✓
Child identifies the letter that stands for a given sound.	✓		✓		
Child produces the most common sound for a given letter.		✓		✓	✓
Child retells or reenacts poems and stories in sequence.				✓	
Child describes, relates to, and uses details and information from books read aloud.	✓	✓	✓		✓
Child asks and answers questions about books read aloud (such as, "Who?" "What?" "Where?").				✓	

Emergent Literacy: Writing

	1	2	3	4	5
Child uses scribbles, shapes, pictures, symbols, and letters to represent language.		✓	✓		
Child writes own name or a reasonable approximation of it.					✓
Child writes some letters or reasonable approximations of letters upon request.		✓			✓
Child experiments with and uses some writing conventions when writing or dictating.	✓			✓	

Mathematics

	1	2	3	4	5
Child demonstrates that, when counting, the last number indicates how many objects were counted.	✓				
Child uses concrete objects or makes a verbal word problem to add up to 5 objects.			✓		
Child measures the length and height of people or objects using standard or non-standard tools.				✓	
Child identifies, duplicates, and creates simple patterns.	✓	✓		✓	✓

Science

	1	2	3	4	5
Child identifies organisms and describes their characteristics.	✓	✓	✓		✓
Child recognizes and selects healthy foods.			✓		

Social Studies

	1	2	3	4	5
Child identifies similarities and differences among people.			✓		
Child identifies similarities and differences in families.			✓		

Fine Arts

	1	2	3	4	5
Child expresses emotions or ideas through art.	✓		✓		
Child expresses ideas, emotions, and moods through individual and collaborative dramatic play.					✓

Physical Development

	1	2	3	4	5
Child develops small-muscle strength and control.		✓			
Child coordinates body movements in a variety of locomotive activities (such as walking, jumping, running, hopping, skipping, climbing).		✓			

Technology Applications

	1	2	3	4	5
Child names and uses various computer parts (such as mouse, keyboard, CD-ROM, microphone, touch screen).		✓			

Materials and Resources

	DAY 1	DAY 2	DAY 3	DAY 4	DAY 5
Program Materials	• Teacher's Treasure Book • Oral Language Development Card 46 • Rhymes and Chants Flip Chart • *Who Is the Beast?* Big Book • ABC Picture Cards • Connecting Cubes • Buliding Blocks Math Activities • Making Good Choices Flip Chart • Math and Science Flip Chart • Home Connections Resource Guide	• Teacher's Treasure Book • Photo Library CD-ROM • Dog Puppet • *Who Is the Beast?* Big Book • ABC Picture Cards • Buliding Blocks Math Activities • Making Good Choices Flip Chart • Math and Science Flip Chart	• Teacher's Treasure Book • Oral Language Development Card 47 • Photo Library CD-ROM • Rhymes and Chants Flip Chart • Concept Big Book 3: *Amazing Animals* • ABC Big Book • Connecting Cubes • Making Good Choices Flip Chart • Dog Puppet • Farm Animal Counters	• Teacher's Treasure Book • Dog Puppets • Connecting Cubes • Flannel Board Patterns for "The Knee-High Man" • ABC Picture Cards • Connecting Cubes • Photo Library CD-ROM • Home Connections Resource Guide	• Teacher's Treasure Book • Rhymes and Chants Flip Chart • *Who Is the Beast?* Big Book • ABC Picture Cards • Math and Science Flip Chart • Pattern Blocks • Making Good Choices Flip Chart • Connecting Cubes
Other Materials	• Fish template • Paper • Scissors • Crayons • Washable markers • Books about animals • Finger paint	• Finger paints • Paper • Clothing cover-ups • Crayons or washable markers • Plastic beverage stirrers • Scissors • Glue • Craft sticks	• Butcher paper • Crayons or washable markers • Scissors • Glue • Paper • Pencils • Books about families • Shoe boxes	• Paper • Crayons or washable markers • Books about real animals • Poster board • Yarn or ribbon • Folk tales and fairy tales featuring make-believe animals • Felt • Tape and scissors	• Construction paper • Crayons or washable markers • String • Glue or stapler • Clothing hangers • Shallow foil pans • Sand or other filler for trays • Plastic beverage stirrers
Home Connection	Remind children to tell families what they learned about how tigers, birds, and fish are the same and how they are different. Send home Weekly Parent Letter, Home Connections Resource Guide, pp. 49–50.	Remind children to show their families examples of patterns they have found or made.	Remind children to talk with families about their culture's celebrations.	Remind children to retell the story "The Knee-High Man" to their families. Send home Story Book 14, Home Connections Resource Guide, pp. 133–136.	Remind children to tell families which animal they played at the party and what the animal did.

Assessment

As you observe children throughout the week, you may fill out an Anecdotal Observational Record Form to document an individual's progress toward a goal or signs indicating the need for developmental or medical evaluation. You may also choose to select work for each child's portfolio. The Anecdotal Observational Record Form and Weekly Assessment rubrics are available in the assessment section of DLMExpressOnline.com.

More Literature Suggestions

- **Bird, Butterfly, Eel** by James Prosek
- **Down on the Farm** by Merrily Kutner
- **Chickens Aren't the Only Ones** by Ruth Heller
- **Tarra and Bella: The Elephant and Dog Who Became Best Friends** by Carol Buckley
- **Lots and Lots of Zebra Stripes: Patterns in Nature** by Stephen Swinburne
- **La vaca que decía oink** por Bernard Most
- **¡Nadie me quiere!** por Raoul Krischanitz
- **El caballo y su sombra** por Arturo Alape
- **Chato y los amigos pachangueros** por Gary Soto
- **Arco iris de animales** por Enrique Martínez

	DAY 1	**DAY 2**
Let's Start the Day **Language Time** `large group`	**Opening Routines** p. 102 **Morning Read Aloud** p. 102 **Oral Language and Vocabulary** p. 102 Compare Fish **Phonological Awareness** p. 102 Produce Rhyming Words	**Opening Routines** p. 108 **Morning Read Aloud** p. 108 **Oral Language and Vocabulary** p. 108 Wild Beasts **Phonological Awareness** p. 108 Provide Rhyming Words
Center Time `small group`	**Focus On:** **Math and Science Center** p. 103 **Library and Listening Center** p. 103	**Focus On:** **ABC Center** p. 109 **Writer's Center** p. 109
Circle Time **Literacy Time** `large group`	**Read Aloud** *Who is the Beast?/¿Quien es la bestia?* p. 104 **Learn About Letters and** **Sounds:** /v/ *Vv*, /ks/ *Xx* p. 104	**Read Aloud** *Who is the Beast?/¿Quien es la bestia?* p. 110 **Learn About Letters and Sounds:** /v/ *Vv*, /ks/ *Xx* p. 110
Math Time `large group`	**Cube Patterns** p. 105	**Count and Move in Patterns** p. 111
Social and **Emotional** **Development** `large group`	**Solving Problems** p. 105	**Solving Problems** p. 111
Content **Connection** `large group`	**Science:** **Oral Language and Academic Vocabulary** p. 106 Introduce a Chart **Observe and Investigate** p. 106 Same and Different Chart	**Math:** **"Oh Dear, What Can the Pattern Be?"** p. 112 **Pattern Strips (The Core)** p. 112
Center Time `small group`	**Focus On:** **Creativity Center** p. 107 **Purposeful Play** p. 107	**Focus On:** **Pretend and Learn Center** p. 113 **Purposeful Play** p. 113
Let's Say **Good-Bye** `large group`	**Read Aloud** p. 107 **Writing** p. 107 **Home Connection** p. 107	**Read Aloud** p. 113 **Writing** p. 113 **Home Connection** p. 113

Focus Question How are animals the same and different?

¿En qué se parecen y diferencian los animales?

DAY 3

Opening Routines p. 114
Morning Read Aloud p. 114
Oral Language and Vocabulary
p. 114 Compare Animal Features
Phonological Awareness
p. 1148 Provide Rhyming Words

Focus On:
Creativity Center p. 115
Writer's Center p. 115

Read Aloud
Amazing Animals/
Animales asombrosos
p. 116
**Learn About Letters
and Sounds:**
/v/ Vv, /ks/ Xx p. 116

Build Cube Stairs p. 117

Solving Problems p. 117

Social Studies:
Oral Language and Academic Vocabulary
p. 118 Talk About Language and Customs
Understand and Participate
p. 118 Look at Family Pictures

Focus On:
Construction Center p. 119
Purposeful Play p. 119

Read Aloud p. 119
Writing p. 119
Home Connection p. 119

DAY 4

Opening Routines p. 120
Morning Read Aloud p. 120
Oral Language and Vocabulary
p. 120 Real or Make-Believe?
Phonological Awareness
p. 120 Provide Rhyming Words

Focus On:
Math and Science Center p. 121
Pretend and Learn Center p. 121

Read Aloud "The Knee-High Man"/
"El hombre que llegaba hasta las rodillas"
p. 122
Learn About Letters and Sounds:
/v/ Vv, /ks/ Xx p. 122

Listen and Copy p. 123

Solving Problems p. 123

Math:
Talk About Core Units p. 124
Cube Patterns p. 124

Focus On:
Library and Listening Center p. 125
Purposeful Play p. 125

Read Aloud p. 125
Writing p. 125
Home Connection p. 125

DAY 5

Opening Routines p. 126
Morning Read Aloud p. 126
Oral Language and Vocabulary
p. 126 Same and Different
Phonological Awareness
p. 126 Provide Rhyming Words

Focus On:
Construction Center p. 127
ABC Center p. 127

Read Aloud *Who is the Beast?/¿Quien es la bestia?* p. 128
Learn About Letters and Sounds:
/v/ Vv, /ks/ Xx p. 128

Pattern Strips (The Core) p. 129

Being Helpful p. 129

Dramatic Play:
Oral Language and Academic Vocabulary
p. 130 Animal Characteristics
Explore and Express p. 130 A Night at the Zoo

Focus On:
Writing Center p. 131
Purposeful Play p. 131

Read Aloud p. 131
Writing p. 131
Home Connection p. 131

Learning Centers

Math and Science Center

Stripes and Spots
Children use a template to trace and cut out two fish. They draw spots on one fish and stripes on the other and then work together to make patterns. See p. 103.

How High is Knee-High?
Children measure their leg up to their knee with Connecting Cubes. They measure classroom objects and compare them with their knee-high measurement. See p. 121.

Long Tails and Short Tails
Children sort pictures of animals into two groups: those with long tails and those with short tails.

Bigger and Smaller
Children fold a sheet of drawing paper and draw an animal that is bigger than they are on one side and an animal that is smaller than they are on the other side.

ABC Center

Xs and Vs
Children use their fingers to form the letters *x* and *v*. Then they finger paint uppercase and lowercase *Xx* and *Vv* in different colors. See p. 109.

Sand Tray Letters
Children take turns tracing *Xx* and *Vv* in the sand as they say the name and sound for each letter. See p. 127.

A Van for *Vv*
Children draw a van on a large piece of construction paper. They write the letters *Vv* on the van and draw pictures of objects whose names begin with /v/v/, such as *vase, vest,* and *violin.*

Creativity Center

Fingerprint Animals
Children dip their thumb in finger paint to make fingerprint animals and use markers to add body parts, such as legs and ears. See p. 107.

Animal Homes
Children work in pairs or threes to draw the setting for an animal home, such as a jungle or an ocean. They draw and cut out pictures of animals to glue on the home. See p. 115.

Paper Bag Puppets
Children draw animal faces on paper bags to create simple hand puppets. They use yarn and felt pieces for ears and whiskers.

Animal Mural
Children use colored chalk to create an animal mural on a large sheet of butcher paper.

Library and Listening Center

Finding Differences

Children look through books about animals and draw a picture of an animal that is not a fish. They pretend to be the animal and tell how they are different from a fish. See p. 103.

Familiar Tales

Children browse through familiar folk and fairy tales and take turns retelling stories using flannel board pieces or characters they make up themselves. See p. 125.

Pet Stories

Partners look through storybooks about children and their pets, such as *Whistle for Willie* by Ezra Jack Keats and *Can I Keep Him?* by Steven Kellogg, and compare the story characters.

Construction Center

Build a Farm

Partners construct a barn from a shoebox by cutting farm doors in the side and drawing windows. They use Connecting Cubes to make fences and animal pens. See p. 119.

Animal Mobiles

Children make mobiles that display animals that are alike in some way, such as wild animals, pets, farm animals, or water animals. See p. 127.

Animal Shelter

Children build an animal shelter, using blocks, boxes, and other materials. They make pets out of clay to place in the shelter.

Writer's Center

Story Captions

Children draw their favorite animal from the book *Who Is the Beast?* and write or dictate a caption for it. See p. 109.

Pet Books

Children fold a sheet of paper in half to make a book, draw their favorite kind of pet on the cover, and draw a picture inside to show what they would do with the pet. See p. 115.

Zoo News

Children recall what they did at their zoo party by drawing pictures of an animal they portrayed and a game they played. They write or dictate to tell about each picture. See page 232.

Animal Talk

Children fold a sheet of paper into four boxes. In each box, they draw an animal that makes a unique sound and label it with the sound word.

Pretend and Learn Center

Stick Puppet Story

Children make stick puppets of animals from *Who Is the Beast?*, and use them to act out the story together. See p. 113.

Real and Make-Believe

Children look through books about animals and choose one to imitate. First, they move and make sounds like a real animal; then they act like an animal in a make-believe story. See p. 121.

Tortoise and Hare

Partners pretend to be the tortoise and hare having a conversation after the race. They take turns playing each role.

Animal Sounds

Children imitate animals by making sounds, such as *meow, moo, quack, oink, baa,* and *tweet,* as others guess what animal they are.

DAY 1

Focus Question
How are animals the same and different?
¿En qué se parecen y diferencian los animales?

✔ Learning Goals

Social and Emotional Development
• Child demonstrates initiative in independent activities; makes independent choices.

Language and Communication
• Child names and describes actual or pictured people, places, things, actions, attributes, and events.

Emergent Literacy: Reading
• Child generates words that rhyme.

Vocabulary

coral	coral	fins	aletas
fish	peces	ocean	océano
scales	escamas	swim	nadar

Differentiated Instruction

👋 Extra Support
Oral Language and Vocabulary
If...children have difficulty explaining how the fish are the same and different,
then...point out that all the fish have fins, and help children find characteristics that are different, such as stripes and spots.

⭐ Enrichment
Phonological Awareness
Challenge children to name other words that rhyme with *whale, day,* and *small.*

Let's Start the Day

▶ **Opening Routines and Transition Tips**
For **Opening Routines** and **Transition Tips** turn to pages 178–181 and visit
DLMExpressOnline.com for more ideas.

📖 Read **"Jump or Jiggle"/¿Quién camina?"** from the *Teacher's Treasure Book,* page 87, for your morning Read Aloud.

Language Time

large group · 15 minutes

👫 **Social and Emotional Development** Encourage children to talk to each other respectfully as they participate in activities and find answers to questions.

Oral Language and Vocabulary

✔ **Can children use a wide variety of words to describe fish?**

Compare Fish Talk about fish. Ask: *Do you know where fish live? ¿Saben dónde viven los peces?* Explain that many fish live in the ocean. *What do fish look like? ¿Cómo son los peces?*

● Display *Oral Language Development Card 46.* Ask: *How are these fish the same? How are they different? ¿En qué se parecen estos peces? ¿En qué se diferencian?* Then follow the suggestions on the back of the card.

Oral Language Development Card 46

Phonological Awareness

✔ **Can children produce rhyming words?**

Produce Rhyming Words Display *Rhymes and Chants Flip Chart,* p. 23. Remind children that rhyming words end with the same sounds. Chant "Animals Protect Themselves." Say the word *well* and ask students for words that rhyme with *well.* Repeat with the word *up.*

ELL Review the uncommon words in the *Rhymes and Chants Flip Chart.* Act out the word *puff* by puffing out your cheeks. Ask: *Does puffing itself up make a fish bigger or smaller?* Act out the word *prickly* by lightly touching a sharpened pencil. Ask: *Are prickly spines easy to touch or hard to touch?*

For additional suggestions on how to meet the needs of children at the Beginning, Intermediate, Advanced, and Advanced-High levels of English proficiency, see pages 184–187.

Rhymes and Chants Flip Chart, page 23

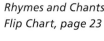

Center Time

 small group · 60–90 minutes

Math and Science Center

 Track children's ability to create patterns.

Materials fish template, paper, scissors, crayons or washable markers

Stripes and Spots Remind children that some fish have spots and some have stripes.

- Provide children with a fish template cut from cardboard. Have them trace and cut out two fish.

- Have children draw spots on one fish and stripes on the other.

- Have children work together to make a pattern with their fish, for example: spots, spots, stripes, spots, spots, stripes, spot, spots, stripes. Then have them count how many fish are in their pattern.

Center Tip

If...children have difficulty cutting with scissors, **then...**place your hand over theirs as you cut together.

Library and Listening Center

 Track children's use of theme-related vocabulary.

Materials books about animals, *Oral Language Development Card 46,* paper, crayons or washable markers

Finding Differences Display *Oral Language Development Card 46* in the center and provide a variety of books with pictures of different animals.

- Tell children to look through the books and draw a picture of an animal that is not a fish.

- Have children pretend to be the animal and use their picture to tell others how they are different from a fish.

Center Tip

If...children have difficulty naming animals they see in the books, **then...** point to and identify the animals and have them repeat the names.

Learning Goals

Mathematics
- Child demonstrates that, when counting, the last number indicates how many objects were counted.
- Child identifies, duplicates, and creates simple patterns.

Science
- Child identifies organisms and describes their characteristics.

Differentiated Instruction

✋ Extra Support
Library and Listening Center
If...children have trouble telling how the animal of their choice is different from a fish, **then...** help them name characteristics of both animals and ask: *What is one thing your animal has that a fish does not? Digan una cosa que tiene su animal y que el pez no tenga.*

⭐ Enrichment
Math and Science Center
Challenge children to also make some plain fish and create a pattern with spotted fish, striped fish, and plain fish.

Accommodations for 3's
Math and Science Center
If...three-year-olds have trouble making patterns, **then...**help them put four of their fish in a row and have them count the fish.

Focus Question

How are animals the same and different?
¿En qué se parecen y diferencian los animales?

Learning Goals

Language and Communication
• Child builds English listening and speaking vocabulary for common objects and phrases. (ELL)

Emergent Literacy: Reading
• Child names most upper- and lowercase letters of the alphabet.

• Child identifies the letter that stands for a given sound.

• Child describes, relates to, and uses details and information from books read aloud.

Vocabulary

beast	bestia	eyes	ojos
legs	patas	stripes	rayas
tail	cola	tracks	huellas
whiskers	bigotes		

Differentiated Instruction

 Extra Support

Learn About Letters and Sounds
If...children have difficulty remembering letter sounds, **then...**practice the sounds with them several times as they trace over the letters on the ABC Picture Cards.

 Enrichment
Read Aloud
After reading aloud the book once, page through the illustrations and have children take turns telling what happens on each page.

Special Needs
Hearing Impairment
Teach all children the signs for some of the animals you will study this week. Display photographs of each animal, and use the sign when talking about a specific animal.

Literacy Time

Read Aloud

✓ **Can children find ways that animals in the story are similar and different?**

Build Background Tell children that they will read a book about wild animals.

● Ask: *Are wild animals pets? Can you name some wild animals? ¿Los animales salvajes son mascotas? ¿Pueden nombrar algunos animales salvajes?*

Listen for Enjoyment Display *Who Is the Beast?* and read the title. Explain that a beast is an animal, but the word *beast* is often used to describe a wild animal that is big and dangerous. Conduct a picture walk.

● Browse through the pages. Name the animals. Ask: *Who do you think the beast is? ¿Quién creen que es la bestia?*

● Read the book aloud. Have children join in on the repetitive phrase *The beast, the beast!* Pause to allow children to provide rhyming words when they can.

● Stop frequently to ask: *How are these animals different? How are they the same? ¿En qué se diferencian estos animales? ¿En qué se parecen?*

Respond to the Story Discuss the story. Ask: *How is the tiger different from the other animals in the story? How is the tiger the same? ¿En qué se diferencia el tigre de los demás animales del cuento? ¿En qué se parece?*

TIP Revisit the illustrations in the book to help children describe how the tiger is different from and similar to the other animals.

ELL As you read aloud, point to details in the illustrations to help children understand words such as *tail, stripes, legs, eyes, whiskers,* and *tracks.* Use gestures and movements for phrases such as *fly by, swing high and low, turn back, buzz along, hide from sight,* and *filled with fear.*

Learn About Letters and Sounds

✓ **Can children identify sounds and letters /v/ spelled *Vv* and /ks/ spelled *Xx*?**

Identify Letters and Sounds /v/*Vv*, /ks/*Xx* Display the ABC Picture Cards for *Vv* and *Xx*.

● Have children write each letter in the air as they name the letter and say the sound. *What is the letter? What sound does it stand for? ¿Cómo se llama la letra? ¿Qué sonido tiene?*

● Have children write *v* and *x* on index cards. Say: *I will say a letter. Hold up your letter card after I say it. Yo voy a decir una letra. Levanten la tarjeta con esa letra después de que yo la diga.* Say the letter names several times in random order.

● Say: *Now I will say the sounds of the letters. Hold up a letter card for each sound. Ahora, voy a decir los sonidos de las letras. Levanten una tarjeta de letra por cada sonido que diga.* Say /v/ and /ks/ several times in random order.

Who Is the Beast?
¿Quién es la bestia?

Vv
violin

Xx
x-ray

large group · 15 minutes

Math Time

Observe and Investigate

✓ **Can children recognize and recreate patterns?**

Cube Patterns Have children sit in a circle, and put a large pile of Connecting Cubes in the center.

- Make a strip of three cubes in a blue/blue/ yellow pattern. You may use other colors as long as you model a pattern.

- Show the cube strip to children; tell students it is the core unit. Have each child recreate it.

- Afterward, help children link all their cube strips to make a cube pattern train. Chant color names as you point to each cube in the train. Repeat with a different core unit, such as yellow/blue/red.

ELL Have children create a "living" cube pattern train. Give each child a square of colored paper. Arrange children in a line to form a pattern. Have children say their colors as you point to them.

Building Blocks

Online Math Activity

Introduce Pattern Planes 2: Duplicate, in which children duplicate a linear (in a line or row) pattern of flags, based on outlines of each flag's shape serving as a guide or model. Each child should complete Pattern Planes 2 this week.

large group · 15 minutes

𝍂𝍂𝍂 Social and Emotional Development

Making Good Choices

✓ **Do children understand how to use problem-solving strategies and seek appropriate help when needed?**

Solving Problems Discuss how children can solve problems and find answers to their questions. Display the *Making Good Choices Flip Chart,* page 23. Point to the girl working with cube patterns.

- Ask: **What problem is the girl trying to solve, or figure out? How might she solve the problem?** *¿Qué problema está intentando resolver la niña? ¿Cómo puede resolverlo?*

- Discuss how the girl can try to solve the problem on her own and what she should do if she still needs help.

- Ask: **When is it okay to ask for help? When is it okay to offer to help someone?** *¿Cuándo está bien pedir ayuda? ¿Cuándo está bien ofrecerle ayuda a alguien?*

Making Good Choices Flip Chart, page 23

✓ Learning Goal

Social and Emotional Development
- Child demonstrates initiative in independent activities; makes independent choices.
- Child demonstrates appropriate conflict-resolution strategies, requesting help when needed.

Mathematics
- Child identifies, duplicates, and creates simple patterns.

Vocabulary

cube	cubo	core unit	unidad
pattern	patrón	problem	problema
solve	solucionar		

Differentiated Instruction

✋ **Extra Support**

Observe and Investigate

If...children struggle when recreating core units, **then...**help them name the colors in the core unit you made and have them say the colors with you as they recreate it.

⭐ **Enrichment**

Observe and Investigate

Have partners build a longer core unit pattern, for example: yellow/blue/blue/yellow. Have them link their cubes together and say the color names. Then have them continue adding to the pattern.

Focus Question

How are animals the same and different?

¿En qué se parecen y diferencian los animales?

 Learning Goals

Language and Communication
• Child exhibits an understanding of instructional terms used in the classroom.

Science
• Child identifies organisms and describes their characteristics.

Vocabulary

bird	pájaro	chart	tabla
column	columna	different	diferente
fish	peces	same	igual
tiger	tigre		

Differentiated Instruction

 Extra Support

Observe and Investigate

If...children have difficulty using the chart, **then...**have them to go the chart, point to the word *Tiger* as you read the word, and run their hand down the chart to look at pictures that give information about tigers. Repeat for the other animals.

Enrichment

Oral Language and Academic Vocabulary
Challenge children to add robust vocabulary to their daily spoken language: **scientist, row, information**.

Science Time

Personal Safety Skills Remind children that they should never approach a strange animal, whether it is a pet or a wild animal, without adult permission and supervision.

Oral Language and Academic Vocabulary

✓ **Do children understand how to use a chart?**

Introduce a Chart Display *Math and Science Flip Chart* page 41. Point to the animal chart.

● Say: *This is a chart. Scientists use charts to show information in a way that is easy to read and understand. Ésta es una tabla. Los científicos usan tablas para mostrar información de manera que sea fácil de leer y entender.*

● Point to and identify the columns on the chart and the column headings. Explain that children can learn about each animal in the chart by looking down the columns.

Observe and Investigate

✓ **Can children identify similarities and differences in animals?**

Same and Different Chart Have children use the chart to find information about animals.

● Ask: *Which animals are shown on this chart? ¿Qué animales se muestran en esta tabla?* Have children point to all the pictures about tigers. Point out the label and explain that all of the information about tigers is in the first column.

● Help children use the chart to answer questions. Ask: *Can you use the chart to find an animal that has fur? Does the bird have fur? Does a fish have feathers? Could any of the animals be pets? ¿Pueden usar la tabla para encontrar un animal que tenga pelo? ¿Tiene pelo el pájaro? ¿Tiene plumas un pez? ¿Son mascotas algunos de estos animales?*

● Have children use the chart to identify each animal's habitat as well as the way it moves.

TIP Remind children that they saw a tiger, birds, and a fish in the book *Who Is the Beast?*

ELL Begin by comparing concrete objects in the classroom, such as two Farm Animal Counters. For children at the Beginning level of proficiency, ask yes or no questions: *Does the horse have legs? Does the sheep have legs? Is the horse purple? Is the sheep purple?* Then ask yes or no questions about animals on the chart.

Math and Science Flip Chart, page 41

Center Time

▶ **Center Rotation** Center Time includes teacher-guided activities and independent activities. Refer to the **Learning Centers** on pages 100–101 for activities in additional centers.

small group · 30 minutes

Creativity Center

☑ **Track children's ability to describe similarities and differences in the fingerprint animals.**

Materials paper, finger paint in different colors, washable markers

Fingerprint Animals Set out shallow bowls of finger paint, paper, and washable markers. Invite children to make fingerprint animals.

- Have children dip a finger or their thumb in paint and make a print on paper. Allow them to practice several times.

- Then have children make animals from their fingerprints. After the fingerprints dry, have children use markers to add body parts such as legs, a tail, and ears.

- Have children tell how their fingerprint animals are the same and different.

Center Tip

If...children have difficulty making clear fingerprints, **then...**help them dip their finger to get the right amount of paint and gently press it on paper.

☑ Learning Goal

Social and Emotional Development
• Child demonstrates appropriate conflict-resolution strategies, requesting help when needed.

Emergent Literacy: Writing
• Child experiments with and uses some writing conventions when writing or dictating.

Fine Arts
• Child expresses emotions or ideas through art.

Writing

Recap the day. Ask children to draw two different animals and write or dictate to tell how they are the same and different.

Purposeful Play

☑ **Observe children appropriately communicating with each other in respectful ways and asking for help when needed.**

Children choose an open center for free playtime. Encourage problem-solving skills by suggesting that they work together to make animal patterns using the Farm Animal Counters.

Let's Say Good-Bye

large group · 15 minutes

 Read Aloud Revisit "Jump or Jiggle"/"¿Quién camina?" for your afternoon Read Aloud. Ask children to act out each movement with you.

 Home Connection Refer to the Home Connections activities listed in the Resources and Materials chart on page 97. Remind children to tell families what they learned about how tigers, birds, and fish are the same and how they are different. Sing the "Good-Bye Song" as children prepare to leave.

Focus Question

How are animals the same and different?

¿En qué se parecen y diferencian los animales?

Opening Routines and Transition Tips

For **Opening Routines** and **Transition Tips** turn to pages 178–181 and visit **DLMExpressOnline.com** for more ideas.

Read **"The Tortoise and the Hare"/**"La tortuga y la liebre" from the *Teacher's Treasure Book*, page 291, for your morning Read Aloud.

✓ Learning Goals

Language and Communication
• Child uses newly learned vocabulary daily in multiple contexts.
• Child speaks in complete sentences of four or more words including a subject, verb, and object.

Emergent Literacy: Reading
• Child generates words that rhyme.

Technology Applications
• Child names and uses various computer parts (such as mouse, keyboard, CD-ROM, microphone, touch screen).

Vocabulary

beast	bestia	claws	garras
dangerous	peligroso	paws	patas
roar	rugido	tiger	tigre
wild	salvaje		

Differentiated Instruction

 Extra Support

Oral Language and Vocabulary
If...children have difficulty comparing and contrasting beasts and pets, **then...**have them compare specific animals, such as a tiger and a house cat or a dog and bear.

 Enrichment

Phonological Awareness
Give partners the Dog Puppets and have them use the puppets to say other words that rhyme.

Language Time

large group   15 minutes

👪 Social and Emotional Development Remind children to try different ways to solve problems before asking for help.

Oral Language and Vocabulary

✓ **Can children use complete sentences to identify and describe animals that might be called beasts?**

Wild Beasts Remind children that they read about wild animals in the book *Who Is the Beast?* Review that the word *beast* is often used to describe a wild animal that is big and dangerous. Say: ***Tigers are often called beasts. What other animals might be called beasts?*** *A los tigres se les suele llamar bestias. ¿A qué otros animales podría llamárseles bestias?*

● Have children take turns naming a wild beast. Ask: ***Is it big? Is it wild? Is it dangerous?*** *¿Es grande? ¿Es salvaje? ¿Es peligroso?*

● Encourage children to compare a wild beast to a pet, using complete sentences. Ask: ***How is a wild beast different from a pet like a cat or a dog?*** *¿En qué se diferencia una bestia salvaje de una mascota, como un gato o un perro?* Encourage children to roar like a beast.

ELL Display animal photos from the *Photo Library CD-ROM*. Choose animals that are wild and large, such as the bear, bobcat, elephant, lion, and rhinoceros. Ask yes and no questions: ***Is it big and wild? Is it a beast? Is it a pet?*** If the photo is accompanied by sound, have children listen and then make the sound of the animal.

Phonological Awareness

✓ **Can children generate rhyming words?**

Provide Rhyming Words Display a Dog Puppet. Have the puppet introduce itself and say: ***Rhyming words end with the same sounds. I know some rhyming words... tall, small; paws, claws; wet, pet.*** *Las palabras que riman terminan con los mismos sonidos. Yo conozco unas palabras que riman: tall, small; paws, claws; wet, pet.* Then have the puppet say the following sentences. Let children give the rhyming words.

● I am small. A giraffe is _____. (tall)

● I have paws. A tiger has _____. (claws)

● A fish is a pet. A fish is _____. (wet)

Who Is the Beast?
¿Quién es la bestia?

Center Time

> ▶ **Center Rotation** Center Time includes teacher-guided activities and independent activities. Refer to the **Learning Centers** on pages 100–101 for activities in additional centers.

 small group 60–90 minutes

ABC Center

	Center Tip
✓ **Track children's formation of letters.** **Materials** finger paints, paper, clothing cover-ups **Xs and Vs** Display the ABC Picture Cards for *Vv* and *Xx*. Point to each letter and have children form the letter with their fingers, making a *v* sign for *v* and crossing index fingers to make an *x*. • Provide finger paint, paper, and cover-ups. Keep the Picture Cards on display and have children finger paint the letters in upper case and lower case forms. Encourage them to make letters in different colors. • As children paint, ask: *What is this letter? What sound does it stand for? ¿Cómo se llama esta letra? ¿Qué sonido tiene?*	**If...**children have difficulty painting the letters, **then...** demonstrate how to hold the brush and make straight lines to form *v* and *x*.

Writer's Center

	Center Tip
✓ **Track children's listening skills and retention of information.** **Materials** drawing paper, crayons or washable markers **Story Captions** Tell children that they will draw and write about their favorite animal in *Who Is the Beast?* • Display the Big Book *Who Is the Beast?* • Play the *Listening Library CD* and have children follow along as they listen. • Have children draw their favorite animal from the story and write a caption for their drawing	**If...**children have difficulty knowing what to write in a caption, **then...**show them books with captions and explain that a caption tells about a picture.

Learning Goals

Emergent Literacy: Reading
• Child names most upper- and lowercase letters of the alphabet.

• Child produces the most common sound for a given letter.

Emergent Literacy: Writing
• Child uses scribbles, shapes, pictures, symbols, and letters to represent language.

• Child writes some letters or reasonable approximations of letters upon request.

Differentiated Instruction

 Extra Support
Writer's Center
If...children have difficulty creating captions for their animal pictures, **then...**provide examples by writing short captions for one or two animals in the story, such as *pretty bird* or *big tiger*.

 Enrichment
ABC Center
Challenge children to include letters *Cc* and *Uu* in their finger painting.

Accommodations for 3's
Writer's Center
If... children randomly scribble words or make circular scribbling, **then...**suggest that they write by starting at the left of their paper (point) and going to the right (point).

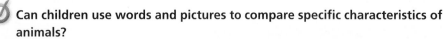
Focus Question

How are animals the same and different?

¿En qué se parecen y diferencian los animales?

 Learning Goals

Emergent Literacy: Reading
- Child names most upper- and lowercase letters of the alphabet.
- Child produces the most common sound for a given letter.
- Child describes, relates to, and uses details and information from books read aloud.

Science
- Child identifies organisms and describes their characteristics.

Vocabulary

beast	bestia	jump	saltar
stripes	rayas	tail	cola
tiger	tigre	whiskers	bigotes

Differentiated Instruction

 Extra Support

Learn About Letters and Sounds

If...children have difficulty forming letters with their bodies, **then...**have them look at the ABC Picture Cards again and work gently to help them place their bodies in the correct position.

 Enrichment

Learn About Letters and Sounds

Teach children how to write and read *fox*. Write the word for children to trace. Sound out the letters with them: /f/ /o/ /ks/. Challenge children to compare a fox to a tiger.

Literacy Time

large group · 15 minutes

📖 Read Aloud

✅ **Can children use words and pictures to compare specific characteristics of animals?**

Build Background Display the Big Book *Who Is the Beast?* Point to the front cover.

- Ask: *Is this the front or back cover? ¿Ésta es la portada o la contraportada?*

- Page through the book and have children point to the beginning of the story and the end.

- Then say: *We read this book together. What do you remember about this book?* *Hemos leído este libro juntos. ¿Qué recuerdan sobre este libro?*

Listen for Understanding As you reread the book, track the print with your hand and point out and name the animals.

- Point out specific similarities and differences in the animals. *I see the tiger's tail in this picture. Does the bird have a tail, too? Does the bird have stripes? Veo la cola del tigre en esta imagen. ¿El pájaro también tiene cola? ¿El pájaro tiene rayas?*

- Ask: *Who is the beast in this book? ¿Quién es la bestia en este libro?*

Respond to the Story Have children make comparisons. Ask: *Which animal has whiskers like the tiger? Which has stripes? Which has a tail? Which animals can jump? How are all the animals the same? ¿Qué animal tiene bigotes como el tigre? ¿Cuál tiene rayas? ¿Cuál tiene una cola? ¿Qué animales pueden saltar? ¿Qué cosas tienen en común todos los animales?*

 TIP As children respond to the story, point to details in the pictures to support their comparisons.

 ELL Engage children and provide group enrichment by asking children to share what the animals are called in their home language.

Learn About Letters and Sounds

✅ **Can children identify sounds and letters /v/ spelled *Vv* and /ks/ spelled *Xx*?**

Identify Letters and Sounds /v/Vv, /ks/Xx Display ABC Picture Cards for *Vv* and *Xx*. Remind children that they painted these letters during Center Time. Point to each letter and ask: *What is the letter? What sound does it stand for? ¿Qué letra es ésta? ¿Qué sonido tiene?*

- Have partners lie on the floor to form the letter *v*. Have children repeat the /v/ sound while in their letter formation.

- Then have children stand up and make an *x* by spreading legs wide apart and reaching arms up and out. Have them say the /ks/ sound.

Who Is the Beast?
¿Quién es la bestia?

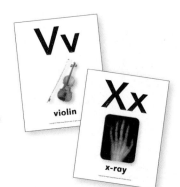

Vv · violin
Xx · x-ray

Math Time

Observe and Investigate

 Can children create patterns?

Count and Move in Patterns Tell children that they will count and move in patterns.

- Count aloud with children to 20 (or more as appropriate) in patterns of 4, such as 1 (clap), 2 (clap), 3 (clap), 4 (hop), 5 (clap), 6 (clap), 7 (clap), 8 (hop).

- Repeat with other motions if you choose. Incorporate animal movements to fit the weekly theme. For example, have students hop like a rabbit, hop like a rabbit, pounce like a tiger, and pounce like a tiger while counting 1 (hop), 2 (hop), 3 (pounce), 4 (pounce), 5 (hop), 6 (hop), 7 (pounce), 8 (pounce) and so on.

👫 Social and Emotional Development

Making Good Choices

 Do children understand how to use problem-solving strategies and seek appropriate help when needed?

Solving Problems Revisit the *Making Good Choices Flip Chart*, page 23, :How Can I Solve Problems?"

- Display a Dog Puppet. Say: ***Tell the puppet about the problem the girl has and how she can solve her problem.*** *Cuenten al títere el problema que tiene la niña. ¿Cómo puede resolverlo?*

- Provide each child a turn to tell the puppet about the girl's problem and how she can solve it herself. Encourage them to tell who the girl can ask for help if she still needs it. Remind children to try to solve problems together during Center Time and to ask politely if they still need help.

 Provide sentence frames for children to use during the conversation with the puppet: ***The girl cannot* _____ . *She can try* _____ . *She can ask* ____ *for help.*** Model completed sentence frames. Then have children complete the frames on their own if they can, or have them repeat your words.

Online Math Activity

Introduce Marching Patterns 2: Extend, in which children extend a linear (in a line or row) pattern by one full repetition of an entire core unit of marching members. Each child should complete Marching Patterns 2 this week.

Making Good Choices Flip Chart, page 23

✔ Learning Goal

Social and Emotional Development
- Child demonstrates initiative in independent activities; makes independent choices.
- Child demonstrates appropriate conflict-resolution strategies, requesting help when needed.

Mathematics
- Child identifies, duplicates, and creates simple patterns.

Physical Development
- Child coordinates body movements in a variety of locomotive activities (such as walking, jumping, running, hopping, skipping, climbing).

Vocabulary

count	contar
pattern	patrón
politely	amablemente
problem	problema
solve	resolver

Differentiated Instruction

✋ Extra Support
Observe and Investigate
If...children have difficulty counting to 20, **then...**count to 12 using patterns of 4.

⭐ Enrichment
Observe and Investigate
Have partners come up with new movements for Count and Move in Patterns. Invite them to demonstrate their new movements to the group.

💜 Special Needs
Delayed Motor Development
If...children become fatigued by engaging in the movement patterns, **then...**invite them to call out movements in a pattern for the other children to follow.

Focus Question
How are animals the same and different?
¿En qué se parecen y diferencian los animales?

Learning Goals

Language and Communication
• Child exhibits an understanding of instructional terms used in the classroom.

Mathematics
• Child identifies, duplicates, and creates simple patterns.

Vocabulary

core	principal	diagonal	diagonal
horizontal	horizontal	pattern	patrón
unit	unidad	vertical	vertical

Differentiated Instruction

Extra Support

Math Time
If...children need help recreating patterns, **then...**verbalize each picture as children copy it.

Enrichment

Math Time
Challenge children to create their own pattern strip by drawing a more complex core unit to extend.

Math Time

 large group / 20 minutes

☑ **Can children identify a core unit?**

"Oh Dear, What Can the Pattern Be?" Sing the following lyrics to the tune of "Oh Dear, What Can the Matter Be?"

> Oh dear, what can the pattern be?   Este patrón me desvive.
> *(Repeat two more times)*
> Let's look at the pattern and see.   Pero yo soy detective.

● Use *Math and Science Flip Chart* page 42 to reintroduce pattern strips to children, emphasizing the idea of the core unit as the set of elements that is repeated. For example, in an ABCCABCCABCC pattern, ABCC is the core unit.

☑ **Can children recreate patterns?**

Pattern Strips (The Core) Point to the first pattern strip on the *Math and Science Flip Chart,* and have children describe its pattern: diagonal/ diagonal/vertical/ diagonal/diagonal/vertical. Ask children what the core pattern of the strip is (diagonal/diagonal/ vertical).

● Have children help you recreate the pattern using flat, plastic beverage stirrers, and then have each child recreate the pattern's core unit once. After you check their work, have children continue to recreate additional core units.

● Repeat with other patterns strips that use positional and shape patterns. Use Pattern Blocks to have children recreate the shape patterns.

TIP Tell children that they will have another chance to work with pattern strips in a few days.

ELL Bring in examples of patterns on clothes, ceramics, and so on. Review the concepts of core units and help children identify them on the objects.

For additional suggestions on how to meet the needs of children at the Beginning, Intermediate, Advanced, and Advanced-High levels of English proficiency, see pages 184–187.

Pattern Strips
Tiras con patrones

Math and Science Flip Chart, page 42

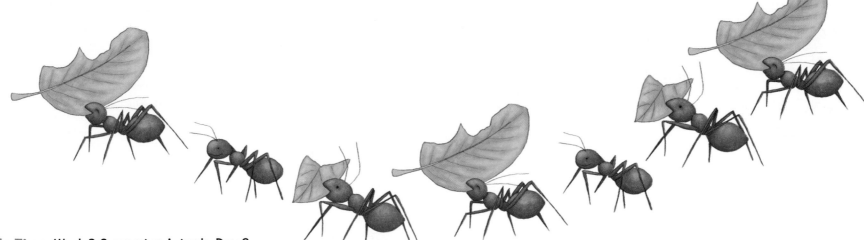

Center Time

▶ **Center Rotation** Center Time includes teacher-guided activities and independent activities. Refer to the **Learning Centers** on pages 100–101 for activities in additional centers.

 small group 30 minutes

Pretend and Learn Center

	Center Tip

☑ **Track children's ability to retell a story in their own words.**

Materials drawing paper, crayons or washable markers, scissors, glue, craft sticks

Stick Puppet Story Have children draw, color, and cut out small pictures of animals from the Big Book *Who Is the Beast?* Suggest that each child create two animals. Check to make sure that all the story animals are represented.

- Help children use glue their animals onto craft sticks to make character puppets.

- Have children use their puppets to act out the story together.

Center Tip

If...children have difficulty creating animals for the puppets, **then...**draw the animals for them and have them color and cut them out.

Purposeful Play

☑ **Observe children sustaining independent play sequences.**

Children choose an open center for free playtime. Encourage initiative and persistence by suggesting that children take turns pantomiming animals in a game of Animal Charades.

Let's Say Good-Bye

 large group 15 minutes

 Read Aloud Revisit the story "The Tortoise and the Hare"/"La tortuga y la liebre" for your afternoon Read Aloud. Ask children to listen for words with the /v/ and /ks/ sounds.

 Home Connection Refer to the Home Connections activities listed in the Resources and Materials chart on page 97. Remind children to show their families examples of patterns they have found or made. Sing the "Good-Bye Song" as children prepare to leave.

✓ Learning Goal

Social and Emotional Development
- Child demonstrates initiative in independent activities; makes independent choices.

Language and Communication
- Child names and describes actual or pictured people, places, things, actions, attributes, and events.

Emergent Literacy: Writing
- Child uses scribbles, shapes, pictures, symbols, and letters to represent language.

Writing

Recap the day. Have children describe the animals in *Who Is The Beast?* Then ask: *What did you learn about the way animals move?* ¿Qué aprendieron sobre la manera en que se mueven los animales? Ask them to draw and label a picture of an animal jumping, running, swimming, or flying.

DAY 3

Let's Start the Day

Focus Question

How are animals the same and different?

¿En qué se parecen y diferencian los animales?

 Learning Goals

Language and Communication
• Child names and describes actual or pictured people, places, things, actions, attributes, and events.

• Child speaks in complete sentences of four or more words including a subject, verb, and object.

Emergent Literacy: Reading
• Child generates words that rhyme.

Vocabulary

ears	orejas	fur	pelaje
hop	saltar	kit	cría
legs	patas	rabbit	conejo

Differentiated Instruction

 Extra Support

Phonological Awareness

If...children have difficulty generating words that rhyme with *hop*, **then**...segment the word. Say: *Listen carefully. /h/ /op/, hop. What sounds do you hear at the end of hop? What other words end with /op/? Escuchen atentamente. /h/ /op/, hop. ¿Qué sonidos escuchan al final de hop? ¿Qué otras palabras terminan en /op/?*

 Enrichment

Phonological Awareness

Ask children what a baby bunny is called. (kit) Challenge them to generate words that rhyme with *kit*.

Accommodations for 3's

Phonological Awareness

If...children have difficulty naming words that rhyme with *hop*, **then**...have them hop around the room until you say *stop*. Ask: *Do hop and stop rhyme? ¿Riman hop y stop?*

 Opening Routines and Transition Tips

For **Opening Routines** and **Transition Tips** turn to pages 178–181 and visit **DLMExpressOnline.com** for more ideas.

Read **"Sammy the Rodeo Sea Horse"/"Omar, el caballito de mar"** from the *Teacher's Treasure Book*, page 223, for your morning Read Aloud.

Language Time

large group · **15 minutes**

Social and Emotional Development Remind children to try to think of answers to questions on their own and to ask for help from peers and then adults when it is needed.

Oral Language and Vocabulary

Can children use a wide variety of words in complete sentences to compare animals?

Compare Animal Features Talk about the coverings that animals have on their bodies. Ask: *What covers a tiger? Is it fur or feathers? What covers a bird? Is it feathers or scales? Is a fish covered with fur, feathers, or scales? ¿Qué es lo que cubre al tigre? ¿Pelaje o plumas? ¿Qué es lo que cubre a un pájaro? ¿Plumas o escamas? ¿Un pez está cubierto de pelaje, plumas o escamas?*

● Display *Oral Language Development Card 47*. Identify the animals as rabbits and point out their fur. Then follow the suggestions on the back of the card.

ELL Display the following images in the *Photo Library CD-ROM*: tiger, rabbit, eagle, trout. Point to and name the covering on each animal as the picture is shown: *fur, fur, feathers, scales*. Then display the images again and have children name each covering.

Phonological Awareness

Can children provide and generate rhyming words?

Provide Rhyming Words Revisit *Rhymes and Chants Flip Chart*, page 23. Remind children that rhyming words end with the same sounds. Chant "Animals Protect Themselves" with children. Say: *These animals protect themselves in a lot of different ways. Another way is to move away. Think about the rabbits we saw. How do rabbits move? Estos animales se protegen de diferentes maneras. Otra forma de protegerse es escapar . Piensen en los conejos que vimos. ¿Cómo se mueven los conejos?* Have children give words that rhyme with *hop*.

Oral Language Development Card 47

Rhymes and Chants Flip Chart, page 23

Center Time

Center Rotation Center Time includes teacher-guided activities and independent activities. Refer to the **Learning Centers** on pages 100–101 for activities in additional centers.

small group 60–90 minutes

Creativity Center

	Center Tip

Track children's knowledge of different animal environments.

Materials butcher paper or other large paper, crayons or washable markers, scissors, glue

Animal Homes Remind children that the animals in *Who Is the Beast?* live in the jungle. In "Animals Protect Themselves," the fish lives in the ocean. Ask: **Where else do animals live?** *¿En qué otros lugares viven los animales?*

- Have children work in pairs or threes to draw the setting for an animal home, such as a jungle, the ocean, or a house. Tell them not to draw any animals in their picture. Encourage each small group to draw a different home.

- Have children share their drawings with each other and then work together to draw and cut out different animals to glue onto the homes.

Center Tip

If...children have difficulty choosing animals to add to their drawings, **then...**display *Who Is the Beast?* and *Concept Big Book 3: Amazing Animals,* and have them choose from animals shown on the pages.

Writer's Center

Center Tip

Track children's ability to describe the characteristics of pets.

Materials paper, pencils, crayons or washable markers.

Pet Books Tell children that they will make a book about their favorite kind of pet.

- Show children how to fold a sheet of paper in half to make a book. Have them draw a picture of their favorite kind of pet on the front of the book and write their name below it.

- On the inside of the book, have children draw and write to tell what they would do with the pet and how they would care for it.

- Have children share their books and discuss how their pets are the same as wild animals and how they are different.

Center Tip

If . . . children have difficulty deciding on a pet to write about, **then . . .** show them pictures of pets in the book *Amazing Animals.*

Learning Goal

Social and Emotional Development
- Child demonstrates initiative in independent activities; makes independent choices.

Emergent Literacy: Writing
- Child uses scribbles, shapes, pictures, symbols, and letters to represent language.

Science
- Child identifies organisms and describes their characteristics.

Fine Arts
- Child expresses emotions or ideas through art.

Differentiated Instruction

Extra Support
Writer's Center
If...children have difficulty writing in detail, **then...**have them dictate ideas to you. Copy words into their book.

Enrichment
Writer's Center
Challenge children to write complete sentences in their book.

Accommodations for 3's
Writer's Center
If...children have difficulty completing a book, **then...**have them draw a picture of their favorite kind of pet and dictate why they like it.

Focus Question

How are animals the same and different?

¿En qué se parecen y diferencian los animales?

Learning Goals

Emergent Literacy: Reading
- Child names most upper- and lowercase letters of the alphabet.
- Child identifies the letter that stands for a given sound.
- Child describes, relates to, and uses details and information from books read aloud.

Science
- Child identifies organisms and describes their characteristics.

Vocabulary

farm	granja	feathers	plumas
fur	pelaje	ocean	océano
scales	escamas	wild	salvaje

Differentiated Instruction

 Extra Support

Read Aloud

If...children have difficulty comparing animals, **then...**give them specific animals to compare: *Is a giraffe or a kitten a pet? Is a bear or a sheep wild? Is a cow or a whale a farm animal? ¿Cuál es una mascota, la jirafa o el gatito? ¿Cuál es un animal salvaje, el oso o la oveja? ¿Cuál es un animal de granja, la vaca o la ballena?*

 Enrichment

Read Aloud

As you read, challenge children to give other examples that could be included in the book, such as: *A tiger has four legs, too. A mouse is small, too. A pet can also be a hamster.*

 Special Needs

Speech/Language Delays

Even if the child does not correctly say or pronounce a letter, don't stop him or her. Repeat the letter correctly, and encourage him or her to repeat it after you.

Literacy Time

 large group · 15 minutes

Read Aloud

✓ **Can children use information in the Concept Big Book to make comparisons?**

Build Background Tell children that you will be rereading a book about amazing animals.

- Ask: *What amazing animals do you remember from this book? ¿Qué animales asombrosos recuerdan de este libro?*

Listen for Understanding Reread *Concept Big Book 3: Amazing Animals*, tracking the print with your hand and pointing to animal characteristics in the pictures. As you read, pause to allow children to answer the questions in the text.

- Ask: *What surprised or amazed you about these animals? ¿Qué los sorprendió sobre estos animales?*

Respond to the Story Help children compare animals in the book. Ask: *Which animals are pets and which are wild? Which are farm animals? Can you name an animal with fur? Can you name an animal with feathers or scales? ¿Qué animales son mascotas y cuáles son salvajes? ¿Cuáles son animales de granja? ¿Pueden nombrar a un animal con pelaje? ¿Pueden nombrar a un animal con plumas o escamas?*

TIP Point out animals in the book to help children make comparisons.

Learn About Letters and Sounds

✓ **Can children identify sounds and letters /v/ spelled *Vv* and /ks/ spelled *Xx*?**

Identify Letters and Sounds *Vv, Xx* Sing the "ABC Song" with children. Ask: *Do v and x come at the beginning of the alphabet or near the end? ¿Las letras v y x están al comienzo del abecedario o cerca del final?*

- Display the *ABC Big Book* and page through it slowly. Have children say *"stop"* when you come to the letter *Vv* and then again at *Xx*.

- Write *van, six, vegetable, vase, mix,* and *box* on the board. Read the words. Then have volunteers circle the *v* or the *x* in each word. Say the /v/ and /ks/ sounds with children as you point to the letters.

- Say: *Listen for the sound of /v/ or /x/ as I read the words again. Escuchen el sonido de /v/ o /x/ mientras vuelvo a leer las palabras.* Encourage children to join in when they can.

ELL Support word meaning. Point out a box and a vase in the classroom. Show pictures of a van and vegetables from the *Photo Library CD-ROM*. Ask children to hold up six fingers and to pretend to mix food in a bowl.

For additional suggestions on how to meet the needs of children at the Beginning, Intermediate, Advanced, and Advanced-High levels of English proficiency, see pages 184–187.

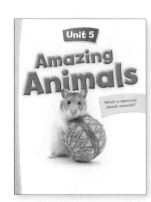

Amazing Animals
Animales asombrosos

ABC Big Book

Math Time

Observe and Investigate

 Can children uses cubes to form a growing pattern?

Build Cube Stairs Remind children how to build cube stairs, and point out that the stairs form a pattern – a growing pattern in which each step is one higher (one more) than the previous one.

- Show children how to link Connecting Cubes, and then show them two steps using the cubes (one cube for the first step, two cubes for the second).

- Ask children how many cubes it will take to make the next step. (three) "Walk" your fingers up the steps, asking children to count "1, 2, 3" with you.

- Children then build their own cube stairs.

ELL Have children count the steps in their home language. Then count in English and have children count with you.

✗✗✗ Social and Emotional Development

Making Good Choices

 Do children understand how to use problem-solving strategies and seek appropriate help when needed?

Solving Problems Display *Making Good Choices Flip Chart* page 23, "How Can I Solve Problems?" Review with children the problem that the girl has and the ways she can solve it, including how she can solve it on her own and who she can ask for help.

- With a Dog Puppet, role play how the girl can ask the boy next to her for help. Then role play how the girl can ask her peers, then the teacher, for help. Model using polite words and communicating in respectful ways.

- After each role play, ask: ***How did I ask for help? What did I say? What else could I have said?*** *¿De qué manera pedí ayuda? ¿Qué dije? ¿Qué otra cosa podría haber dicho?*

- Play the song "Everybody Needs Help Sometimes"/"Todos necesitan ayuda alguna vez" from the Making Good Choices Audio CD. Ask children why it is important to ask for help when they need it.

Online Math Activity

Children can complete Pattern Planes 2 and Marching Patterns 2 during computer time or Center Time.

Making Good Choices Flip chart, page 23

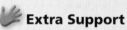

✓ Learning Goal

Mathematics
- Child uses concrete objects or makes a verbal word problem to add up to 5 objects.

Social and Emotional Development
- Child demonstrates appropriate conflict-resolution strategies, requesting help when needed.

Vocabulary

cube	cubo	higher	más alto
pattern	patrón	problem	problema
solve	resolver	stairs	escaleras

Differentiated Instruction

✋ Extra Support

Observe and Investigate
If...children need help building their own cube stairs, **then...**continue to verbalize and provide hands-on assistance until they can work on their own.

⭐ Enrichment

Social and Emotional Development
Have partners use the dog puppets to role play the girl and the boy. Then have them role play the girl and the teacher.

Accommodations for 3's

Observe and Investigate
If...children need help making cube stairs, **then...**have them form three steps as you guide their hands and count with them "1, 2, 3."

Learning Goals

Language and Communication
• Child names and describes actual or pictured people, places, things, actions, attributes, and events.

Science
• Child recognizes and selects healthy foods.

Social Studies
• Child identifies similarities and differences among people.

• Child identifies similarities and differences in families.

Vocabulary

celebrate	celebrar	country	país
holiday	día festivo	language	idioma
world	mundo		

Differentiated Instruction

 Extra Support

Understand and Participate

If...children have difficulty choosing an item to draw, **then...**invite them to look through the books you provided again. Ask questions such as: *Does this look like fun? Is this something you would like to eat? What do you like about this piece of clothing? ¿Esto parece divertido? ¿Les gustaría comer esto? ¿Qué es lo que les gusta de esta prenda de vestir?*

 Enrichment

Understand and Participate

Challenge children to create a chart that shows a food, a holiday, and an article of clothing from this country in the first row and a food, a holiday, and an article of clothing from another culture in the second row.

Social Studies Time

 large group 20 minutes

Health Skills During the discussion, help children name foods from other cultures that are healthy and nutritious.

Oral Language and Academic Vocabulary

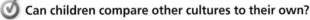

✓ **Can children identify languages and customs?**

Talk About Language and Customs Remind children that animals live in many different parts of the world. Explain that people live in many different parts of the world, too.

● Tell students that people in different parts of the world have their own language, or special way of speaking, and their own special ways of doing things, such as celebrating holidays.

● Ask: *What languages do we use in this country? What are some ways we celebrate special days at school? How do families in this country celebrate holidays? ¿Qué idiomas hablamos en este país? ¿Cómo celebramos los días festivos en la escuela? ¿Cómo celebran las familias los días festivos?*

Understand and Participate

✓ **Can children compare other cultures to their own?**

Look at Family Pictures Display books depicting families from around the world. Make sure some of the photos show special occasions.

● Page through the books with children, pointing out unique clothing, customs, or foods.

● Ask: *What are some things that are different about families in other parts of the world? What are some things that are the same? ¿Qué cosas son diferentes en las familias que viven en otras partes del mundo? ¿Qué cosas son similares?*

● Continue the discussion by talking about foods from different cultures. Ask: *Have you ever eaten food that people in other countries eat? What are some different kids of foods from different countries? How was it like food at your house or how was it different? ¿Alguna vez han comido comida de otros países? ¿Qué tipos de comida de otros países conocen? ¿En qué se parece y en qué se diferencia de la comida que comen en sus casas?*

● Have children draw something that they like from another culture, such as a food, a custom, or an item of clothing. Post the pictures in the classroom to celebrate cultural differences.

TIP Maintain a comfortable environment in which children can share by asking for only general details about families.

ELL Use the *Photo Library CD-ROM* pictures and the language translation feature to teach children words associated with food.

Center Time

Center Rotation Center Time includes teacher-guided activities and independent activities. Refer to the **Learning Centers** on pages 100–101 for activities in additional centers.

   small group 30 minutes

Construction Center

	Center Tip

✓ **Track children's knowledge of how farm animals are the same and different.**

Materials shoe boxes, scissors, crayons or washable markers, Farm Animal Counters

Build a Farm Remind children that they learned about farm animals in *Amazing Animals*. Then have partners construct a barn from a shoe box by cutting farm doors in the side and drawing or cutting out windows. Have children use Connecting Cubes to make fences and animal pens.

- Encourage cooperation between partners as they design and create their barn.

- Provide Farm Animal counters and have partners use the manipulatives to act out farm activities. Ask: *What animals do you have on your farm? What do the farm animals do?* ¿Qué animales tienen en su granja? ¿Qué hacen los animales de granja?

Center Tip

If...children need help creating their barn, **then...**draw barn doors on the shoebox for them to cut. Make initial cuts for the windows and have them finish the task.

Learning Goal

Social and Emotional Development
- Child demonstrates initiative in independent activities; makes independent choices.

Language and Communication
- Child names and describes actual or pictured people, places, things, actions, attributes, and events.

Emergent Literacy: Writing
- Child uses scribbles, shapes, pictures, symbols, and letters to represent language.

Science
- Child identifies organisms and describes their characteristics.

Social Studies
- Child identifies similarities and differences in families.

Purposeful Play

✓ **Observe children as they cooperate to work in groups.**

Children choose an open center for free playtime. Encourage cooperation skills by suggesting that children place their farms on a large table and act out stories about different farm families and the holidays they celebrate on their farms.

Writing

Recap the day. Ask: *What new things did you learn about animals today? What new things did you learn about people?* ¿Qué cosas nuevas aprendieron hoy acerca de los animales? ¿Qué cosas nuevas aprendieron sobre las personas? Record answers on chart paper. Share the pen by having children write letters and words they know.

Let's Say Good-Bye

   large group 15 minutes

 Read Aloud Revisit "Sammy the Rodeo Sea Horse"/"Omar, el caballito de mar" for your afternoon Read Aloud. Ask children to listen for the names of different kinds of animals.

 Home Connection Refer to the Home Connections activities listed in the Resources and Materials chart on page 97. Remind children to talk with families about their culture's celebrations. Sing the "Good-Bye Song" as children prepare to leave.

DAY 4

Focus Question

How are animals the same and different?
¿En qué se parecen y diferencian los animales?

Let's Start the Day

▶ **Opening Routines and Transition Tips**
For **Opening Routines** and **Transition Tips** turn to pages 178–181 and visit DLMExpressOnline.com for more ideas.

📖 Read **"Old Gray Cat"/"El viejo gato gris"** from the *Teacher's Treasure Book*, page 208, for your morning Read Aloud.

Language Time

large group | 15 minutes

👪 **Social and Emotional Development** Encourage children to remember the plan for how to handle prolems when they are working on their own: Try to solve it yourself. Ask someone nearby for help. Ask an adult for help.

Oral Language and Vocabulary

✓ **Can children engage in conversations with make-believe characters?**

Real or Make-Believe? Talk about the animals that children read about this week: Ask: *Which animals are very big? Which are small? Which of the animals have you seen in real life? ¿Qué animales son muy grandes? ¿Cuáles son pequeños? ¿Cuáles de estos animales han visto ustedes en la vida real?*

- Explain that some stories have make-believe animals that can talk like people.

- Ask: *What would you say to an animal if you could talk to it? ¿Qué le dirían a un animal si pudieran hablar con él?*

- Model talking to an animal such as a tiger and asking questions: *Hello, Mr. Tiger. Can you teach me how to roar like you? Hola, Sr. Tigre. ¿Me enseñaría a gruñir como usted?* Then have children give questions that they would ask animals.

ELL Use the Big Books *Who Is the Beast?* and *Amazing Animals,* and have children point to an animal and complete sentence frames: *Hello Mr. _____. Can you teach me how to _____?*

Phonological Awareness

✓ **Can children generate rhyming words?**

Provide Rhyming Words Display the Dog Puppets. Have one puppet say: *Listen to my word: cat. Can you say a word that rhymes? Escuchen esta palabra: cat. ¿Conocen una palabra que rime con cat?* Have the other puppet say: *I can say a word that rhymes with cat: bat! Puedo decir una palabra que rima con cat: ¡bat!* Repeat with other rhyming words: **fox/box, bee/see, fish/wish, snake/bake.** Then have pairs take turns saying a word and asking their partner for a word that rhymes.

Who Is the Beast?
¿Quién es la bestia?

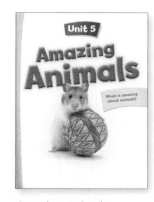

Amazing Animals
Animales asombrosos

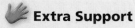
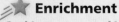

Center Time

▶ **Center Rotation** Center Time includes teacher-guided activities and independent activities. Refer to the **Learning Centers** on pages 100–101 for activities in additional centers.

 small group 60–90 minutes

Math and Science Center | Center Tip

☑ **Track children's ability to compare measurements accurately.**

Materials Connecting Cubes, paper, crayons or washable markers

How High is Knee-High? Have children use Connecting Cubes to measure their leg up to their knee. Ask: *How many cubes did you connect to make a knee-high strip of cubes? ¿Cuántos cubos usaron para llegar hasta la altura de la rodilla?*

- Have children compare their cube strip or their leg to things in the classroom. Ask: *Which things are higher than your knee? Which are not as high? Which are about as high? ¿Qué cosas son más altas que su rodilla? ¿Cuáles no son tan altas? ¿Cuáles son casi tan altas?*

- Have children draw and share a picture of something that is as high as their knee, not as high as their knee, and about as high.

Center Tip

If...children have difficulty counting their Connecting Cubes, **then...**count with them as you point to each cube.

Pretend and Learn Center | Center Tip

☑ **Track children's ability to portray both real and make-believe animals.**

Materials poster board, crayons or washable markers, poster board, yarn or ribbon

Real and Make Believe Have children choose an animal to act out and draw their animal on a square of poster board. Help them attach yarn or ribbon to the poster board to make a wearable sign.

- Say: *Now act like real animals. Move and make sounds like real animals. Remember, no talking! Ahora, actúen como animales reales. Muévanse y hagan sonido como los de los animales reales. ¡Recuerden que no deben hablar!*

- After children interact like real animals, have them switch to make-believe. Say: *Now, act like animals in a make-believe story. You can talk and ask each other questions. Ahora, actúen como los animales de un cuento fantástico. Pueden hablar entre ustedes y hacerse preguntas.*

- Ask: *Which was more fun to act out, a real animal or a make-believe animal? ¿Qué fue más divertido actuar: un animal real o uno fantástico?* Have children tell why.

Center Tip

If...children have difficulty remembering not to speak when acting out real animals, **then...**remind them by giving nonverbal signals such as putting your finger to your lips and shaking your head "no."

☑ Learning Goal

Language and Communication
- Child uses oral language for a variety of purposes.

Emergent Literacy: Reading
- Child enjoys and chooses reading-related activities.

Mathematics
- Child measures the length and height of people or objects using standard or non-standard tools.

Differentiated Instruction

 Extra Support

Math and Science Center

If...children struggle making a Connecting Cube strip that is as high as their knee, **then...**have them make a smaller strip that is as long as their hand or have partners make strips together.

 Enrichment

Math and Science Center

Challenge children to use a ruler or yardstick to measure their leg to the knee and then use the ruler or yardstick to measure things in the classroom.

Accommodations for 3's

Pretend and Learn Center

If...children struggle to participate in the pretend activity, **then...**create a picture sign for them with a familiar animal, such as a pet or a farm animal, and have them join in.

Circle Time

Focus Question

How are animals the same and different?

¿En qué se parecen y diferencian los animales?

Learning Goals

Language and Communication
- Child demonstrates an understanding of oral language by responding appropriately.

Emergent Literacy: Reading
- Child names most upper- and lowercase letters of the alphabet.
- Child produces the most common sound for a given letter.
- Child asks and answers questions about books read aloud (such as, "Who?" "What?" "Where?").

Vocabulary

bull	toro
horse	yegua
knee-high	a la altura de la rodilla
owl	lechuza
pig	cerdo
size	tamaño

Differentiated Instruction

 Extra Support

Learn About Letters and Sounds

If...children have difficulty repeating the /v/ and /ks/ sounds in the chant, **then**...show them the correct mouth positions for the letters and have them practice saying the sounds slowly.

Enrichment

Read Aloud

Have children use the flannel characters to retell the story on the flannel board.

Literacy Time

large group — 15 minutes

📖 Read Aloud

☑ **Can children understand the events in a folk tale?**

Build Background Tell children that you will be reading about a man who is only knee-high, and some animals that tell him how he can grow.

- Ask: *Do you think this will be a make-believe story? Why or why not? ¿Creen que este cuento va a ser fantástico? ¿Por qué sí o por qué no?*

Listen for Enjoyment Read the story "The Knee-High Man"/"El hombre que llegaba hasta las rodillas" from *Teacher's Treasure Book* page 323. Display the flannel board patterns (pages 431-432).

- Before you read and act out the story, show children the characters. Say: *This is the knee-high man. These are the animals he talks to. As I read, listen carefully to what the animals tell the man. Éste es el hombre que llegaba hasta las rodillas. Éstos son los animales con los que habla. Mientras leo, escuchen con atención lo que dicen los animales.*

Respond to the Story Discuss the story. Have children recall the animals in the story as you point to them on the flannel board. Ask: *Who was the smartest animal of all? What did that animal tell the knee-high man? ¿Cuál fue el más listo de todos los animales? ¿Qué le dijo ese animal al hombre que llegaba hasta las rodillas?*

TIP Use animal noises to enhance the storytelling. Oink for the pig, whinny for the horse, snort for the bull, and hoot for the owl.

ELL Retell the story on the flannel board, pausing often to point to characters and ask questions: *What did the man do? What did the animal say?* Use sentence frames to help children phrase responses: *The man asked the _____ how to grow. The* (animal name) *said _____.*

Learn About Letters and Sounds

☑ **Can children identify sounds and letters /v/ spelled *Vv* and /ks/ spelled *Xx*?**

Identify Letters and Sounds *Vv* and *Xx* Display the ABC Picture Cards for letters *Vv* and *Xx*. Point to each letter. *What is the name of this letter? Do you remember the sound? ¿Cuál es el nombre de esta letra? ¿Recuerdan que sonido tiene?*

- Have children recite the following chant with you as you point to the cards:
  V, v, v! I know the sound of *v*.
  The sound of v is /v/.
  /v/, /v/, /v/!
  X, x, x! I know the sound of *x*.
  The sound of x is /ks/.
  /ks/, /ks/, /ks/!

- Repeat the chant and have children trace the letters *x* and *v* in the air with their finger as they say them.

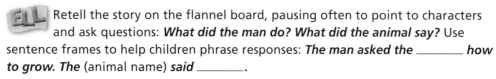

Teacher's Treasure Book page 323

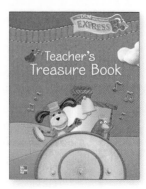

ABC Picture Cards

Building Blocks

Online Math Activity

Children can complete Pattern Planes 2 and Marching Patterns 2 during computer time or Center Time.

large group · 15 minutes

Math Time

Observe and Investigate

 Can children recognize and recreate patterns?

Listen and Copy Tell children that you will clap in patterns and they will name the patterns and repeat them.

- Clap in patterns a certain number of times. For example: clap, clap, pause, clap, long pause, clap, clap, pause, clap, long pause, and so on. Keep pauses distinct. Ask children to name the patterns (two claps and then one or AAB).

- Increase the number of claps, and do rhythmic patterns, such as two medium-paced claps, a pause, three fast claps, and so on. Remember to complete at least three repetitions of a pattern's core unit before asking children to repeat the pattern.

- Use this activity as a way to get children's attention during the day. For example, when they hear a clapping pattern, children stop what they are doing and repeat the pattern.

large group · 15 minutes

Social and Emotional Development

Making Good Choices

 Do children understand how to use problem-solving strategies and seek appropriate help when needed?

Solving Problems Tell children that you will use the puppets to act out a problem and how it can be solved.

- Display the Dog Puppets and tell children that the puppets want to clap in patterns. Model a scenario in which one puppet tries several times to clap in a pattern, but cannot. End with that puppet asking the other puppet for help.

- Ask: *What problem did the puppet have? How did the puppet solve the problem?*
  ¿Qué problema enfrentó el títere? ¿Cómo resolvió el problema el títere?

- Remind children that when they have a problem or a question, they should try several times to solve it on their own. Then they can ask another child or the teacher for help.

  ELL As you work with the puppets, model polite language and appropriate ways to ask for help.

Learning Goal

Social and Emotional Development
- Child demonstrates initiative in independent activities; makes independent choices.
- Child demonstrates appropriate conflict-resolution strategies, requesting help when needed.

Mathematics
- Child identifies, duplicates, and creates simple patterns.

Vocabulary

copy	copiar	clap	palmada
listen	escuchar	pattern	patrón
problem	problema	solve	resolver

Differentiated Instruction

Extra Support
Observe and Investigate
If...children have difficulty with clapping in patterns, **then...**clap the core unit once and have children repeat. Then complete two and three repetitions of the core unit.

Enrichment
Observe and Investigate
Have partners come up with new clapping patterns of their own and present them to the group.

Special Needs
Behavioral Social/Emotional
Noise can be very offensive to children with certain types of disabilities. Adapt the clapping activities accordingly.

Learning Goals

Language and Communication
• Child demonstrates an understanding of oral language by responding appropriately.

Mathematics
• Child identifies, duplicates, and creates simple patterns.

Vocabulary

cube	cubo	core unit	unidad principal
pattern	patrón	smallest	más pequeño
train	tren		

Differentiated Instruction

 Extra Support

Math Time

If...children need help recreating core units, **then...**say the color names as children put cubes together, for example as: *blue, blue, yellow* or *yellow, blue, red.*

 Enrichment

Math Time

Challenge partners to make their own cube pattern train, trade it with a partner, and recreate their partner's pattern train.

Math Time

large group   20 minutes

✓ **Can children understand the concept of a core unit?**

Talk About Core Units Review core units with children. Use Connecting Cubes to make a pattern. Point to the core unit.

● Say: **This is the smallest part of the pattern that repeats. It is the core unit.** *Ésta es la parte más pequeña del patrón. Es la unidad principal.*

✓ **Can children recreate patterns?**

Cube Patterns This lesson is a variation of the activity introduced on Day 1.

● Have children sit in a circle, and put a large pile of Connecting Cubes in the center.

● Make a strip of three cubes in a blue/blue/ yellow pattern. You may use other colors as long as you model a pattern. Show the cube strip to children; it is the core unit. Have children recreate it.

● Help children then link all cube strips to make a cube pattern train. Chant color names as you point to each cube in the train. Repeat with a different core unit such as yellow/blue/red.

● Afterward, show children a pattern train you made previously, and ask them what the smallest part (core unit) is that they could use to extend the train.

● Select a child to create a core pattern. Have the rest of the children create a pattern train using that pattern. Repeat as time permits.

TIP Tell children that they can say the colors in the model core unit to quietly themselves as they recreate it.

ELL Review color names using Colors and Shapes pictures in the *Photo Library CD-ROM*. Access the translation tool so that children can hear the color names in English and their home language.

For additional suggestions on how to meet the needs of children at the Beginning, Intermediate, Advanced, and Advanced-High levels of English proficiency, see pages 184–187.

Center Time

▶ **Center Rotation** Center Time includes teacher-guided activities and independent activities. Refer to the **Learning Centers** on pages 100–101 for activities in additional centers.

small group 30 minutes

Library and Listening Center

✓ **Track children's ability to retell familiar stories.**

Materials familiar folk tales and fairy tales with make-believe animal characters, paper or felt, washable markers, tape, scissors

Familiar Tales Tell children that they will read other stories about make-believe animals.

- Collect familiar tales with make-believe animals and place them in the center.

- Have children choose stories and take turns retelling them.

- Invite children to use the flannel board to retell the stories if they wish. Have them use existing flannel board pieces or characters they make themselves from paper or felt.

Center Tip

If...children make paper pieces for the flannel board, **then...**help them put double-sided tape on the back of each piece so that it will stick to the board.

Purposeful Play

✓ **Observe children communicating with each other in respectful ways.**

Children choose an open center for free playtime. Encourage cooperation skills by suggesting they draw a make-believe animal and take turns telling each other what their animal would say.

Let's Say Good-Bye

large group 15 minutes

Read Aloud Revisit "Old Gray Cat"/"El viejo gato gris" for your afternoon Read Aloud. Ask children to tell whether the animals in the story are real or make believe, and why they think so.

Home Connection Refer to the Home Connections activities listed in the Resources and Materials chart on page 97. Remind children to retell the story "The Knee-High Man" to their families. Sing the "Good-Bye Song" as children prepare to leave.

✓ Learning Goal

Social and Emotional Development
• Child demonstrates appropriate conflict-resolution strategies, requesting help when needed.

Emergent Literacy: Reading
• Child retells or reenacts poems and stories in sequence.

Emergent Literacy: Writing
• Child experiments with and uses some writing conventions when writing or dictating.

✏ Writing

Recap the day. Say: *Let's quickly retell the story "The Knee-High Man."* *Vamos a volver a contar rápidamente el cuento "El hombre que llegaba hasta las rodillas."* Encourage children to retell the story in complete sentences. Write their responses, pointing out the way that you write from left to right and leave spaces between words.

Let's Start the Day

Focus Question
How are animals the same and different?
¿En qué se parecen y diferencian los animales?

 Learning Goals

Social and Emotional Development
• Child demonstrates initiative in independent activities; makes independent choices.

Language and Communication
• Child uses newly learned vocabulary daily in multiple contexts.

• Child understands and uses sentences of increasing length and complexity.

Emergent Literacy: Reading
• Child generates words that rhyme.

Vocabulary

blend	mezclar	different	diferente
prickly	espinoso	puff	inflarse
same	igual		

Differentiated Instruction

 Extra Support
Oral Language and Vocabulary
If...children have difficulty identifying animal characteristics, **then**...use the *Photo Library CD-ROM* to show images of two animals in succession. Ask how each pair is the same and different.

Enrichment
Oral Language and Vocabulary
Invite partners to play a game in the *Photo Library CD-ROM*. To play, click on **Game Time!** Select **Animals**. Play "Select the Correct Picture." Have children do the activity on a touch screen or whiteboard, if possible.

 Opening Routines and Transition Tips
For **Opening Routines** and **Transition Tips** turn to pages 178–181 and visit DLMExpressOnline.com for more ideas.

Read **"Rabbit: A Mayan Legend"**/"El conejo: una leyenda maya" from the *Teacher's Treasure Book*, page 251, for your morning Read Aloud.

Language Time

  large group 15 minutes

Social and Emotional Development Encourage children to participate in all activities. Say: *Remember, when there's a job to do on your own, do your best to do it on your own. If you have a problem, ask someone around you for help before you ask an adult.* *Recuerden que cuando tienen que hacer un trabajo solos, tienen que intentar hacerlo por su cuenta. Si tienen un problema, antes de llamar a un adulto pidan ayuda a algún compañero.*

Oral Language and Vocabulary

✓ **Can children tell how animals are the same and different?**

Same and Different Talk with children about their work with animals this week. Say: *This week we learned how some animals are the same. What else did we learn?* *Esta semana aprendimos en qué se parecen algunos animales. ¿Qué más aprendimos?* Help children recognize that they also learned how animals are different.

● Display *Rhymes and Chants Flip Chart*, p. 23. Chant "Animals Protect Themselves" with children. Ask: *How are the ways in which animals protect themselves different? Which animal makes itself bigger? Which animal makes itself prickly?* *¿De qué diferentes maneras se protegen los animales? ¿Qué animal se hace más grande? ¿Qué animal se eriza?*

Phonological Awareness

✓ **Can children provide rhyming words?**

Provide Rhyming Words Remind children that rhyming words end with the same sounds. Then use *Rhymes and Chants Flip Chart*, p. 23 to chant "Animals Protect Themselves" again with children. Say: **Well rhymes with tell. What else rhymes with well?** *Well rima con tell. ¿Qué otra palabra rima con* well?

ELL Tell children to clap every time they hear a word that rhymes with well. Say: *smell, wish, bell, tell, swim, sell.* Repeat with *small* and *hall, tall, door, call, long, fall.*

Animals Protect Themselves
(to the tune of "London Bridge")

Animals protect themselves
Very well, very well.
Animals protect themselves
For survival.

There's a fish that puffs way up
So it can't be eaten up.
Porcupines have prickly spines
For survival.

Animals with spots or stripes
Blend in so they're out of sight.
Some can change their colors too
For survival.

Rhymes and Chants Flip Chart, page 23

Center Time

▶ **Center Rotation** Center Time includes teacher-guided activities and independent activities. Refer to the **Learning Centers** on pages 100–101 for activities in additional centers.

 small group · 60–90 minutes

✓ Learning Goal

Emergent Literacy: Reading
• Child names most upper- and lowercase letters of the alphabet.

• Child produces the most common sound for a given letter.

Emergent Literacy: Writing
• Child writes some letters or reasonable approximations of letters upon request.

Science
• Child identifies organisms and describes their characteristics.

Construction Center

✓ Track children's knowledge of animal similarities.

Materials construction paper, crayons or washable markers, string, glue or stapler, clothing hangers

Animal Mobiles Have children make an animal mobile that depicts animals that are the same in some way, such as wild animals, pets, farm animals, animals with fur, big animals, or water animals.

● Tell children to draw and cut out at least four animals in their category. Then have them cut a piece of string for each animal. Suggest that the strings be different lengths.

● Have children glue each animal to a string and then tie it to a hanger to construct an animal mobile. Hang the mobiles for children.

Center Tip

If...children have difficulty constructing their mobiles, **then...**help them attach the pictures to the string and have them show you where to tie the pictures on the hanger.

ABC Center

✓ Track children's ability to recognize and write letters.

Materials shallow foil pans, sand or other filler for sand trays

Sand Tray Letters Display the ABC Picture Cards *Vv* and *Xx* and review the sounds of the letters with children.

● Fill shallow trays with sand or another material in which children can trace letters.

● Have partners take turns tracing *v*'s and *x*'s in the sand as they say the name and sound for each letter.

Center Tip

If...children have difficulty recalling letter sounds, **then...**have them trace *v*'s in the sand as they say /v/ with you. Repeat with /ks/*x*.

Differentiated Instruction

✋ Extra Support
Construction Center
If...children have difficulty choosing animals for their mobile, **then...**display the read alouds and the Rhymes and Chants Flip Chart for the week and have them choose animals from them.

★ Enrichment
ABC Center
Challenge children to make a pattern of *x*'s and *v*'s in the sand tray.

Accommodations for 3's
ABC Center
If...children have difficulty writing letters in the sand tray, **then...**lightly trace the letter in the sand and have them trace over it as they say the letter sounds with you.

Focus Question

How are animals the same and different?
¿En qué se parecen y diferencian los animales?

Learning Goals

Emergent Literacy: Reading
• Child names most upper- and lowercase letters of the alphabet.
• Child produces the most common sound for a given letter.
• Child describes, relates to, and uses details and information from books read aloud.

Science
• Child identifies organisms and describes their characteristics.

Vocabulary

beast	bestia	jump	saltar
stripes	rayas	tall	alto
tiger	tigre	whiskers	bigotes

Differentiated Instruction

 Extra Support

Letter and Word Knowledge
If...children have difficulty forming straight lines to write *v* and *x*, **then...**give them chenille sticks and have them bend one stick to form a v and cross two sticks to form an x.

 Enrichment

Letter and Word Knowledge
Challenge children to write a pattern with x's and v's, such as *x, x, v, x, x, v, x, x, v*. Ask them to "read" their pattern by pointing to each letter and saying the sound.

 Special Needs

Cognitive Challenges
Limit the comparison of the animals in the book to two specific animals. Ask questions to help elicit specific responses.

Literacy Time

 large group · 15 minutes

📖 Read Aloud

✓ **Can children use information from the book to compare animal characteristics?**

Build Background Tell children that you will be rereading the book *Who Is the Beast?* Display the Big Book.

● Ask: *What animals did we read about in this book? ¿Sobre qué animales leímos en este libro?*

Listen for Understanding Reread the book to review how the animals are the same and different.

● Let children provide rhyming words if they can and encourage them to join in on the repetitive words, *The beast, the beast!*

● Pause as you read to let children tell you ways that animals are the same and different. *What animals do you see on this page? How are they the same? How are they different? ¿Qué animales ven en esta página? ¿En qué se parecen? ¿En qué se diferencian?*

Respond and Connect Have children connect their new learning to their daily lives. Ask: *What will you look for the next time you see an animal? La próxima vez que vean un animal, ¿qué cosas van a buscar?*

TIP Make sure children recognize the difference in animals coverings – fur, feathers, skin, and scales. Model as needed.

Learn About Letters and Sounds

✓ **Can children identify letters and sounds?**

Review Letters and Sounds Vv, Xx Display ABC Picture Cards for *Vv* and *Xx*. Say the name of each letter and its sound as you point to it. Have children repeat: *The letter is v. The sound is /v/. The letter is x. The sound is /ks/. La letra es v. El sonido es /v/. La letra es x. El sonido es /ks/.*

● Ask children to trace each letter in the air as they say the sound.

● Have children form each letter with their fingers as they say its sound. Children can make a v sign for v and cross index fingers to make x.

● Have children write each letter on paper as they say the letter sound.

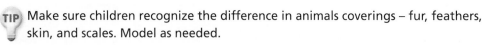 Give children extra practice saying the /v/ and /ks/ sounds. Have children repeat *van, vase, very,* and *vent* and listen for /v/ at the beginning. Then have them repeat *box, wax, fox,* and *mix* and listen for /ks/ at the end.

For additional suggestions on how to meet the needs of children at the Beginning, Intermediate, Advanced, and Advanced-High levels of English proficiency, see pages 320–323.

Who Is the Beast?
¿Quien es la bestia?

ABC Picture Cards

Math Time

small group 15 minutes

Observe and Investigate

✓ **Can children identify and recreate patterns?**

Pattern Strips (The Core) This is a small-group version of the activity done on Day 2. Display *Math and Science Flip Chart* page 42.

- Have children choose a pattern strip to describe its pattern and identify its core unit, and then use the corresponding material (flat, plastic beverage stirrers or Pattern Blocks) to recreate the pattern.

- If children struggle, have them isolate the core unit first and then build on it to mimic the pattern. Have children describe the pattern. Use fingers to simultaneously point to each element of the core unit, such as pointing with three fingers to ABC, and then moving the same fingers to the next ABC, and so on. During discussion, put the word *and* between the core units, such as yellow/green *and* yellow/green.

- Check whether children can identify and reproduce a pattern's core unit or are merely matching it piece by piece.

⚙ Online Math Activity

Children can complete Pattern Planes 2 and Marching Patterns 2 during computer time or Center Time.

Pattern Strips
Tiras con patrones

Math and Science Flip Chart, page 42

large group 15 minutes

⁂ Social and Emotional Development

Making Good Choices

✓ **Do children understand why problem-solving strategies are important?**

Being Helpful Display *Making Good Choices Flip Chart*, page 23, "How Can I Solve Problems?"

- Point to the flip chart illustration. Ask: *How can we solve problems in the classroom? Who can we ask for help? What are some polite words we can use? ¿Cómo podemos resolver problemas en el salón de clase? ¿A quién le podemos pedir ayuda? ¿Qué palabras amables podemos usar?*

- Give partners Connecting Cubes. Say: *Pretend that you're trying to make a pattern. You've tried one or two times, but you are still confused. Show what you can do to solve your problem. Imaginen que uno de ustedes intenta hacer un patrón. Lo han intentado una o dos veces, pero aún están confundidos. Su compañero debe mostrar ahora lo que pueden hacer para resolver el problema* Have one partner role play the child who needs help and the other role play the child who has the answers. Then have partners switch roles and act out the problem and solution again.

 ELL Pair children with proficient partners who can model polite words to use when asking for help.

Making Good Choices Flip Chart, page 23

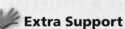

✓ Learning Goal

Social and Emotional Development
- Child demonstrates appropriate conflict-resolution strategies, requesting help when needed.

Language and Communication
- Child matches language to social setting.

Mathematics
- Child identifies, duplicates, and creates simple patterns.

Vocabulary

core unit	unidad principal		
diagonal	diagonal	horizontal	horizontal
pattern	patrón	problem	problema
solve	resolver	vertical	vertical

Differentiated Instruction

✋ Extra Support

Observe and Investigate
If...children need help working with the pattern strips, **then...**model step-by-step patterning. For example, place several AB units next to each other but with a clear space between, and chant the pattern together while pointing to corresponding materials (stirrers or blocks), and then move the units closer to each other, chanting the pattern again.

⭐ Enrichment

Observe and Investigate
Challenge children to work on more complex core units, such as one that begins and ends with the same element (ABBCA).

Learning Goals

Social and Emotional Development
• Child initiates play scenarios with peers that share a common plan and goal.

Science
• Child identifies organisms and describes their characteristics.

Fine Arts
• Child expresses ideas, emotions, and moods through individual and collaborative dramatic play.

Vocabulary

different	diferente	move	moverse
same	igual	similar	similar
sound	sonido	zoo	zoológico

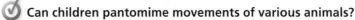 **Differentiated Instruction**

 Extra Support

Explore and Express
If...children have difficulty choosing an animal to pantomime, **then...**review the pictures in *Who Is the Beast?* and have children choose one of those animals.

Enrichment

Explore and Express
Invite children to think of a snack that their animal could bring to the party and pretend to present it to the group, such as honey from a bee, nuts and seeds from a bird, bananas from a monkey, or striped cookies from a tiger.

Dramatic Play Time

 large group 20 minutes

👪 Social and Emotional Development Skills Model positive interactions by engaging with children during their dramatic play and addressing them as their animal characters.

Oral Language and Academic

☑ **Can children name characteristics of animals?**

Animal Characteristics Remind children that they learned how animals are the same and different.

● Ask: *How do animals move? What sounds do they make? ¿Cómo se mueven los animales? ¿Qué sonidos hacen?*

● Ask: *If you could be any animal in the zoo, what would you be? How would you be different from other animals? Si pudieran ser cualquier animal del zoológico, ¿cuál serían? ¿En qué serían diferentes de los demás animales?*

● Have children discuss specific details.

Explore and Express

☑ **Can children pantomime movements of various animals?**

A Night at the Zoo Tell children that they will act out a make-believe scene at a zoo. Tell them to pretend that it is night time at the zoo. All the people are gone and the animals have come out to have a party together.

● Tell children to choose an animal to act out.

● Have children gather together as their animal characters to sing, dance, and play games such as follow the leader, leap frog, and duck, duck, goose.

● Encourage children stay to stay in character during the animal party.

TIP Tell children that even though they are pretend animals that can talk, they should try to move and make noises like real animals.

ELL Have children pair up with English proficient partners. Children can act out the same kind of animal and go to the zoo party as twins or siblings.

Center Time

Center Rotation Center Time includes teacher-guided activities and independent activities. Refer to the **Learning Centers** on pages 100–101 for activities in additional centers.

 small group 30 minutes

Writing Center

✓ **Track children's ability to recall and describe events.**

Materials paper, crayons or washable markers

Zoo News Have children write to describe what they did at their zoo party.

- Show children how to fold a sheet of drawing paper in half to make two writing "pages."

- On one half of the paper have children draw the animal they acted out at the zoo party. On the other half, have them draw a game they played.

- Have children write or dictate to tell about each picture.

Center Tip

If...children need help writing to tell about their pictures, **then...**have them dictate words to you that they can copy.

✓ Learning Goal

Language and Communication
• Child names and describes actual or pictured people, places, things, actions, attributes, and events.

Emergent Literacy: Writing
• Child writes own name or a reasonable approximation of it.

Writing

Recap the day and week. Say: *Name two animals. Tell me one way they are the same and one way they are different.* *Nombren dos animales. Díganme una cosa en la que se parecen y otra en la que se diferencian esos animales.* Record responses on chart paper. Share the pen with children and have them write their name or first initial next to their entry.

Purposeful Play

✓ **Observe children describing experiences.**

Children choose an open center for free playtime. Encourage cooperation skills by suggesting children display the writing done in the Writing Center and take turns telling each other about their pictures.

Let's Say Good-Bye

 large group 15 minutes

 Read Aloud Revisit the story "Rabbit: A Mayan Legend"/"El conejo: una leyenda maya" for your afternoon Read Aloud. Ask children to listen for words that describe the animals.

 Home Connection Refer to the Home Connections activities listed in the Resources and Materials chart on page 97. Remind children to tell families which animal they played at the party and what the animal did. Sing the "Good-Bye Song" as children prepare to leave.

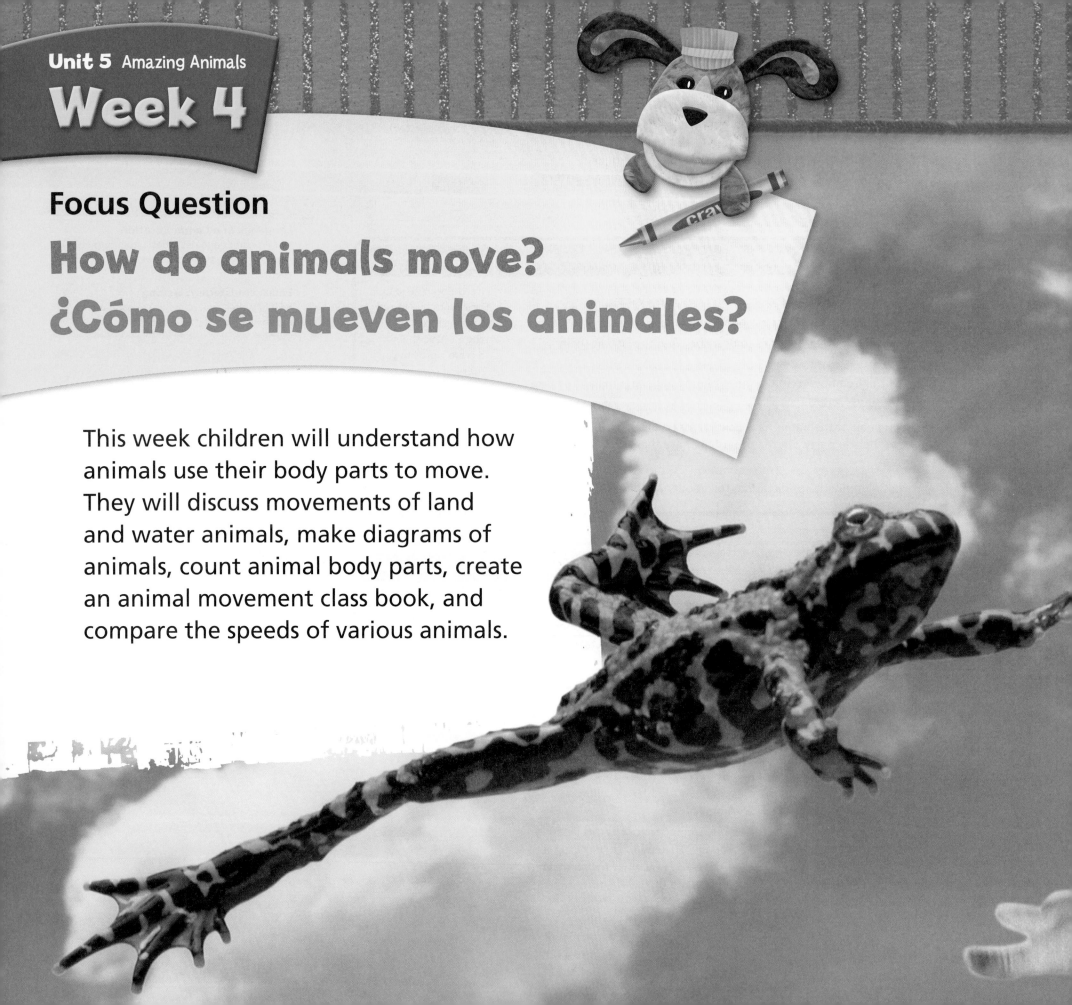

Week 4

Focus Question

How do animals move?
¿Cómo se mueven los animales?

This week children will understand how animals use their body parts to move. They will discuss movements of land and water animals, make diagrams of animals, count animal body parts, create an animal movement class book, and compare the speeds of various animals.

Social and Emotional Development	DAY				
	1	2	3	4	5
Child initiates interactions with others in work and play situations.				✓	
Child demonstrates appropriate conflict-resolution strategies, requesting help when needed.	✓	✓	✓	✓	✓

Language and Communication	DAY				
	1	2	3	4	5
Child demonstrates an understanding of oral language by responding appropriately.		✓	✓	✓	
Child follows two- and three-step oral directions.				✓	
Child begins and ends conversations appropriately.					✓
Child follows basic rules for conversations (taking turns, staying on topic, listening actively).				✓	
Child experiments with and produces a growing number of sounds in English words. (ELL)				✓	
Child names and describes actual or pictured people, places, things, actions, attributes, and events.	✓	✓	✓	✓	✓
Child understands or knows the meaning of many thousands of words, many more than he or she uses.	✓				
Child uses newly learned vocabulary daily in multiple contexts.			✓	✓	

Emergent Literacy: Reading	DAY				
	1	2	3	4	5
Child enjoys and chooses reading-related activities.				✓	
Child generates words that rhyme.	✓	✓		✓	✓
Child names most upper- and lowercase letters of the alphabet.	✓	✓	✓	✓	✓
Child identifies the letter that stands for a given sound.	✓	✓	✓	✓	✓
Child produces the most common sound for a given letter.		✓	✓		
Child describes, relates to, and uses details and information from books read aloud.	✓	✓		✓	✓

Emergent Literacy: Writing	DAY				
	1	2	3	4	5
Child participates in free drawing and writing activities to deliver information.			✓		
Child uses scribbles, shapes, pictures, symbols, and letters to represent language.					✓

Mathematics	DAY				
	1	2	3	4	5
Child counts 1–10 concrete objects correctly.	✓	✓		✓	
Child demonstrates that the numerical counting sequence is always the same.	✓	✓			
Child tells how many are in a group of up to 5 objects without counting.		✓		✓	
Child recognizes and names numerals 0 through 9.	✓			✓	
Child recognizes, names, describes, matches, compares, and sorts common two-dimensional shapes (such as circle, square, rectangle, triangle, rhombus).					✓
Child sorts objects and explains how the sorting was done.		✓			
Child collects, organizes, and records data using a graphic representation.	✓				
Child identifies, duplicates, and creates simple patterns.			✓		

Science	DAY				
	1	2	3	4	5
Child identifies organisms and describes their characteristics.	✓	✓	✓		✓
Child observes, understands, and discusses the relationship of plants and animals to their environments.	✓				✓

Social Studies	DAY				
	1	2	3	4	5
Child understands and discusses roles, responsibilities, and services provided by community workers.			✓		
Child identifies common areas and features of home, school, and community.			✓		

Fine Arts	DAY				
	1	2	3	4	5
Child uses and experiments with a variety of art materials and tools in various art activities.			✓		

Physical Development	DAY				
	1	2	3	4	5
Child coordinates body movements in a variety of locomotive activities (such as walking, jumping, running, hopping, skipping, climbing).	✓				✓
Child develops small-muscle strength and control.			✓		

Technology Applications	DAY				
	1	2	3	4	5
Child names and uses various computer parts (such as mouse, keyboard, CD-ROM, microphone, touch screen).			✓		

Materials and Resources

DAY 1	DAY 2	DAY 3	DAY 4	DAY 5

Program Materials

DAY 1	DAY 2	DAY 3	DAY 4	DAY 5
• Teacher's Treasure Book • Oral Language Development Cards 48, 49 • Rhymes and Chants Flip Chart • *Move!* Big Book • ABC Picture Cards • Numeral Cards • Building Blocks Math Activities • Making Good Choices Flip Chart • Math and Science Flip Chart • Home Connections Resource Guide	• Teacher's Treasure Book • Dog Puppets • Photo Library CD-ROM • Alphabet/Letter Tiles • Two-Color Counters • *Move!* Big Book • ABC Big Book • Shape Sets • Building Blocks Math Activities • Making Good Choices Flip Chart • Math and Science Flip Chart • Counting Cards	• Teacher's Treasure Book • Oral Language Development Card 50 • Sequence Cards: "Building a Home" • Rhymes and Chants Flip Chart • Concept Big Book 3: *Amazing Animals* • ABC Big Book • ABC Picture Cards • Making Good Choices Flip Chart • Photo Library CD-ROM	• Teacher's Treasure Book • Dog Puppets • Photo Library CD-ROM • ABC Big Book • ABC Picture Cards • Dot Cards • Numeral Cards • Math and Science Flip Chart • Farm Animal Counters • Home Connections Resource Guide	• Teacher's Treasure Book • Rhymes and Chants Flip Chart • Photo Library CD-ROM • Alphabet/Letter tiles • *Move!* Big Book • ABC Picture Cards • Shape Sets or Pattern Blocks • Making Good Choices Flip Chart • Farm Animal Counters

Other Materials

DAY 1	DAY 2	DAY 3	DAY 4	DAY 5
• Books about animals • Paper • Crayons • Photos of animals • Mural paper • Scissors • Paste	• Small box or can • Cardboard squares • Paper plates • Crayons • Yarn • Glue • Pieces of felt or construction paper • Craft sticks	• Drawing paper and crayons • Paper plates • Construction paper • Glue • Assorted art supplies • Books about community workers • Blocks • Miniature figures of community workers and their vehicles	• Different versions of several folk tales and fairy tales • Paper	• Magazines • Glue • Paper • Crayons or markers • Puppet (Mr. Mixup) • Blocks • Construction paper • Animal toys

Home Connection

DAY 1	DAY 2	DAY 3	DAY 4	DAY 5
Remind children to tell families about animals that live on water, land, or both. Send home Weekly Parent Letter, Home Connections Resource Guide, pp. 51–52.	Remind children to show families how they can count objects around the house.	Remind children to tell families about the important jobs community workers do.	Remind children to tell families a story about animals. Send home Story Book 15, Home Connections Resource Guide pp. 137–140.	Remind children to show families the different ways they moved today and to tell families what they learned this week about the ways animals move.

Assessment

As you observe children throughout the week, you may fill out an Anecdotal Observational Record Form to document an individual's progress toward a goal or signs indicating the need for developmental or medical evaluation. You may also choose to select work for each child's portfolio. The Anecdotal Observational Record Form and Weekly Assessment rubrics are available in the assessment section of DLMExpressOnline.com.

More Literature Suggestions

- **The Three Little Gators** by Helen Ketteman
- **Birds** by Kevin Henkes
- **Carry Me** by Susan Stokdale
- **What Do You Do With a Tail Like This?** by Robin Page and Steve Jenkins
- **Fish Eyes: A Book You Can Count On** by Lois Ehlert

- **Nadarín** por Leo Lionni
- **Harquin: el zorro que bajó al valle** por John Burningham
- **El pingüino Pedro y sus nuevos amigos** por Marcus Pfister
- **Spot va a la escuela** por Eric Hill
- **En el coche** por Claude Ponti

Daily Planner

		DAY 1	DAY 2
Let's Start the Day Language Time	large group	**Opening Routines** p. 140 **Morning Read Aloud** p. 140 **Oral Language and Vocabulary** p. 140 Animal Body Parts and Animal Places **Phonological Awareness** p. 140 Recognize Rhyming Words	**Opening Routines** p. 146 **Morning Read Aloud** p. 146 **Oral Language and Vocabulary** p. 146 How Pets Move **Phonological Awareness** p. 146 Recognize Rhyming Word
Center Time	small group	**Focus On:** **Library and Listening Center** p. 141 **Pretend and Learn Center** p. 141	**Focus On:** **ABC Center** p. 147 **Creativity Center** p. 147
Circle Time Literacy Time	large group	**Read Aloud** *Move!/¡A moverse!* p. 142 **Learn About Letters and Sounds: Review Letters** *Cc, Uu, Xx, Vv* p. 142	**Read Aloud** *Move!/¡A moverse!* p. 148 **Learn About Letters and Sounds: Review Letters** *Cc, Uu, Xx, Vv* p.148
Math Time	large group	**Number Jump** p. 143	**Guess My Rule** p. 149
Social and Emotional Development	large group	**Solving Problems** p. 143	**Being Helpful** p. 149
Content Connection	large group	**Science:** **Oral Language and Academic Vocabulary** p. 144 Talking About Land and Water Animals **Observe and Investigate** p. 144 Which Animal Is It?	**Math:** **Snapshots** p. 150 **Draw Farm Animals** p. 150
Center Time	small group	**Focus On:** **Math and Science Center** p. 145 **Purposeful Play** p. 145	**Focus On:** **Math and Science Center** p. 151 **Purposeful Play** p. 151
Let's Say Good-Bye	large group	**Read Aloud** p.145 **Writing** p. 145 **Home Connection** p. 145	**Read Aloud** p. 151 **Writing** p. 151 **Home Connection** p. 151

DAY 3

Opening Routines p. 152
Morning Read Aloud p. 152
Oral Language and Vocabulary
p. 152 Animal Body Parts and Animal Places
Phonological Awareness
p. 152 Recognize Rhyming Words

Focus On:
Writer's Center p. 153
Creativity Center p. 153

Read Aloud
Amazing Animals/
Animales asombrosos
p. 154
Learn About Letters and Sounds: Review Letters
Cc, Uu, Xx, Vv p. 154

 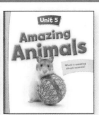

Listen and Copy p. 155

Being Helpful p. 155

Social Studies:
Oral Language and Academic Vocabulary
p. 156 Talking About Community Workers
Understand and Participate
p. 156 Learning About Community Workers

Focus On:
Construction Center p. 157
Purposeful Play p.157

Read Aloud p.157
Writing p. 157
Home Connection p.157

DAY 4

Opening Routines p. 158 Morning Read Aloud p. 282
Oral Language and Vocabulary
p. 158 Animal Friends
Phonological Awareness
p. 158 Recognize Rhyming Words

Focus On:
Library and Listening Center p. 159
Pretend and Learn Center p. 159

Read Aloud
"Tortoise Wins a Race"/
"*La tortuga gana la carrera*" p. 160
Learn About Letters and Sounds: Review Letters
Cc, Uu, Xx, Vv p. 160

Memory Number p. 161

Being Helpful p. 161

Math:
Counting Farm Animals p. 162
Count and Move p. 162

Focus On:
Math and Science Center p. 163
Purposeful Play p. 163

Read Aloud p. 163
Writing p. 163
Home Connection p. 163

DAY 5

Opening Routines p. 164
Morning Read Aloud p. 164
Oral Language and Vocabulary
p. 164 How Animals Move
Phonological Awareness
p. 164 Recognize Rhyming Words

Focus On:
Writer's Center p. 165
ABC Center p. 165

Read Aloud *Move!/¡A moverse!* p. 166
Learn About Letters and Sounds: Cc, Uu, Xx, Vv p. 166

Mr. Mixup (Shapes) p. 167

Being Helpful p. 167

Outdoor Play:
Oral Language and Academic Vocabulary
p. 168 All Living Things Move
Explore Movement p. 168 Hop, Skip, and Jump

Focus On:
Construction Center p. 169
Purposeful Play p. 169

Read Aloud p. 169
Writing p. 169
Home Connection p. 169

Learning Centers

Math and Science Center

Observing Animals
Children complete a chart with the headings, *0 Legs, 2 Legs, 4 Legs,* and *6 Legs* by drawing pictures of animals and pasting them in the correct columns. See p. 145.

X-Ray Vision
Partners place Counting Cards 1–10 facedown in order and take turns pointing to a card and telling what it is. Then they match the correct number of counters to each card. See p. 151.

Count and Compare
Each partner creates a set of 1–10 animal counters. Children count each set and determine which set has more. See p. 163.

Do You Remember?
Partners display a set of 4–5 different counters. One partner covers his/her eyes as the other removes a counter. The first child tells which counter was removed.

ABC Center

Letter Bingo
Children use bingo cards with the letters *C, c, U, u, X, x, V,* and *v* written in the squares. When a letter is called, children cover it on their card. The first child to cover a row wins. See p. 147.

Matching Letters
Children match uppercase and lowercase forms of *Cc, Uu, Xx,* and *Vv* as they chant the sound of each letter. Then they write each letter with a crayon or marker. See p. 165.

Birdseed Letters
Children use glue to write the letters *Cc, Uu, Xx,* and *Vv,* and then sprinkle birdseed over the glue.

Creativity Center

Paper Plate Pet Puppets
Children create pet puppets by drawing or gluing features on a paper plate and attaching a craft stick to the back of it. See p. 147.

Birds in a Nest
Children use half a paper plate and construction paper to create birds in a nest. They use colored tissue for feathers. See p. 153.

Bunny Tail Art
Children use cotton balls and finger paint to make bunny prints by dabbing the cotton balls in paint and pressing them against paper in the shape of a rabbit.

Bird Feeder
Children tie a piece of string around a pinecone, spread peanut butter on the pinecone, and roll it in birdseed. Hang it in a tree and see what happens.

Library and Listening Center

Browsing Animal Books
Children browse through animal books and choose an animal. They draw a diagram of that animal and use arrows to point to three or four of its body parts. See p. 141.

Browsing Stories and Tales
Children browse through different versions of folk tales and fairy tales to see that the same story can vary. They talk about how the stories are alike and different. See p. 159.

Favorite Book
Partners look through books they have heard or read this week, identify which one they like best, and explain why it is their favorite.

Construction Center

Build a Community
Partners use blocks to build a community that includes buildings such as a police station, hospital, post office, and school, and shows community workers doing their jobs. See p. 157.

Build a Running Track
Children use blocks and other art materials to build a running track for animals. They pretend two animals are having a race and discuss which animal is faster. See p. 169.

Build a Petting Farm
Children use blocks and Connecting Cubes to build a petting farm. They use plastic animals or make them from clay.

Writer's Center

Matching Movement and Rhyme
Children draw pictures of animals that show specific action words, such as *run*, *hop*, and *fly*. Then they match the action word with a rhyming word. See p. 153.

Animals Move
Children create a class book called "Animals Like to Move." They draw a picture of an animal and write or dictate words that tell how it moves. See p. 165.

Amazing Animals
Children choose an animal that they think is amazing, draw a picture of it, and write or dictate to tell why it is so special.

Pretend and Learn Center

Moving Like a Monkey
Children use what they have learned about monkeys to move in a variety of ways. Partners then guess and describe what the "monkey" is doing. See p. 141.

Create a New Version of a Song
Children create a new version of "Old MacDonald Had a Farm," such as "Old MacDonald Had a Zoo," and perform the song for the class. See p. 159.

A Visit to the Vet
Children set up a veterinarian's office, using stuffed animals, bandages, and other props. They take turns playing the veterinarian and pet owner.

Can It Be?
A child says something about an animal that is true or false, such as, "hens lay eggs" or "dogs can fly." Other children tell whether the statement is true or not.

Let's Start the Day

Focus Question

How do animals move?
¿Cómo se mueven los animales?

✓ Learning Goals

Social and Emotional Development
• Child demonstrates appropriate conflict-resolution strategies, requesting help when needed.

Language and Communication
• Child understands or knows the meaning of many thousands of words, many more than he or she uses.

Emergent Literacy: Reading
• Child generates words that rhyme.

Vocabulary

arm	brazo	branch	rama
head	cabeza	monkey	mono
throat	cuello	tree	arbol

Differentiated Instruction

 Extra Support

Phonological Awareness
If...children have difficulty recognizing words that rhyme, **then...**say a series of word pairs, some of which rhyme and some of which do not. Say: *Raise your hand if you hear two words that rhyme: cat/bat, cat/fox, fox/box, box/hen, hen/pen, pig/wig* Levanten la mano si escuchan dos palabras que riman: cat/bat, cat/fox, fox/box, box/hen, hen/pen, pig/wig. Point out the same ending sounds in the rhyming pairs.

 ★ **Enrichment**

Phonological Awareness
Challenge children to suggest words that rhyme with *hop, stomp, snap,* and *waddle.* (*pop, mop, top; chomp, clomp, swamp; tap, clap, map; model, toddle.*)

▶ **Opening Routines and Transition Tips**
For **Opening Routines** and **Transition Tips** turn to pages 178–181 and visit **DLMExpressOnline.com** for more ideas.

 Read **"The Zanzibar Zoo"/**"El zoológico de Zanzíbar" from the *Teacher's Treasure Book,* page 305, for your morning Read Aloud.

Language Time

 large group / 15 minutes

👥 **Social and Emotional Development** Remind children that if they are not sure what to do, they may ask their classmates for help as they work. They may also ask you for help whenever necessary.

Oral Language and Vocabulary

✓ **Can children use words that name an animal's body parts and places where it lives?**

Animal Body Parts and Animal Places Talk about familiar animals, such as birds, insects, pets, or farm animals. Ask: *Can you name the parts of a bird? Where does a bird live? ¿Qué partes del cuerpo de los pájaros conocen? ¿Dónde viven los pájaros?*

• Display *Oral Language Development Card 48.* Name the animals (monkeys) and point out their body parts and where they are resting. Then follow the suggestions on the back of the card.

Oral Language Development Card 48

Phonological Awareness

✓ **Can children identify words that rhyme?**

Recognize Rhyming Words Display *Rhymes and Chants Flip Chart,* page 24. Tell children that rhyming words end with the same sounds. For example, *run* and *fun* both end in *-un.*

Recite "At the Zoo" in a lively voice. Guide children to find the rhyming words *kangaroo, zoo, do,* and *too.*

ELL Use the *Rhymes and Chants Flip Chart* to revisit the action words *hop, stomp, snap,* and *waddle.* Say each word and pantomime the action for children. Then have children pantomime the action with you as they say the word.

For additional suggestions on how to meet the needs of children at the Beginning, Intermediate, Advanced, and Advanced-High levels of English proficiency, see pages 184–187.

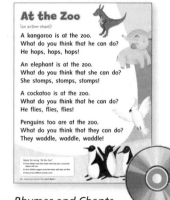

Rhymes and Chants Flip Chart, page 24

Center Time

> **Center Rotation** Center Time includes teacher-guided activities and independent activities. Refer to the **Learning Centers** on pages 138–139 for activities in additional centers.

 small group 60–90 minutes

Library and Listening Center

Center Tip

☑ Track the use of names of animal body parts as children share diagrams of chosen animals and identify body parts.

Materials animal books, paper, crayons

Browsing Animal Books Have children browse through animal books to choose an animal for their diagram.

● Have children draw a picture of the animal and draw arrows to show three or four body parts.

● Ask: **Which body part helps the animal move?** *¿Qué parte ayuda al animal a moverse?*

● Have children share their diagrams with a partner, pointing to each body part as they name it.

 If...children have difficulty recalling the name of a body part, **then...**offer them a clue by saying a word that rhymes with the part (e.g., *begs/legs; sings/wings; mail/tail; red/head.*)

Pretend and Learn Center

Center Tip

☑ Look for examples of children solving problems and figuring things out together. Compliment them for helping each other out.

Moving Like a Monkey Have children use what they learned about monkeys to move in a variety of ways.

● Partners take turns pantomiming a movement, while the other partner guesses what the action is (e.g., climb, run, swing, eat, sit, rest, and sleep).

● Encourage children to speak in complete sentences to describe what the monkey is doing, for example: *The monkey climbs a tree.*

 If...children have difficulty coming up with actions to pantomime, **then...**offer suggestions or display *Oral Language Development Card 48.*

Learning Goals

Social and Emotional Development
● Child demonstrates appropriate conflict-resolution strategies, requesting help when needed.

Language and Communication
● Child understands or knows the meaning of many thousands of words, many more than he or she uses.

Physical Development
● Child coordinates body movements in a variety of locomotive activities (such as walking, jumping, running, hopping, skipping, climbing).

Differentiated Instruction

✋ **Extra Support**

Library and Listening Center
If...children have difficulty drawing a picture of an animal, **then...**have them use the animal's picture in the book and name the body parts.

⭐ **Enrichment**

Library and Listening Center
Challenge children to describe the different ways the animal can move.

Focus Question

How do animals move?

¿Cómo se mueven los animales?

 Learning Goals

Emergent Literacy: Reading

• Child names most upper- and lowercase letters of the alphabet.

• Child identifies the letter that stands for a given sound.

• Child describes, relates to, and uses details and information from books read aloud.

Science

• Child identifies organisms and describes their characteristics.

Vocabulary

colony	colonia	float	flotar
leap	saltar	move	moverse
prey	presa	slither	deslizarse
snag	atrapar	startled	asustar

 Differentiated Instruction

Extra Support

Learn About Letters and Sounds

If...children have difficulty "writing" the letters *Cc, Uu, Xx,* and *Vv* with a wet paintbrush, **then...**have them dip their finger in water and trace letters that you have written on the chalkboard.

Enrichment

Learn About Letters and Sounds

Challenge children to find words and names that begin with *Cc, Uu,* and *Vv* or end with *Xx* around the classroom. Have them choose a word or name and use Alphabet/Letter Tiles to build it. Have children read the words they build.

Literacy Time

 large group · 15 minutes

📖 Read Aloud

✓ **Can children categorize information learned from a book?**

Build Background Tell children that you will be reading a book about amazing animals and the different ways they can move.

● Ask: *Can you name animals that run? Can you name animals that fly?* ¿Qué animales corren? ¿Cuáles vuelan?

Listen for Enjoyment Display the cover of the book *Move!* and read the title. Conduct a picture walk.

● Browse through the pages. Name each animal and describe how it moves.

● Say: *Some animals move in the same way. For example, a gibbon can walk. What other animals walk?* Algunos animales se mueven de la misma manera. Por ejemplo, los gibones caminan. ¿Qué otros animales caminan?

Respond to the Story Have children talk about how different animals move and which animals move in the same way. Ask: *Which animals can swim? Which animals can fly?* ¿Qué animales nadan? ¿Cuáles vuelan?

TIP Be sure children can use information in the book to categorize how animals move. Say: *A crocodile slithers in the water. Which animal slithers on land?* Un cocodrilo se desliza en el agua. ¿Qué animal se desliza por la tierra?

ELL As you leaf through *Move!*, point out characteristics of the animals, such as the long legs of a jacana. Encourage children to point out and describe features they notice. Explain that a gibbon is a type of monkey and that jacana, roadrunner, and penguin are types of birds.

Learn About Letters and Sounds

✓ **Can children identify the sounds /k/, /u/, /ks/, and /v/, spelled *Cc, Uu, Xx,* and *Vv*?**

Review Letters *Cc, Uu, Xx, Vv* Use the ABC Picture Cards to review the letters. Point to the cake on the ABC Picture Card for *Cc.* Say: *The word* cake *begins with the letter Cc. The letter* c *makes the sound /k/. What sound does the letter Cc make?* La palabra cake comienza con la letra Cc. La letra c tiene el sonido /k/. ¿Qué sonido tiene la letra Cc?

● Point to the upper case and lower case *Cc,* trace them on the card, and then write the letters on the chalkboard. Have children use a paintbrush dipped in water to "write" their own upper case and lower case *Cc* on the chalkboard.

● Repeat for the letters *Uu, Xx,* and *Vv.* Point out how the upper case and lower case letters are similar.

Move!
¡A moverse!

ABC Picture Cards

Math Time

Observe and Investigate

✓ Can children identify numbers and count?

Number Jump Show a Numeral Card from 1 to 9 (*Teacher's Treasure Book,* pages 510–511). Have children jump safely or move in another way that many times.

● Show children Numeral Card 5. Say: **What number is this? Let's pretend we are kangaroos and jump five times.** *¿Qué número es éste? Imaginemos que somos canguros y saltamos cinco veces.* As children jump, count the jumps together. Repeat with other numerals.

● Change jumping to another animal movement, such as hopping like a rabbit. Show children Numeral Card 7, and say: **Let's hop like a rabbit this many times. A rabbit hops fast.** *Vamos a saltar como conejos. Un conejo salta rápido.* Repeat with other numerals and have children walk slowly like an ant or a turtle.

 Give children many opportunities to practice counting throughout the day, for example: **How many books are on the table? Let's count them: 1, 2, 3, 4.**

Building Blocks

Online Math Activity

Introduce Party Time 3: Produce Groups, in which children are told how many guests are attending a party and then asked to set out that many items. Each child should complete the activity this week.

👫 Social and Emotional Development

Making Good Choices

✓ Do children show a desire to solve problems independently?

Solving Problems Discuss how problems can come up between friends. Display the *Making Good Choices Flip Chart*, page 24. Point to the two children who have reached for the same puzzle.

● Ask: **What is happening in the picture? Is there a problem? What do you think it is? What's a good idea to help solve the problem?** *¿Qué sucede en la ilustración? ¿Hay algún problema? ¿Cuál creen que sea? ¿Qué idea se les ocurre para solucionar el problema?*

● Then discuss the solutions the children have suggested plus any you add. For example, the children might do the puzzle together or take turns doing the puzzle.

● Play the song "Pushy, Pushy, Pushy"/"La cancion del empujon" from the Making Good Choices Audio CD. Ask children whether being pushy is a good way to solve the problem of two people wanting to use the same toy.

Making Good Choices Flip Chart, page 24

Learning Goals

Social and Emotional Desvelopment
● Child demonstrates appropriate conflict-resolution strategies, requesting help when needed.

Mathematics
● Child counts 1–10 concrete objects correctly.
● Child demonstrates that the numerical counting sequence is always the same.
● Child recognizes and names numerals 0 through 9.

Vocabulary

count	contar	fast	rápido
number	número	slow	lento

Differentiated Instruction

✋ **Extra Support**

Observe and Investigate
If...children struggle with counting from 1 to 9, **then...**focus on mastering Numeral Cards 1 to 5 before progressing further.

⭐ **Enrichment**

Observe and Investigate
Children who have mastered counting from 1 to 9 can be introduced to numerals 10, 11, and 12.

Accommodations for 3's

Observe and Investigate
If...children struggle with counting, **then...**focus on counting 1, 2, and 3 objects.

Science Time

large group 🕐 20 minutes

Oral Language and Academic Vocabulary

✔ Can children categorize animals that live and move in water and on land?

Talking About Land and Water Animals Point to the *Math and Science Flip Chart.* Ask: *What animals do you see? What are they doing? ¿Qué animales ven? ¿Qué están haciendo?*

● Point to the turtle in the water. Ask: *What kind of animal is this? What is it doing? Where else do you see a turtle? ¿Qué tipo de animal es éste? ¿Qué está haciendo? ¿En qué otro lugar pueden ver una tortuga?* Have children point to the turtle on land. Ask: *How do turtles move on land? ¿Cómo se mueven las tortugas en la tierra?* Help children recognize that turtles move very slowly.

● Discuss that ducks and frogs can swim in water and move on land. Say: *Ducks waddle when they walk on land. Can you think of another animal that waddles?* (penguin) *Los patos se balancean cuando caminan sobre la tierra. ¿Qué otros animales se balancean al caminar? (los pingüinos)*

● Explain that fish must live in water. They cannot live or move on land. Display *Oral Language Card 49.* Name the animal (manatee). Explain that this animal lives in the water all the time. In that way, it is like a fish. Emphasize that a manatee is not a fish, though, and that It looks and behaves very differently from the ways fish do. Then follow the suggestions on the back of the card.

● Ask: *Which animals can only swim and live in water? Which animals can swim in water and move on land? ¿Qué animales pueden nadar y vivir en el agua? ¿Cuáles pueden nadar en el agua y moverse sobre la tierra?*

ELL Make sure children understand the meanings of the words *land* and *water.* Point to the water on the chart, make swimming motions, and say: *This is water.* Point to the land and say: *This is land. Animals and people walk on land.*

Observe and Investigate

✔ Can children match animals and their movements when given clues?

Which Animal Is It? Tell children that you will give them clues about animals they have learned about. They will figure out the animal(s) that match the clue.

● Say: *I'm thinking of a very large animal that swims in the water. It does not live on land. What is it?* (manatee) *Estoy pensando en un animal muy grande que nada en el agua. No vive en la tierra. ¿Cuál es? (manatí)*

● Say: *I'm thinking of two animals that swim in water and move on land. They both have a dark green color. What are they?* (frog and turtle) *Estoy pensando en dos animales que nadan en el agua y se mueven en la tierra. Ambos tienen un color verde oscuro. ¿Cuáles son? (rana y tortuga)*

Math and Science Flip Chart page 43

Oral Language Development Card 49

Center Time

▶ **Center Rotation** Center Time includes teacher-guided activities and independent activities. Refer to the **Learning Centers** on pages 138–139 for activities in additional centers.

small group — 30 minutes

Math and Science Center

✓ **Encourage children to identify how many legs an animal has.**

Materials picture books about animals or photos of animals, a large sheet of mural paper, scissors, paste

Observing Animals Divide a large sheet of mural paper into four columns with these headings: *0 Legs, 2 Legs, 4 Legs*, and *6 Legs*. Say: **We are going to draw pictures of animals and count the number of legs they have. Then we will paste the pictures in the correct columns.** *Vamos a dibujar animales y a contar el número de patas que tienen. Después, pegaremos los dibujos en la columna correcta.*

● Have children use the books and photos to help them select an animal to draw. Watch as they observe and draw the animal.

● Have children cut out their picture, count the number of legs on the animal, and then paste the picture in the correct column.

Center Tip

If...children need help counting the legs on their animal, **then**...count with them and help them match the number to the correct column.

Purposeful Play

✓ **Observe children taking turns and communicating in respectful ways.**

Children choose an open center for free playtime. Encourage appropriate behavior and problem-solving skills by suggesting they take turns to pantomime the movements of the animal whose picture they pasted on the chart.

Let's Say Good-Bye

large group — 15 minutes

 Read Aloud Revisit the story "The Zanzibar Zoo"/"El zoológico de Zanzíbar" for your afternoon Read Aloud. Ask children to listen for words with the sounds /k/ and /u/.

 Home Connection Refer to the Home Connections activities listed in the Resources and Materials chart on page 135. Remind children to tell families about animals that live in water, on land, or both. Sing the "Good-Bye Song" as children prepare to leave.

✓ Learning Goals

Social and Emotional Development
• Child demonstrates appropriate conflict-resolution strategies, requesting help when needed.

Language and Communication
• Child names and describes actual or pictured people, places, things, actions, attributes, and events.

Mathematics
• Child collects, organizes, and records data using a graphic representation.

Science
• Child identifies organisms and describes their characteristics.

Writing

Recap the day. Have children discuss the animals they learned about. Ask: **Which animals move on land and swim in water? Which animals can swim only in water?** *¿Qué animales se mueven en la tierra y nadan en el agua? ¿Qué animales solamente nadan en el agua?* Record their answers. Read them back as you track the print, and emphasize the correspondence between speech and print.

Focus Question

How do animals move?
¿Cómo se mueven los animales?

 Learning Goals

Language and Communication
• Child names and describes actual or pictured people, places, things, actions, attributes, and events.

Emergent Literacy: Reading
• Child generates words that rhyme.

Vocabulary

climb	trepar	crawl	arrastrarse
leap	saltar	run	correr
swim	nadar	walk	caminar

Differentiated Instruction

 Extra Support

Oral Language and Vocabulary
If...children have difficulty describing how a pet moves, **then...**offer a picture stimulus, and ask: *What is the puppy doing? How is it moving?* *¿Qué hace el perrito? ¿Cómo se mueve?*

Enrichment

Oral Language and Vocabulary
Expand children's vocabularies during the discussion by adding action words such as *prance, dance, spring, pounce,* and *creep.* Briefly define each word and reinforce during Center Time play.

Let's Start the Day

 Opening Routines and Transition Tips
For **Opening Routines** and **Transition Tips** turn to pages 178–181 and visit DLMExpressOnline.com for more ideas.

Read **"Monkey See, Monkey Do"/"Como los monos"** from the *Teacher's Treasure Book,* page 224, for your morning Read Aloud.

Language Time

large group   15 minutes

Social and Emotional Development Remind children to take turns as they talk about pets.

Oral Language and Vocabulary

Can children identify that an animal can move in several ways?

How Pets Move Have children talk about their pets or pets they have seen. Ask: *What kinds of pets do you have or would you like to have? What kinds of pets do you know about? How do these pets get from one place to another? ¿Qué tipos de mascotas tienen? ¿Qué tipo de mascotas conocen? ¿Cómo se mueven esas mascotas?*

● Have children name a pet and describe the different ways it can move around. Help them recognize that a pet, such as a cat, can move in a number of ways. For example, it can walk, run, and climb. Ask: *How many different ways can your pet move? Do you think it could run faster than you can? ¿De cuántas maneras se pueden mover sus mascotas? ¿Pueden correr más rápido que ustedes?*

● Encourage children to name some ways that a pet can move, using appropriate action words. Choose a few children to demonstrate how their pets move from one place to another.

Phonological Awareness

Can children identify words that rhyme?

Recognize Rhyming Words Display the Dog Puppets. Tell children that each puppet will say a word. If the words rhyme, children should flap their arms like a bird. Remind them that rhyming words end with the same sound, such as *walk* and *talk.* Have the puppets say these and other word pairs: *climb/time, run/eat, jump/bump, swim/him, leap/keep, fly/see, float/boat.*

 Display animal photos from the *Photo Library CD-ROM.* Choose pets, such as parakeet, hamster, and rabbit. Then ask simple questions about each animal, for example: *Can a rabbit walk? Can a rabbit run? Can a rabbit fly?* Have children answer your questions with complete sentences.

For additional suggestions on how to meet the needs of children at the Beginning, Intermediate, Advanced, and Advanced-High levels of English proficiency, see pages 184-187.

Center Time

▶ **Center Rotation** Center Time includes teacher-guided activities and independent activities. Refer to the **Learning Centers** on pages 138–139 for activities in additional centers.

 small group 60–90 minutes

ABC Center

 Review the letters and sounds for *Cc, Uu, Xx,* and *Vv.*

Materials Alphabet/Letter Tiles for *C, c, U, u, X, x, V, v*; Two-Color Counters; a small box or can; a cardboard square for each child, divided into nine small squares with the letters *C, c, U, u, X, x, V,* and *v* written randomly in the squares. (Note that one letter will be written twice.)

Letter Bingo Place the Alphabet/Letter Tiles in a box or can. Give each child a card.

- Choose an Alphabet/Letter Tile from the box. Ask: ***What is the name of this letter? What sound does the letter make?*** *¿Cuál es el nombre de esta letra? ¿Qué sonido tiene?*

- Have children say the name of the letter and identify its sound. Then have them find it on their cards, and cover it with a counter.

- The first child to cover a row across or down wins the game. Play a few times.

Center Tip

If...children have difficulty distinguishing between upper case and lower case letters on their card, **then...**remind them that the upper case letters are larger than their lower case counterparts.

Creativity Center

 Listen for words children use to describe their pet's movements as they act them out with puppets.

Materials paper plates, crayons, yarn, glue, pieces of felt or construction paper, craft sticks

Paper Plate Pet Puppets Tell children that they will use paper plates to create pet puppets.

- Distribute the paper plates. Have children draw features on the plates or glue art materials on them to represent their pet's features. Say: ***Think about what your pet looks like.*** *Piensen en cómo se ve su mascota.*

- Then glue a wide craft stick to the back of the plate. Have children show how their pet puppets walk, run, climb, and swim. Say: ***Show me how your puppets can move.*** *Cuenten y muestren cómo se mueven sus mascotas.*

Center Tip

If...children are not sure where on the plate to glue or draw each feature, **then...**draw a small "x" to indicate where a feature should be placed.

✓ Learning Goals

Emergent Literacy: Reading
- Child names most upper- and lowercase letters of the alphabet.
- Child produces the most common sound for a given letter.

Science
- Child identifies organisms and describes their characteristics.

Differentiated Instruction

✋ Extra Support
ABC Center
If...children have difficulty remembering the sound of a letter, **then...**have them echo the sound after you say it.

★ Enrichment
ABC Center
Challenge children to name words that begin with the sounds /k/, /u/, and /v/. They may also name words that end with the sound /ks/.

Accommodations for 3's
ABC Center
If...children have difficulty finding a letter from among the other letters, **then...**play the game with only two letters at a time, such as *Cc* and *Uu,* and use cards that have only six squares.

Focus Question

How do animals move?
¿Cómo se mueven los animales?

✓ Learning Goals

Emergent Literacy: Reading
• Child names most upper- and lowercase letters of the alphabet.
• Child identifies the letter that stands for a given sound.
• Child produces the most common sound for a given letter.
• Child describes, relates to, and uses details and information from books read aloud.

Science
• Child identifies organisms and describes their characteristics.

Vocabulary

climb	trepar	different	diferente
dive	zambullirse	run	correr
same	igual	swim	nadar
walk	caminar		

Differentiated Instruction

 Extra Support

Learn About Letters and Sounds
If...children have difficulty writing the letters *Cc, Uu, Xx,* and *Vv,* **then...**have them use clay to form the letters and then trace them with their finger.

 Enrichment

Learn About Letters and Sounds
Tell children there are several words that begin with the letter *c* and one word that begins with the letter *u* in the book *Move!* (catch, crocodile, climb, climbs, colony; up). Have children find the words and flag them with sticky notes.

Literacy Time

 large group ⏱ 15 minutes

📖 Read Aloud

✓ **Can children categorize information learned from a book?**

Build Background Tell children that you will be reading a book about amazing animals and the different ways they can move.

● Ask: *What animals do you know that like to swim? What animals like to climb?*
¿Saben a qué animales les gusta nadar? ¿A cuáles les gusta trepar?

Listen for Understanding Display the cover of the book *Move!* and read the title.

● Turn to the first page of the book. Say: *This is the first page of the book. The first page is where the book begins. Ésta es la primera página. En la primera página es donde comienza el libro.*Then turn to the last page of the book, and say: *This is the last page of the book. It is where the book ends. Ésta es la última página del libro. Aquí es donde termina el libro.*

● Say: *Now let's read to learn about different animals that move in the same way.*
Ahora vamos a leer para aprender acerca de diferentes animales que se mueven de la misma manera.

Respond to the Story Have children name animals from the book that move in the same way. Ask: *Which animals can climb? Which animals can run? ¿Qué animales pueden trepar? ¿Cuáles pueden correr?*

💡TIP Be sure children use both the words and pictures in the book to categorize animals that can move in the same way.

ELL As you read *Move!,* point to specific illustrations, and ask questions, such as: *Is the whale walking or swimming? Is the snake climbing or running?* Have children answer the questions with complete sentences.

Learn About Letters and Sounds

✓ **Can children identify sounds /k/, /u/, /ks/, and /v/, spelled *Cc, Uu, Xx,* and *Vv*?**

Review Letters *Cc, Uu, Xx, Vv* Sing the "ABC Song" with children as you turn the pages of the *ABC Big Book.* Stop when you come to a letter that is being reviewed this week. For example, for *Cc,* stop at the page for *cake, cat,* and *crayon* Remind children that these words begin with the letter *Cc* and the sound /k/. Ask: *What sound do you hear at the beginning of cake, cat, and crayon? What letter makes the sound /k/? ¿Qué sonido escuchan al comienzo de cake, cat, and crayon? ¿Qué letra tiene el sonido /k/?*

● Model how to write upper case and lower case *Cc* on the chalkboard. Have children "write" upper case and lower case *Cc* on a partner's back with their finger.

● Repeat the same procedure, in turn, to review the letters *Uu, Vv,* and *Xx.* Encourage children to say the sound the letter makes as they "write" it on their partner's back.

Move!
¡A moverse!

ABC Big Book

Math Time

Observe and Investigate

 Can children name and sort common shapes?

Guess My Rule Tell children to watch carefully as you sort Shape Set shapes into piles based on something that makes them alike. Ask them to silently guess your sorting rule, such as squares versus all other shapes. Sort shapes one at a time, continuing until there are at least two in each pile.

- Signal "shhh," and pick up a new shape. Gesture to indicate that children should point to the pile where the shape belongs. Then place it in the correct pile. Repeat until many shapes are sorted.

- Ask children to tell a classmate what your sorting rule was. Encourage their discussion by asking: *Why did you guess that rule? How do you know? Show me how the shapes match your rule.* *¿Cómo adivinaron esta regla? ¿Cómo lo saben? Muéstrenme cómo las figuras corresponden a esta regla.*

𝕏𝕏𝕏 Social and Emotional Development

Making Good Choices

 Do children show a desire to solve problems independently?

Being Helpful Revisit the *Making Good Choices Flip Chart* page 24, "How Do Friends Solve Problems?"

- Display the dog puppet. Say: *Tell the puppet about the girl and boy who want to use the same puzzle and how they can solve the problem.* *Cuéntenle al títere sobre la niña y el niño que querían utilizar el mismo rompecabezas y cómo solucionaron el problema.*

- Provide each child a turn to tell the puppet about a way to solve the problem, such as, they could work on the puzzle together or they could take turns using the puzzle. Remind children that friends should always look for ways to solve a problem

  ELL Provide sentence frames to help during the conversation with the dog puppet. Use these and others: *The girl and boy want to _____. They can _____.* Model the use of each frame. Have children repeat, and then use their own words. Some children may feel more comfortable just repeating the completed frame you provided.

Building Blocks

Online Math Activity

Introduce Memory Number 2: Counting Cards to Numerals, in which children match one set of cards to another set with numerals only. Each child should complete Memory Number 2 this week.

Making Good Choices Flip Chart page 24

 Learning Goals

Social and Emotional Development
- Child demonstrates appropriate conflict-resolution strategies, requesting help when needed.

Mathematics
- Child sorts objects and explains how the sorting was done.

Vocabulary

alike	igual	rule	regla
shape	figura	sort	clasificar

Differentiated Instruction

✋ Extra Support

Observe and Investigate

If...children struggle with sorting shapes during the activity, **then...**reduce the number of shapes they are sorting to three or four.

⭐ Enrichment

Observe and Investigate

Have children find alternative ways to sort the shapes. Challenge them to make up their own sorting rules.

Focus Question

How do animals move?
¿Cómo se mueven los animales?

 Learning Goals

Language and Communication
• Child demonstrates an understanding of oral language by responding appropriately.

Mathematics
• Child counts 1–10 concrete objects correctly.
• Child tells how many are in a group of up to 5 objects without counting.

Vocabulary

counters	fichas	cover	cubrir
hidden	esconder	uncover	descubrir

 Differentiated Instruction

 Extra Support

Math Time

If...children struggle to identify the number of counters, **then...**reduce the number of counters or show the counters for a longer time.

Enrichment

Math Time

Challenge children by increasing the number of counters and by placing the counters in random arrangements.

Special Needs

Vision Loss

Children can participate in the Snapshots activity if they are allowed to feel the pattern, then recreate it.

Math Time

✓ **Can children identify the number of objects shown without counting?**

Snapshots Have three counters prepared on a paper plate (or a piece of construction paper), and cover the plate with a cloth you cannot see through. Show children the covered plate, and explain that counters are hidden under the cloth.

● Tell children to watch carefully and quietly with hands in their laps as you quickly uncover the plate to show the counters. Uncover the plate for two seconds, and cover it again.

● Have children show with their fingers how many counters they saw. Then say: **Now tell me how many counters you saw.** *Ahora díganme cuántas fichas vieron.* Uncover the plate again, if needed.

● Repeat the activity using other numbers of counters and have children show and then tell their answers.

✓ **Can children draw a number of objects and label with the numeral?**

Draw Farm Animals Tell children that they will draw a picture of farm animals and label it with a number.

● Display *Math and Science Flip Chart* page 44, "Count the Farm Animals." Talk about the animals on the chart and how many there are of each kind.

● Say: **Now let's draw our own pictures.** *Vamos a hacer nuestros propios dibujos.* Have children choose a farm animal that is not on the chart, such as a cow or goat. Have them draw any number of animals from 1 to 10.

● Discuss other kinds of farm animals that children could draw, such as rabbits, roosters, donkeys, lambs, or ducks. Remind them to write a number on their picture.

TIP Encourage children to write the name of their animal on the label, such as "5 cows".

ELL Provide animal photos of a cow, goat, lamb, duck, and so on for children to use as models to create their own pictures. Point to each animal and have children repeat its name after you.

Math and Science Flip Chart page 44

Center Time

▶ **Center Rotation** Center Time includes teacher-guided activities and independent activities. Refer to the **Learning Centers** on pages 138–139 for activities in additional centers.

small group · 30 minutes

Math and Science Center

✓ **Observe children as they use Counting Cards to count from 1 to 10.**

Materials Counting Cards 1–10; Two-Color Counters

X-Ray Vision Have children work in pairs. Help them place Counting Cards 1-10 facedown in numerical order. Say: *You can use your "X-ray vision" to tell which card it is. Pueden usar su "visión de rayos X" para decirme qué tarjeta es.*

● Have children take turns pointing to a card and telling which card it is. Children flip their card to show whether they are correct, and replace their card facedown. Observe strategies as children work. Do they count with their fingers, count backward, or use eyes only?

● After all cards have been identified, have children turn the cards over. Then have children count the correct number of Two-Color Counters to go with each card.

Center Tip

If...children have difficulty counting from 1 to 10, **then...**have them practice with Counting Cards 1–5 until they are proficient.

Purposeful Play

✓ **Observe children taking turns and communicating respectfully.**

Children choose an open center for free playtime. Encourage cooperation skills by suggesting that children work together to create a show or story with their farm animal pictures and that they can ask for and offer help at any time during the activity.

Let's Say Good-Bye

large group · 15 minutes

 Read Aloud Revisit "Monkey See, Monkey Do"/"Como los monos" for your afternoon Read Aloud. Remind children to act out the different ways the monkeys move.

 Home Connection Refer to the Home Connections activities listed in the Resources and Materials chart on page 135. Remind children to show families how they can count objects around the house. Sing the "Good-bye Song" as children prepare to leave.

✓ Learning Goals

Social and Emotional Development
• Child demonstrates appropriate conflict-resolution strategies, requesting help when needed.

Language and Communication
• Child names and describes actual or pictured people, places, things, actions, attributes, and events.

Mathematics
• Child counts 1–10 concrete objects correctly.
• Child demonstrates that the numerical counting sequence is always the same.

Writing

Recap the day. Have children name animals that can climb. Ask: *What are some other ways that animals move? ¿De qué otras maneras pueden moverse los animales?* Ask them to draw a picture of an animal in motion and label it.

DAY 3

Focus Question
How do animals move?
¿Cómo se mueven los animales?

Learning Goals

Language and Communication
• Child uses newly learned vocabulary daily in multiple contexts.

Emergent Literacy: Reading
• Child generates words that rhyme.

Vocabulary

beak	pico	feathers	plumas
fly	volar	nest	nido
robin	petirrojo	twigs	ramitas

Differentiated Instruction

 Extra Support
Phonological Awareness
If...children have difficulty recognizing words that rhyme, **then...**emphasize the ending sound that rhyming words share. Say: *The words* zoo *and* do *rhyme because they both end with* /ü/. *Does the word* boo *end with the sound* /ü/? *Las palabras* zoo y do *riman porque ambas terminan con* /ü/. *La palabra* boo, *¿termina con el sonido* /ü/?

⭐ **Enrichment**
Phonological Awareness
Challenge children to generate rhyming words for *run, skip,* and *jump.*

Accommodations for 3's
Phonological Awareness
If...children have difficulty recognizing words that rhyme, **then...**spend time each day reciting simple nursery rhymes, such as "Jack and Jill," or "Hickory, Dickory, Dock." Recite the rhymes together and identify the words that rhyme.

Let's Start the Day

 Opening Routines and Transition Tips
For **Opening Routines** and **Transition Tips** turn to pages 178–181 and visit DLMExpressOnline.com for more ideas.

📖 Read **"Fish"/"Pececitos"** from the *Teacher's Treasure Book,* page 91, for your morning Read Aloud.

Language Time

large group | 15 minutes

👥 **Social and Emotional Development** Remind children to sit quietly and listen politely as each child takes turns speaking. Praise children for listening politely without interrupting.

Oral Language and Vocabulary

✓ **Can children use words that name an animal's body parts and places where it lives?**

Animal Body Parts and Animal Places Talk about birds that children have seen around their neighborhood. Ask: *What do the birds look like? How do they move? ¿Cómo son los pájaros? ¿Cómo se mueven?*

● Display *Oral Language Development Card 50.* Name the birds (robins) and point out that they are in a nest, which is their home. Then follow the suggestions on the back of the card. Use the Sequence Card set "Building a Home" to illustrate how birds build their nests.

Oral Language Development Card 50

Phonological Awareness

✓ **Can children identify words that rhyme?**

Recognize Rhyming Words Revisit *Rhymes and Chants Flip Chart,* page 24. Remind children that rhyming words end with the same sound.

Have children join in as you chant "At the Zoo." Ask children to find the rhyming words *kangaroo/zoo/do/too.* Say: *If you hear a word that rhymes with zoo and do, then flap your arms like a bird. If the word does not rhyme, then stand still. Si escuchan una palabra que rima con zoo y do, aleteen como pajaritos. Si no riman, quédense quietos.* Say other words slowly, such as *boo, chew, run, flew, hop, new,* and *true.*

🗣 Use the chant to revisit the words that name movement: *hop, stomp, fly,* and *waddle.* Pantomime the movement as you say each word, for example, stomping like an elephant. Have children follow your action and repeat the word.

Rhymes and Chants Flip Chart, page 24

Center Time

▶ **Center Rotation** Center Time includes teacher-guided activities and independent activities. Refer to the **Learning Centers** on pages 138–139 for activities in additional centers.

 small group 60–90 minutes

Writer's Center

Center Tip

☑ **Track children's ability to identify rhyming words.**

Materials drawing paper, crayons

Matching Movement and Rhyme Assign an action word to half the children in the class: *run, hop, fly,* or *dive*. Assign a rhyming word to the rest: *sun, bun; mop, shop; sky, cry; five, hive.*

- Tell children with action words to choose an animal and draw it doing that action. Say: *If your word is* run, *draw an animal running. Si su palabra es* run, *dibujen un animal corriendo.*

- Tell children with rhyming words to draw a picture that shows their word. Their picture might show an object (sun) or an action (cry).

- Tell children to label their pictures, and assist them as necessary.

- Have children with the same action words compare animals. Have children with rhyming words join the correct group. Invite each group to show and tell their action and rhyming words.

If...children have difficulty illustrating the rhyming words, **then...**display pictures for reference and discuss them. For example, say: **This is a hive. Bees live in a hive.**

Creativity Center

Center Tip

☑ **Track children's ability to describe a bird and its nest.**

Materials paper plates, construction paper, glue, assorted art supplies (crayons, yarn, string, tissue paper or felt cut in small pieces, sequins)

Birds in a Nest Tell children that they will make special pictures of birds in a nest. Give each child half a paper plate and construction paper.

- Have children glue the edges of their plate on paper to form a pocket. The plate is the nest. On their paper, have children draw an outline of three baby birds and a mother bird. Have them glue colored tissue or felt pieces on the birds as their feathers. Have them draw faces and use sequins for eyes.

- Have children glue pieces of brown felt, tissue paper, yarn, and string to cover the plate.

- Ask children to describe their birds in a nest.

If...children have difficulty remembering a bird's features, **then...**show photos as a reference.

 Learning Goal

Emergent Literacy: Writing
- Child participates in free drawing and writing activities to deliver information.

Fine Arts
- Child uses and experiments with a variety of art materials and tools in various art activities.

Differentiated Instruction

 Extra Support
Creativity Center
If...children have difficulty using glue to attach materials, **then...**show them how much glue to use, how to spread the glue evenly, and how to hold the two pieces firmly together.

 Enrichment
Creativity Center
Challenge children to describe how a mother bird builds her nest, and how she feeds and takes care of her babies.

Accommodations for 3's
Writer's Center
If...children have difficulty writing letters for a label, **then...**write the first letter of the word and have them trace it.

Focus Question

How do animals move? ¿Cómo se mueven los animales?

Learning Goals

Language and Communication
• Child demonstrates an understanding of oral language by responding appropriately.

Emergent Literacy: Reading
• Child names most upper- and lowercase letters of the alphabet.
• Child produces the most common sound for a given letter.

Science
• Child identifies organisms and describes their characteristics.

Vocabulary

fast	veloces	grass	pasto
ocean	mar	sky	cielo
slither	deslizar	slow	lentos

Differentiated Instruction

 Extra Support

Read Aloud

If...children have difficulty categorizing the animals in the *Concept Big Book* fast or slow, **then...**ask the question about each animal: *Does a tortoise move fast or slowly? Does a bird move fast or slowly? ¿Las tortugas se mueven rápida o lentamente? ¿Los pájaros se mueven rápida o lentamente?*

 Enrichment

Read Aloud

Challenge children to draw pictures of the animals in the book in their natural habitats, such as the seal by the ocean or the snake in the grass. Help children label their pictures.

📖 Read Aloud

✓ **Can children categorize animals by their movements?**

Build Background Tell children that you will read more information about amazing animals—both wild animals and pets.

● Ask: *What are some different ways that animals move? ¿De qué distintas maneras se pueden mover los animales?*

Listen for Understanding Display *Concept Big Book 3: Amazing Animals*, page 5, and read the title.

● Read pages 14–16. Point to the labels in the photographs and read them after reading the main text.

● Ask: *How do seals move? Where do they live? ¿Cómo se mueven las focas? ¿Dónde viven?*

Respond to the Story Have children name the animals they read about. Ask: *Which animals move fast? Which animals move slowly? Which animals live on land? Which live in the ocean? Which animal can fly? ¿Qué animales son veloces? ¿Qué animales son muy lentos? ¿Cuáles viven en la tierra? ¿Cuáles viven en el mar? ¿Qué animal puede volar?*

TIP Be sure children can categorize animals by the speed of their movements as well as where they live. Remind them that they can learn information from pictures and words.

ELL As you browse the book, point to specific places in the photos as you say the animal names and characteristics. Encourage children to point to the photos and name things they know.

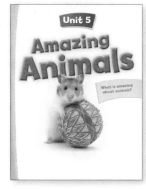

Amazing Animals
Animales asombrosos

large group • 15 minutes

Literacy Time

Learn About Letters and Sounds

✓ **Can children identify the sounds made by Cc, Uu, Xx, and Vv?**

Review the Letters *Cc, Uu, Xx, Vv* Sing the "ABC Song" with children as you page through the *ABC Big Book*, stopping when you get to each target letter. Review the pictures for each letter and the sound each letter makes: /k/, /u/, /ks/, and /v/.

● Model how to write the upper case and lower case letters *Cc* using the ABC Picture Card. Have children trace the letters with their finger.

● While one child is tracing, the other children can be writing the letter in the air or on a piece of carpet, using their finger. Have them say /k/ each time they write the letter.

● Repeat for upper case and lower case letters *Uu, Xx,* and *Vv.*

ABC Big Book

Online Math Activity

Children can complete Party Time 3 and Memory Number 2 during computer time or Center Time.

Math Time

Observe and Investigate

 Can children copy a pattern of actions?

Listen and Copy Clap a certain number of times, for example, up to 6, or another appropriate number. Have children follow by clapping the same number of times.

- Vary the activity by clapping slowly, quickly, or in a pattern, such as clap, clap, pause, clap, clap, pause, and so on. Make sure that all pauses are distinct so that children are able to follow.

- If children can follow you easily, then create a more difficult pattern that uses actions, for example: "clap, stamp, clap, stamp" or "clap, clap, stamp, clap, clap, stamp."

- Invite volunteers to lead the group. This activity may also be used during transition time as you go from one activity to another.

ELL During the activity, name the actions the children are performing (clapping, stamping, and so forth) so that children can associate the word with the action. Reinforce how the action is being done by emphasizing the words *quickly* and *slowly*.

Making Good Choices Flip Chart page 24

✖✖✖ Social and Emotional Development

Making Good Choices

 Do children show a desire to solve problems independently?

Being Helpful Display *Making Good Choices Flip Chart* page 24, "How Do Friends Solve Problems?" Review with children some of the ways the girl and boy can solve their problem with the puzzle. Ask for and write down children's ideas for how to help and solve the problem.

- Using a Dog Puppet, role-play other situations to model how friends solve problems. For example, explain that the puppet took your pencil by mistake and put it in a box that's not yours. Model what you would say to the puppet, as well as how you would say it, to explain that the puppet took your pencil.

- After each role-play, ask: *How did I solve the problem? What did I say? How did I say it? What else might you say or do to solve the problem? ¿Cómo resolví el problema? ¿Qué dije? ¿Cómo lo dije? ¿Qué más dirían o harían ustedes para resolver el problema?*

Learning Goals

Language and Communication
• Child names and describes actual or pictured people, places, things, actions, attributes, and events.

Social Studies
• Child understands and discusses roles, responsibilities, and services provided by community workers.

Technology Applications
• Child names and uses various computer parts (such as mouse, keyboard, CD-ROM, microphone, touch screen).

Vocabulary

bus driver	conductor
community worker	trabajador comunitario
doctor	médico
firefighter	bombero
mail carrier	cartero
police officer	policía
veterinarian	veterinario

Differentiated Instruction

 Extra Support

Oral Language and Vocabulary
If...children have difficulty identifying the names of community workers, **then...**display the pictures from the *Photo Library CD-ROM* (Occupations). Ask: *Who is this worker? What job does he or she do? ¿Quién es este trabajador? ¿Cuál es su trabajo?*

 Enrichment

Understand and Participate
Have partners create community worker riddles for others to answer. Have them give at least two clues.

Social Studies Time

large group   20 minutes

Oral Language and Academic Vocabulary

✓ **Can children identify community workers and the jobs they do?**

Talking About Community Workers Ask children to name some jobs that people in the community have. Prompt children by asking: *Who works to keep us safe? Who delivers our mail? Who keeps our school clean? ¿Quién trabaja para que estemos seguros? ¿Quién nos entrega el correo? ¿Quién mantiene limpia nuestra escuela?*

- Have children share what they know about police officers, mail carriers, and custodians.

- Say: *What other community workers can you name? Today we will learn about these important people. ¿Qué otros trabajadores comunitarios pueden nombrar? Hoy vamos a aprender sobre estas personas tan importantes para nuestra comunidad.*

Understand and Participate

✓ **Can children match descriptions of work with the names of those jobs?**

Learning About Community Workers Display books about community workers as well as *Photo Library CD-ROM* pictures (Occupations: bus driver, veterinarian, doctor, nurse, paramedic, teacher, and school crossing guard).

- Use the *Photo Library* pictures as a starting off point. Page through the books with children to learn information about police officers, firefighters, and mail carriers.

- Discuss each community worker's job. When appropriate, compare and contrast it to another job. Ask: *What does a veterinarian do? Why is it an important job? How are a veterinarian's job and a doctor's job alike? How are they different? What would happen if there were no doctors or veterinarians in a community? ¿Qué hace el veterinario? ¿Por qué es importante su trabajo? ¿En qué se parece su trabajo al de un doctor? ¿En qué se diferencian? ¿Qué pasaría si no hubiera doctores ni veterinarios en una comunidad?*

- Continue the discussion by pointing out that many community workers wear special uniforms, drive special vehicles, or use special tools to perform their job. Point out the special tools that mail carriers and firefighters use. Guide children to recognize that community workers provide useful services that every community needs.

TIP Tell children that volunteers are community workers who give their time and work without pay to help others. Volunteers work in many places, such as hospitals, schools, and libraries.

ELL Have children use the *Photo Library CD-ROM* pictures and browse through the books with a fluent partner to learn the names of community workers and to talk about their jobs. For additional suggestions on how to meet the needs of children at the Beginning, Intermediate, Advanced, and Advanced-High levels of English proficiency, see pages 184-187.

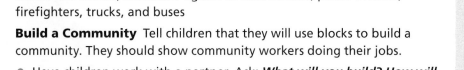

Center Time

▶ **Center Rotation** Center Time includes teacher-guided activities and independent activities. Refer to the **Learning Centers** on pages 138–139 for activities in additional centers.

small group 30 minutes

Construction Center

| | Center Tip |

✓ **Monitor children as they build a community with blocks and show what community workers do.**

Materials blocks, miniature figures of mail carriers, police officers, firefighters, trucks, and buses

Build a Community Tell children that they will use blocks to build a community. They should show community workers doing their jobs.

● Have children work with a partner. Ask: **What will you build? How will you and your partner work together? Do you have a plan?** *¿Qué van a construir? ¿Cómo van a trabajar juntos? ¿Tienen un plan?*

● Have children describe their community and the jobs the community workers perform. Ask: **Which community workers do their jobs in a library?** *¿Cuáles son los trabajadores comunitarios que trabajan en una biblioteca?*

Center Tip

If...children need help sharing the blocks and working together,
then...suggest roles for each child in the building of the community. For example, one child can build the post office while another builds the hospital.

Purposeful Play

✓ **Observe children as they work in pairs or small groups.**

Children choose an open center for free playtime. Encourage problem-solving skills by suggesting they work together to create a play about community helpers who work together to solve a problem in a community, such as a flood.

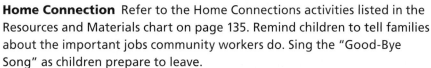

Let's Say Good-Bye

large group 15 minutes

Read Aloud Revisit "Fish"/"Pececitos" for your afternoon Read Aloud. Ask children to act out the ways that fish move in the rhyme.

Home Connection Refer to the Home Connections activities listed in the Resources and Materials chart on page 135. Remind children to tell families about the important jobs community workers do. Sing the "Good-Bye Song" as children prepare to leave.

✓ Learning Goal

Social and Emotional Development
● Child demonstrates appropriate conflict-resolution strategies, requesting help when needed.

Language and Communication
● Child names and describes actual or pictured people, places, things, actions, attributes, and events.

Social Studies
● Child understands and discusses roles, responsibilities, and services provided by community workers.

● Child identifies common areas and features of home, school, and community.

✍ Writing

Recap the day. Have children name the community workers they learned about. Ask: **What are some of the important jobs they do?** *¿Cuáles son algunos de los trabajos importante que hacen?* Record their answers on chart paper. Share the pen by having children write letters and words they know. Ask children to draw a picture to illustrate each sentence.

Let's Start the Day

 Opening Routines and Transition Tips
For **Opening Routines** and **Transition Tips** turn to pages 178–181 and visit
DLMExpressOnline.com for more ideas.

Read **"Five Dancing Dolphins"/**"Cinco delfines bailarines" from
the *Teacher's Treasure Book,* page 237, for your morning Read Aloud.

Focus Question
How do animals move?
¿Cómo se mueven los animales?

 **Learning Goals**

Language and Communication
• Child follows basic rules for conversations (taking turns, staying on topic, listening actively).

Emergent Literacy: Reading
• Child generates words that rhyme.
• Child describes, relates to, and uses details and information from books read aloud.

Vocabulary

different	diferente
ending	final
folktale	cuento folclórico
retell	volver a contar
same	igual

Differentiated Instruction

 Extra Support

Oral Language and Vocabulary
If...children have difficulty understanding that different versions of a story can exist, **then...** read them two versions of a popular fairy tale, such as "Little Red Riding Hood."

Enrichment

Oral Language and Vocabulary
Challenge children to change the ending of a familiar story, such as "The Little Red Hen."

Language Time

large group 15 minutes

🧑‍🤝‍🧑 **Social and Emotional Development** Remind children to listen carefully and wait until their classmate has finished speaking before they speak.

Oral Language and Vocabulary

✅ **Do children recognize that many folktales have different versions?**

Animal Friends Talk about folktales that children are familiar with, such as "The Little Red Hen" and "The Lion and the Mouse." Say: ***These stories are very old. They have been told again and again by many people for many years.*** *Estos cuentos son muy antiguos. Han sido contados una y otra vez por muchas personas durante muchos años.*

● Discuss how sometimes the same story can be told in different ways. Say: ***One retelling of "The Little Red Hen" may have a different ending than another. That is because over the years people add things to a story or change parts of a story.*** *Una versión de "La gallinita roja" puede tener un final diferente al de otra versión. Esto es así porque, con el paso de los años, la gente añade cosas al cuento o cambia algunas partes.*

● Ask: ***Have you ever heard the same story told in a slightly different way? What story was it?*** *¿Alguna vez han oído el mismo cuento, pero contado de una manera ligeramente distinta? ¿Qué cuento fue?* If possible, read children "The Tortoise and the Hare"/"La tortuga y la liebre" from the *Teacher's Treasure Book,* page 291, so they will be able to understand how stories can differ when they listen to "Tortoise Wins a Race" during Read Aloud time.

Phonological Awareness

✅ **Can children identify words that rhyme?**

Recognize Rhyming Words Hold one Dog Puppet and give the second one to a child. Have your puppet "say" a word, such as *run,* and tell the other puppet to say a word that rhymes with *run.* The other child's puppet then says a rhyming word, such as *fun.* Continue until each child has had a turn to use the puppet and say a rhyming word. Remind children that rhyming words end with the same sound.

ELL Display *Photo Library CD-ROM* pictures for *fish, cat, duck, goat, mouse,* and *fox.* Have children say the each animal name with you. Then display pictures of these objects, or the objects themselves: *dish, hat, truck, coat, box, house.* Have children say the name of each object with you. Then have them match the Photo Library picture with the object whose name rhymes.

Center Time

▶ **Center Rotation** Center Time includes teacher-guided activities and independent activities. Refer to the **Learning Centers** on pages 138–139 for activities in additional centers.

small group 60–90 minutes

Learning Goal

Social and Emotional Development
• Child demonstrates appropriate conflict-resolution strategies, requesting help when needed.

Language and Communication
• Child uses newly learned vocabulary daily in multiple contexts.

Emergent Literacy: Reading
• Child enjoys and chooses reading-related activities.

Library and Listening Center

✔ Track children's ability to recognize that stories have different versions.

Materials different versions of several traditional folk tale and fairy tale books

Browsing Stories and Tales Have children browse through folk and fairy tale books to see that the same story can vary.

● Say: *Look carefully at the illustrations. You can see that the animal characters do not look the same in different versions. You can also see that one version may be longer than another. Miren con atención las ilustraciones. Pueden ver que los personajes de los animales no se ven igual en las diferentes versiones. También pueden ver que una versión sea más larga que otra.*

● Read different versions of a story to children. Have them discuss how they are alike and different.

Center Tip

If...children have difficulty noticing differences between stories, **then...**ask specific questions to direct their thinking, for example: *What does the lion say to the mouse at the end of each story? ¿Qué le dice el león al ratón al final de cada cuento?*

Differentiated Instruction

 Extra Support
Pretend and Learn Center
If...children have difficulty thinking of animals for their verses, **then...**have them think of a place, such as an animal shelter, where they have seen different kinds of animals.

 Enrichment
Pretend and Learn Center
Challenge children to adapt other songs and finger plays, such as "The Itsy Bitsy Spider."

Accommodations for 3's
Pretend and Learn Center
If...children have difficulty creating a new version, **then...**have them add verses to the traditional version of "Old MacDonald Had a Farm."

Pretend and Learn Center

✔ Track how well children can change a song to create a new version.

Create a New Version of a Song Explain to children that they will create a new version of "Old MacDonald Had a Farm."

● Sing several verses of "Old MacDonald Had a Farm" with children so they remember it. Have children form groups, and tell them to make up a new song about Old MacDonald and his animals.

● Give children a few suggestions, such as "Old MacDonald Had a Zoo," "Old MacDonald Had a Lake," and "Old MacDonald Had a Cave."

● Have each group perform their new version of the song.

Center Tip

If...children have difficulty coming up with verses, **then...** brainstorm with them by asking questions such as: *What animals can be found in a cave?* (bats, bears, insects) *¿Qué animales pueden encontrar en una cueva?* (murciélagos, osos e insectos)

Circle Time

Literacy Time

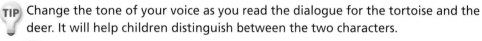 Read Aloud

✓ **Can children answer questions about a story that is read aloud?**

Build Background Tell children that you will be reading a folk tale about a tortoise and a deer.

● Ask: *Which animal moves faster—a tortoise or a deer?* *¿Qué animal se mueve más rápido, la tortuga o el venado?*

Listen for Enjoyment Read aloud *Teacher Treasure Book* page 293, "Tortoise Wins a Race"/"La tortuga gana la carrera."

● Tell children to listen carefully to what happens in the story.

● Ask: *Why does the deer believe he can win the race? Why is the tortoise scared?* *¿Por qué el venado creía que podía ganar la carrera? ¿Por qué la tortuga tenía miedo?*

Respond to the Story Have children explain how the tortoise tricked the deer. Ask: *Do you think the tortoise could have won the race without tricking the deer?* *¿Piensan que la tortuga podría haber ganado la carrera si no hubiera engañado al venado?*

TIP Change the tone of your voice as you read the dialogue for the tortoise and the deer. It will help children distinguish between the two characters.

ELL Focus on the concepts of *faster* and *slower*. Ask: *Which animal moves faster––a horse or a dog?* Have children answer in a complete sentence using this frame: *A [horse] moves faster than a [dog].*

For additional suggestions on how to meet the needs of children at the Beginning, Intermediate, Advanced, and Advanced-High levels of English proficiency, see pages 184-187.

Learn About Letters and Sounds

✓ **Can children identify the sounds /k/, /u/, /ks/, and /v/ for Cc, Uu, Xx, and Vv?**

Review Letters *Cc, Uu, Xx, Vv* Sing the "ABC Song" with children as you page through the *ABC Big Book,* stopping when you get to each target letter. Say the names of the pictures for each letter. Then chant the letter sound. For example, have children say "/v/ /v/ /v/ a very nice violin" as they pretend to play a violin.

● Model how to write the upper case and lower case forms of each letter using the ABC PIcture Cards. Have children trace the letters using their finger.

● While one child is tracing, the other children can be writing the letter in the air or on their palm with their finger. Have them say the sound of the letter each time they "write" it.

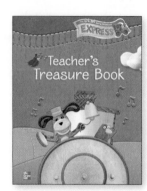

Teacher's Treasure Book, page 293

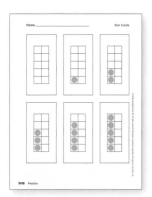

Teacher's Treasure
Book, pages 508–511

Online Math Activity

Children can complete Party Time 3 and Memory Number 2 during computer time or Center Time.

large group 15 minutes

Math Time

Observe and Investigate

 Can children match numbers of objects with their numerals?

Memory Number Tell children that they will play a game with a partner in which they match Dot Cards with Numeral Cards (*Teacher's Treasure Book*, pages 508–511).

● Place a set of Dot and Numeral Cards facedown, each in their own array. Player One turns over a card from each array. If the cards match, that player keeps them and takes another turn.

● If the cards do not match, they are replaced facedown, and Player Two takes a turn. Say: **The game is over when all of the cards have been matched. The player who has more cards wins.** *El juego termina cuando todas las cartas han sido relacionadas. Gana el jugador que tenga más cartas.*

● Point out to children that it is important to try to remember the placement of the cards as the game progresses.

✦✦✦ Social and Emotional Development

Making Good Choices

 Do children show a desire to solve problems independently?

Being Helpful Display the Dog Puppets and a library book. Tell children the puppets want to read the same library book. Model a dialogue between the puppets that ends with the puppets agreeing to read the book together.

● Ask: **What problem did the puppets have? How did they solve their problem?**
¿Cuál es el problema que enfrentaron los títeres? ¿Cómo resolvieron su problema?

● Remind children that sharing is a good way to solve the problem when two friends want to read the same book. Another way is to take turns. First, one person reads the book. Then the other person reads it.

ELL Some children may have difficulty following the conversation between the dog puppets. While role-playing, act out how both dogs pick up the same book. Then show the puppets having fun reading the book together. Use clear dialogue as you perform each action, such as: *Let's share the book. We can read together!*

 Learning Goal

Social and Emotional Development
• Child demonstrates appropriate conflict-resolution strategies, requesting help when needed.

Mathematics
• Child tells how many are in a group of up to 5 objects without counting.

• Child recognizes and names numerals 0 through 9.

Vocabulary

match	relacionar	memory	memoria
more	más	number	cifra
numeral	número	remember	recordar

Differentiated Instruction

 Extra Support
Observe and Investigate
If...children struggle to match Dot and Numeral Cards, **then...**reduce the number of cards for children to match to five sets or fewer.

Enrichment
Observe and Investigate
After children match a Dot and Numeral Card, have them show the number in another way, such as holding up their fingers or clapping.

 Special Needs
Delayed Motor Development
To help children to play the "Memory Number" game, either get a buddy to help the child turn over the cards, or design some way to adapt the cards. Ways to adapt the cards include using clothespns, large paper clips, or even tongue depressors.

Focus Question
How do animals move?
¿Cómo se mueven los animales?

Learning Goals

Language and Communication
• Child follows two- and three-step oral directions.
• Child names and describes actual or pictured people, places, things, actions, attributes, and events.

Mathematics
• Child counts 1–10 concrete objects correctly.
• Child recognizes and names numerals 0 through 9.

Vocabulary

amount	cantidad	count	contar
match	relacionar	number	cifra
numeral	número		

Differentiated Instruction

 Extra Support

Math Time

If...children have difficulty writing a numeral on a sticky note, **then...**write the numeral lightly on the sticky note and have them trace it.

 Enrichment

Math Time

Point out that there are more than 10 boards on the barn in the Flip Chart. Challenge children to count as many as they can.

Math Time

large group   20 minutes

✓ **Can children count and match the number of items in a group with a numeral?**

Counting Farm Animals Display the *Math and Science Flip Chart,* page 44, "Count the Farm Animals." Review with children the different kinds of animals on the chart: hens, sheep, horses, pigs, and birds.

• Say: *First, we are going to count each kind of animal. Primero, vamos a contar cada tipo de animal.* Count the hens with children. Then ask a volunteer to write the numeral on a sticky note (4) and place it on the Flip Chart near the hens.

• Repeat for each type of animal. As children place the sticky note on the chart, have them tell how many animals there are, for example: *There are 8 baby chicks.*

• Have children tell stories about the animals in the Flip Chart scene, focusing especially on number words. You may want to use this as an opportunity to record children's stories, integrating language and math skills.

ELL Focus on animal names and number words. Keep the Flip Chart on display, so that throughout the day you can ask questions such as: *What is the name of this animal? How many horses do you see? How many birds are flying?*

✓ **Can children count and match the number of movements with a numeral?**

Count and Move Ask children to take another look at the farm animals on the Flip Chart. Say: *Did you notice that the animals are moving in different ways? Let's talk about how they are moving. ¿Se dieron cuenta de que los animales se mueven de diferentes maneras? Hablemos sobre cómo se mueven.*

• Discuss how the animals are moving. For example, the horses are galloping. Ask children to use the number on the sticky note (3) to pretend they are horses, galloping 3 times.

• Have children pantomime other animal movements, using the numbers on the sticky notes. For example, they may take 4 steps for 4 hens or flap their arms 7 times for 7 birds.

TIP Tell children that they can count other items in the picture, such as bales of hay, doors, and pickets on the picket fence. They may also hunt for shapes in the picture.

Count the Farm Animals
Contar los animales
de la granja

Math and Science Flip Chart, page 44

Center Time

▶ **Center Rotation** Center Time includes teacher-guided activities and independent activities. Refer to the **Learning Centers** on pages 138–139 for activities in additional centers.

small group   30 minutes

Math and Science Center

✓ **Track children's ability to create sets of items, count them, and compare the sets.**

Materials Farm Animal Counters, paper

Count and Compare Tell children that they will work with a partner to create and count sets of animals.

● Have each child create a set of animal counters without looking at what their partner is doing. Say: **Choose a number from 1 to 10 and create a set of that number of farm animals.** *Escoge un número del 1 al 10 y forma un conjunto de animales de granja.*

● After both children have created sets, have them count the number of animals in their partner's set. Then have partners determine together which set has more animals.

Center Tip

If...children need help determining which set has more, **then...** have them match the animals in the two sets, and see which set has additional animals.

Purposeful Play

✓ **Observe children appropriately handling classroom materials.**

Children choose an open center for free playtime. Encourage cooperation skills by suggesting they work together to create a large farm scene using the Farm Animal Counters.

Let's Say Good-Bye

large group   15 minutes

 Read Aloud Revisit the story "Five Dancing Dolphins"/"*Cinco delfines bailarines*" for your afternoon Read Aloud. Ask children to listen for ways the animals move.

 Home Connection Refer to the Home Connections activities listed in the Resources and Materials chart on page 135. Remind children to tell families a story about animals. Sing the "Good-Bye Song" as children prepare to leave.

✓ Learning Goal

Social and Emotional Development
● Child initiates interactions with others in work and play situations.

Language and Communication
● Child names and describes actual or pictured people, places, things, actions, attributes, and events.

Mathematics
● Child counts 1–10 concrete objects correctly.

Writing

Recap the day. Have children tell about animals that move fast and animals that move slowly. Have them tell how the tortoise won the race in the folktale. Ask: **How did the tortoise trick the deer in the folk tale you heard?** *¿Cómo engañó la tortuga al venado en el cuento folclórico que oyeron?* Record their answers in a list. Read them back as you track the print, and emphasize the correspondence between speech and print.

Let's Start the Day

Focus Question

**How do animals move?
¿Cómo se mueven los animales?**

 Learning Goals

Social and Emotional Development
• Child demonstrates appropriate conflict-resolution strategies, requesting help when needed.

Language and Communication
• Child begins and ends conversations appropriately.

Emergent Literacy: Reading
• Child generates words that rhyme.

Vocabulary

fly	volar	hop	saltar
kangaroo	canguro	stomp	pisar
waddle	balancearse		

Differentiated Instruction

 Extra Support

Oral Language and Vocabulary
If...children have difficulty describing how animals move, **then...**use the animal pictures on the *Photo Library CD-ROM*. Pantomime with children each animal's movements. Then ask: *Can this animal run? Can it fly? ¿Puede este animal correr? ¿Puede volar?*

Enrichment

Oral Language and Vocabulary
Use the animal photos on the *Photo Library CD-ROM* to teach the names and movements of other less familiar animals, such as the camel, octopus, and rhinoceros.

▶ **Opening Routines and Transition Tips**
For **Opening Routines** and **Transition Tips** turn to pages 178–181 and visit **DLMExpressOnline.com** for more ideas.

 Read **"A Fuzzy Caterpillar"/"Lomo arriba y lomo abajo"** from the *Teacher's Treasure Book*, page 117, for your morning Read Aloud.

Language Time

  large group 15 minutes

Social and Emotional Development Remind children to listen carefully as their classmates share or ask questions. Suggest that, in turn, they want their classmates to listen to them when they speak.

Oral Language and Vocabulary

✓ **Can children share what they know about the way animals move?**

How Animals Move Talk about what children have learned this week about the way animals move. Ask: *How do fish move? How do birds move? How do cats move?*
¿Cómo se mueven los peces? ¿Cómo se mueven los pájaros? ¿Cómo se mueven los gatos?

● Display *Rhymes and Chants Flip Chart* page 24. Chant "At the Zoo" with children. Ask: *How do kangaroos move? What do elephants do? What do cockatoos do? How do penguins move? ¿Cómo se mueven los canguros? ¿Cómo lo hacen los elefantes? ¿Cómo se mueven las cacatúas? ¿Cómo se mueven los pingüinos?*

Phonological Awareness

✓ **Can children identify words that rhyme?**

Recognize Rhyming Words Using *Rhymes and Chants Flip Chart* page 24, chant "At the Zoo" once more with children. Remind children that rhyming words end with the same sound.

Point to the kangaroo in the picture. Ask: *Which words in the chant rhyme with* **kangaroo**? *Can you think of a word that rhymes with* **hop**? *Do the words* **fly** *and* **try** *rhyme? What other words can you think of that rhyme with* **fly**? *¿Qué palabras de la canción riman con* kangaroo? *¿Se les ocurre una palabra que rime con* hop? *¿Riman las palabras* fly *y* try? *¿Qué otras palabras conocen que rimen con* fly?

 Use some animal pictures from the *Photo Library CD-ROM*. Name each animal. Then ask questions about how that animal moves. For example: *Does this bird fly? Does this bird walk? Does this bird swim?* Have children answer in complete sentences. Model as needed.

For additional suggestions on how to meet the needs of children at the Beginning, Intermediate, Advanced, and Advanced-High levels of English proficiency, see pages 184–187.

At the Zoo
(an action chant)

A kangaroo is at the zoo.
What do you think that he can do?
He hops, hops, hops!

An elephant is at the zoo.
What do you think that she can do?
She stomps, stomps, stomps!

A cockatoo is at the zoo.
What do you think that he can do?
He flies, flies, flies!

Penguins too are at the zoo.
What do you think that they can do?
They waddle, waddle, waddle!

Rhymes and Chants Flip Chart, page 24

Center Time

▶ **Center Rotation** Center Time includes teacher-guided activities and independent activities. Refer to the **Learning Centers** on pages 138–139 for activities in additional centers.

small group   60–90 minutes

Writer's Center

✓ **Track the use of action/movement words as children tell about their animal.**

Materials magazines, glue, paper, crayons

Animals Move Have children create a class book with the title "Animals Like to Move."

● Have children cut out and glue an animal picture to a sheet of paper.

● Ask: *How does this animal move?* Help children write this question at the top of the page with the picture of the animal.

● Have children write on another sheet of paper the different ways the animal can move. Children may dictate what they know so that you may record it.

● Each child contributes two pages to the class book. One page asks the question, and the second page answers the question.

Center Tip

If...children are not sure how their animal moves, **then...**provide picture books of animals in the Learning Center so that children are able to answer the question.

ABC Center

✓ **Track children's ability to match upper and lower case letters.**

Materials letter cards, letter tiles, or magnetic letters; drawing paper, crayons or markers

Matching Letters Explain to children that they will match the upper case and lower case forms of the letters they reviewed this week. Remind them of the sound each letter stands for, as well.

● As children match the letter forms, have them chant the sound, for example: "/k/ /k/ /k/ as in *cake* and *cat*."

● Have children write each letter with a crayon or marker. Encourage them to add drawings of objects whose names begin with that letter and sound.

Center Tip

If...children have difficulty recalling the sound the letter stands for, **then...**display the ABC Picture Card and have children say the name of the letter and its sound.

✓ Learning Goal

Language and Communication
• Child names and describes actual or pictured people, places, things, actions, attributes, and events.

Emergent Literacy: Reading
• Child names most upper- and lowercase letters of the alphabet.

• Child identifies the letter that stands for a given sound.

Emergent Literacy: Writing
• Child uses scribbles, shapes, pictures, symbols, and letters to represent language.

Differentiated Instruction

 Extra Support
Writer's Center
If...children have difficulty answering the question, **then...**help them formulate an answer by discussing where the animal lives or where it finds its food.

 Enrichment
Writer's Center
Challenge children to make additional pages for their Animal Book, showing such things as the animal's habitat and the food it eats.

Accommodations for 3's
Writer's Center
If...children have difficulty cutting out small animal pictures, **then...**trace a large shape around the image and help children cut the larger area.

large group 15 minutes

Focus Question

How do animals move?
¿Cómo se mueven los animales?

Learning Goals

Emergent Literacy: Reading
• Child names most upper- and lowercase letters of the alphabet.
• Child identifies the letter that stands for a given sound.
• Child describes, relates to, and uses details and information from books read aloud.

Science
• Child identifies organisms and describes their characteristics.

Vocabulary

float	flotar	leap	saltar
move	moverse	slither	deslizarse
snag	atrapar	startled	asustado
waddle	balancearse		

Differentiated Instruction

Extra Support

Learn About Letters and Sounds
If...children have difficulty writing this week's letters, **then**...have them use large muscle groups to paint the letters on an easel with a paintbrush.

Enrichment

Learn About Letters and Sounds
Display the ABC Picture Cards for all of the letters children have learned so far this year. Have children name each letter. Challenge them to also name the sound each letter stands for.

Literacy Time

 Read Aloud

 Can children categorize information about the ways animals move?

Build Background Tell children that you will be rereading the book *Move!*, about amazing animals and how they move.

● Ask: *What did we learn about how some birds move? What did we learn about how penguins move? ¿Qué aprendimos sobre cómo se mueven algunos pájaros? ¿Qué aprendimos sobre cómo se mueven los pingüinos?*

Listen for Understanding Display *Move!* and read the title.

● Reread the pages about the whale. Ask: *What are two ways that a whale moves? What other animal in the book dives? ¿Cuáles son las dos maneras en que se mueve la ballena? ¿Qué otro animal del libro puede nadar?*

● Reread the pages about the snake. Ask: *What are two ways that a snake moves? What other animal in the book slithers? ¿Cómo son las dos maneras en que se mueve la serpiente? ¿Qué otro animal del libro se desliza?*

Respond and Connect Point out to children that the book teaches us two ways that each animal can move. Say: *It also teaches us that some animals can move in the same way*. *También nos enseña que algunos animales se mueven de la misma manera.*

TIP Be sure children realize that both the words and pictures teach how each animal moves.

ELL Provide sentence frames to help children talk about the pictures in *Move!* Use frames such as *A praying mantis can _____. A spider can _____.* Model using each frame, then have children repeat.

Learn About Letters and Sounds

 Can children identify letters and sounds?

Review Letters *Cc, Uu, Xx, Vv* Place ABC Picture Cards for *Cc, Uu, Xx,* and *Vv* on the floor in a path. Have children hop the path as they say the name of each letter.

● Then display pictures of words beginning with *Cc, Uu,* and *Vv*, and ending with *Xx*. These include *cat, camel, cow, vest, van,* and *fox* from the *Photo Library CD-ROM* Also include *X-ray* and *umbrella* ABC Picture Cards.

● Say a picture name. Have children match the beginning sound of the picture name to an ABC Picture Card. (For *fox*, children will match the ending sound.) Ask: *Does cat begin with the letter Cc? Listen, /k/ /k/ cat. ¿La palabra cat comienza con la letra Cc? Escuchen, /k/ /k/ cat.*

Move!
¡A moverse!

ABC Picture Cards

Building Blocks

Online Math Activity

Children can complete Party Time 3 and Memory Number 2 during computer time or Center Time.

Math Time

Observe and Investigate

✓ **Can children identify common shapes?**

Mr. Mixup (Shapes) Tell children that they are going to help Mr. Mixup name shapes. Remind them that each time Mr. Mixup makes a mistake, they should stop him right then to correct him.

- To begin the activity, have Mr. Mixup confuse the names of a triangle and rectangle, using Shape Set shapes or Pattern Blocks.

- After children have named the shapes correctly, ask: **How are a triangle and a rectangle different?** *¿En qué se diferencian un triángulo y un rectángulo?* Count with the children to show that a triangle has three sides and a rectangle has four sides.

- Repeat with other shapes, including rhombuses and hexagons.

ELL Name a shape, such as a rectangle, and have children repeat using the following sentence frame: **This shape is a rectangle.** Have children practice naming shapes with a partner for a few minutes each day.

✕✕✕ Social and Emotional Development

Making Good Choices

✓ **Do children show a desire to solve problems independently?**

Being Helpful Display *Making Good Choices Flip Chart* page 24, "How Do Friends Solve Problems?"

- Point to the flip chart illustration. Ask: **What did we learn about solving a problem with a friend?** *¿Qué aprendimos sobre cómo resolver un problema con un amigo?*

- Place an assortment of puzzles and library books on the table. Say: **Let's pretend that you and a friend want to read the same book or work on the same puzzle. Let's show what we can do to solve the problem.** *Imaginemos que dos de ustedes quieren leer el mismo libro o armar el mismo rompecabezas. Vamos a mostrar lo que podemos hacer para resolver el problema.* Encourage children to suggest working in pairs or taking turns using the puzzles and books.

- Remind children that friends should always try to work together and find ways to solve a problem.

Making Good Choices Flip Chart, page 24

Focus Question
How do animals move?
¿Cómo se mueven los animales?

Learning Goals

Language and Communication
• Child understands or knows the meaning of many thousands of words, many more than he or she uses.

Physical Development
• Child coordinates body movements in a variety of locomotive activities (such as walking, jumping, running, hopping, skipping, climbing).

Vocabulary

hop	brincar	jump	saltar
run	correr	skip	botar
walk	caminar		

Differentiated Instruction

 **Extra Support**

Explore Movement
If...children have difficulty skipping, **then**... allow them to do a step-hop pattern instead.

 **Enrichment**

Explore Movement
Have pairs of children who are confident join hands and skip together.

 **Special Needs**

Behavioral Social/Emotional
Sometimes, children get carried away when moving and don't know when to stop. Work out a special signal so the child knows to slow down and stop.

Outdoor Play Time

large group / 20 minutes

Oral Language and Academic Vocabulary

✓ **Can children describe the different ways they are able to move?**

All Living Things Move Remind children that they learned about different kinds of animals and the way they move. Say: *Today we will talk about and show the different ways we can move. Hoy vamos a hablar y mostrar las diferentes maneras en que nosotros podemos movernos.*

● Ask: *What are some ways you can move? Are there times you move quickly? When? ¿Cómo pueden moverse? ¿Hay ocasiones en que ustedes se mueven más rápido? ¿Cuándo?*

● Ask: *Are there times you move slowly? When do you want to do that? ¿Hay ocasiones en que se mueven más despacio? ¿Cuándo quieren hacerlo?*

● As children share, write a list on chart paper. Next to each item, draw a little picture to show the movement that is being discussed.

Explore Movement

✓ **Can children perform a variety of movements outdoors?**

Hop, Skip, and Jump Take children outside to the schoolyard or playground. Tell them they will practice moving in different ways.

● Ask children to show whether they are able to skip. Give children a starting point and then move approximately 20 feet away. Say: *Show me how you can skip to me. Muéstrenme si pueden saltar hasta aquí.* Have children skip back and forth several times.

● Have children take turns showing other ways to move, such as walking, running, jumping, and hopping.

● Note how well children are able to move. You may want to make notes as they move, so that you can see their progress by the end of the year.

TIP Encourage children to have a good time as they move in different ways.

ELL Display the following photos from the Photo Library CD-ROM: *walking, running, climbing, swimming,* and *diving.* Ask questions, such as: *What are the people doing in this picture?* Have children answer with a complete sentence: *The people are walking.*

Center Time

> **Center Rotation** Center Time includes teacher-guided activities and independent activities. Refer to the **Learning Centers** on pages 242–243 for activities in additional centers.

small group 30 minutes

Refer to the **Learning Centers** on pages 242–243

Construction Center

☑ **Monitor children as they make a park with a running track.**

Materials blocks, Farm Animal Counters, construction paper, animal toys

Build a Running Track Tell children that they will use blocks and other art materials to build a running track for animals.

- Have children work with a partner. Ask: *What will your track look like? Which animals will use the track? ¿Cómo sera su pista? ¿Qué animales van a usar esa pista?*

- Have children describe their finished track and then pretend that two animals are having a race. Ask: *Which animal do you think will win the race if the animals follow the rules? ¿Qué animal creen que va a ganar si ambos siguen las reglas?* Have children speculate about which animal might be the fastest runner.

Center Tip

If...children need to be reminded about sharing the materials and working together,
then...suggest roles for each child in the building of the animal home.

Learning Goal

Language and Communication
- Child names and describes actual or pictured people, places, things, actions, attributes, and events.

Science
- Child observes, understands, and discusses the relationship of plants and animals to their environments.

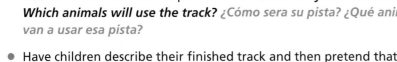

Writing

Recap the day and week. Say: *Tell me something that you learned this week about how animals move. Díganme algo que hayan aprendido esta semana sobre cómo se mueven los animales.* Record children's answers on chart paper. Share the marker with children as you write. Have children write their names beside their entries.

Purposeful Play

☑ **Observe children sharing classroom materials and working cooperatively.**

Children choose an open center for free playtime. Encourage cooperation skills by suggesting they play "Follow the Leader," using animal movements.

Let's Say Good-Bye

large group 15 minutes

 Read Aloud Revisit the story "A Fuzzy Caterpillar"/"Lomo arriba y lomo abajo" for your afternoon Read Aloud. Ask children to act out the way the caterpillar moves.

 Home Connection Refer to the Home Connections activities listed in the Resources and Materials chart on page 135. Remind children to show families the different ways they moved today and to tell what they learned this week about the ways animals move. Sing the "Good-Bye Song" as children prepare to leave.

In general, the purpose of assessing young children in the early childhood classroom is to collect information necessary to make important decisions about their developmental and educational needs. Because assessment is crucial to making informed teaching decisions, it is necessarily a vital component of *DLM Early Childhood Express.* The guidelines and forms found online allow the teacher to implement assessment necessary in the pre-kindergarten classroom.

Effective assessment is an ongoing process that always enhances opportunities for optimal growth, development, and learning. The process of determining individual developmental and educational needs tailors early childhood education practices and provides a template for setting individual and program goals.

Pre-kindergarten assessment should be authentic; that is, it should be a natural, environmental extension of the classroom. Assessments should be incorporated into classroom activities whenever possible, not completed as separate, pull-out activities in which the teacher evaluates the student one-on-one. Whenever possible, assessment should evaluate children's real knowledge in the process of completing real activities. For example, observing children as they equally distribute snacks would be a better assessment of their ability to make groups than observing an exercise in which children group counters would be.

It is also important to note that assessments should be administered over time, as environmental influences can greatly impact single outcomes. If a pre-kindergarten child is tired or ill, for example, the child may not demonstrate knowledge of a skill that has actually been mastered. It is also important to consider the length of assessment for children of this age, as attention spans are still developing and can vary greatly based on environmental influences. Most assessments should be completed within half an hour.

If possible, use multiple types of assessment for the same content area when working with pre-kindergarten children. Some children may be able to demonstrate mastery kinesthetically if they are not able to use expressive language well; others may not process auditory instruction adequately, but will be able to complete an assessment after observing someone model the task. It is vital that the assessment process should never make the child anxious or scared.

Informal Assessment

INFORMAL assessments rely heavily on observational and work-sampling techniques that continually focus on child performance, processes, and product over selected periods of time and in a variety of contexts.

ANECDOTAL assessments are written descriptions that provide a short, objective account of an event or an incident. Only the facts are reported—where, what, when, and how. Anecdotal records are especially helpful when trying to understand a child's behavior or use of skills. These recordings can be used to share the progress of individual children and to develop and individualize curriculum.

The Anecdotal Observational Record Form can be used at any time to document an individual child's progress toward a goal or signs indicating the need for developmental or medical evaluation. Observations can reflect the focused skills for the week, but are not limited to those skills. You may pair the form with video or audio recordings of the child to complete an anecdotal record.

Anecdotal Observational Record Form

CHECKLISTS are lists of skills or behaviors arranged into disciplines or developmental domains and are used to determine how a child exhibits the behaviors or skills listed. Teachers can quickly and easily observe groups of children and check the behaviors or skills each child is demonstrating at the moment.

Weekly Assessment

Weekly Assessments measure progress toward specific guidelines that are addressed in the weekly curriculum. The Performance Assessment Checklist measures progress toward the guidelines of the entire curriculum. It is intended to be used three times per year.

Performance Assessment Checklist

When using either type of checklist, it is important to remember that the skills and behaviors on the list are only guidelines. Each child is unique and has his or her own developmental timetable. It is also important to remember that the checklist only documents the presence or absence of a specific skill or behavior during the time of observation. It does not necessarily mean the skill is consistently present or lacking, though consistency may be noted when the skill has been observed over time.

PORTFOLIO assessments are collections of thoughtfully selected work samples, or artifacts, and accompanying reflections indicative of the child's learning experiences, efforts, and progress toward and/ or attainment of established curriculum goals. They are an authentic, performance-based method to allow teachers to analyze progress over time. As children choose work samples for their portfolios, they become involved in their own learning and assessment and begin to develop the concept of evaluating their own work.

Although early childhood activities tend to focus on processes as opposed to products, there are numerous opportunities to collect samples of children's work. Items to collect include drawings, tracings, cuttings, attempts to print their names, and paintings. You may also include informal assessments of a child's ability to recognize letters, shapes, numbers, and rhyming words.

Formal Assessment

FORMAL assessments involve the use of standardized tests. They are administered in a prescribed manner and may require completion within a specified amount of time. Standardized tests result in scores that are usually compared to the scores of a normative group. These tests generally fall into the following categories: achievement tests, readiness tests, developmental screening tests, intelligence tests, and diagnostic tests.

Assessing Children with Special Needs

Children with special needs may require a more thorough initial assessment, more frequent on-going assessments, and continuous adaptation of activities. Assessment is essentially the first task for the teacher or caregiver in developing the individualized instruction program required for children with disabilities.

Assessing Children Who Are English Language Learners

Whenever possible, assessments should be given in both the child's first language and in English.

Celebrate the Unit

Animal Expert Convention

Hold an Animal Expert Convention in the Classroom

- Invite children to hold an Animal Expert Convention, or meeting, in the classroom. Explain that they will act as animal experts and use what they learned in the unit to tell each other about animals.

- Before the convention, record children making animal noises. Suggest that children imitate the animals that they learned about in the unit. Play the recording during the Animal Expert Convention.

- Organize the classroom into four areas, focusing each area on one of the weekly themes for the unit: I Know Animals, Animals At Home, Comparing Animals, and How Animals Move. In each area, display the appropriate focus question and have children display examples of their completed work, such as:

  animal homes

  leaf prints

  fish patterns

  animal diagrams

  writing pieces, drawings, and other creative work

- Have children form "Animal Expert Groups" and walk from area to area. Encourage children to use their work to tell other group members what they know about animals.

- Provide "animal snacks" for children to enjoy after the convention, such as animal crackers, jungle juice (fruit juice), and "ants on a log" made from raisins, celery sticks, and peanut butter. Check for food allergies before serving snacks.

Evaluate and Inform

- ✓ Review the informal observation notes you recorded for each child during the four weeks of the unit. Identify areas in which individual children will need additional support.

- ✓ Send a summary of your observation notes home with children. Encourage parents to respond to the summary with questions or comments.

- ✓ Review dated samples of children's work in their portfolios. Copy some of these samples to send home to families along with the observation summary.

- ✓ Send home the Unit 5 My Library Book, *Hello, Animals!*, for children to read with their families.

Celebrar la unidad

Pregunta esencial

¿Qué tienen de asombrosos los animales?

Convención de expertos en animales

Organice en el salón una Convención de expertos en animales

- Invite a los niños a participar en una Convención de expertos en animales, o reunión, en el salón de clases. Explíqueles que actuarán como expertos en animales y usarán lo que aprendieron en toda la unidad para hablar entre ellos sobre animales.

- Antes de la convención, grabe a los niños haciendo sonidos de animales. Sugiérales que imiten aquellos animales que estudiaron en la unidad. Reproduzca la grabación durante la Convención de expertos en animales.

- Organice a la clase en cuatro áreas, asignándole a cada área uno de los temas semanales de la unidad: Conozco a los animales, Animales en el hogar, Comparar animales y Cómo se mueven los animales. En cada área, presente la pregunta de enfoque correspondiente y pídales a los niños que exhiban ejemplos de sus trabajos completados, como:

  casas de animales

  impresiones de hojas

  patrones con peces

  diagramas de animales

  piezas de escritura, dibujos y otros trabajos creativos

- Pida a los niños que formen "Grupos de expertos en animales" y que pasen de un área a otra. Anímelos a basarse en sus trabajos para decirles a los miembros de los demás grupos lo que saben sobre animales.

- Deles a los niños "bocadillos de animales" para que los disfruten después de la convención, como galletas de animalitos, jugo de la selva (jugo de alguna fruta) y "hormigas en la rama", hechas con pasitas, tallos de apio y mantequilla de maní. Antes de servir los bocadillos, verifique que no haya alergias a ciertos alimentos entre la clase.

Evaluar e informar

- Revise las observaciones informales que anotó para cada niño durante las cuatro semanas de la unidad. Identifique las áreas en las que cada niño podría requerir un apoyo adicional.

- Deles a los padres de los niños el resumen respectivo de sus observaciones. Insístales que respondan a este informe con preguntas o comentarios.

- Revise las muestras fechadas que hay en el portafolios de trabajo de cada niño. Haga copias de algunas de estas muestras para que las vean sus padres junto con el resumen de observaciones.

- Deles a los niños el librito de la Unidad 5, *¡Hola, animales!,* para leer con sus familias.

Appendix

About the Authors

NELL K. DUKE, ED.D., is Professor of Teacher Education and Educational Psychology and Co-Director of the Literacy Achievement Research Center at Michigan State University. Nell Duke's expertise lies in early literacy development, particularly among children living in poverty, and integrating literacy into content instruction. She is the recipient of a number of awards for her research and is co-author of several books including *Literacy and the Youngest Learner: Best Practices for Educators of Children from Birth to 5* and *Beyond Bedtime Stories: A Parent's Guide to Promoting Reading, Writing, and Other Literacy Skills From Birth to 5.*

DOUG CLEMENTS is SUNY Distinguished Professor of Education at the University of Buffalo, SUNY. Previously a preschool and kindergarten teacher, Clements currently researchs the learning and teaching of early mathematics and computer applications. He has published over 100 research studies, 8 books, 50 chapters, and 250 additional publications, including co-authoring the reports of President Bush's National Mathematics Advisory Panel and the National Research Council's book on early mathematics. He has directed twenty projects funded by the National Science Foundation and Department of Education's Institute of Education Sciences.

JULIE SARAMA Associate Professor at the University at Buffalo (SUNY), has taught high school mathematics and computer science, gifted and talented classes, and early childhood mathematics. She directs several projects funded by the National Science Foundation and the Institute of Education Sciences. Author of over 50 refereed articles, 4 books, 30 chapters, 20 computer programs, and more than 70 additional publications, she helped develop the Building Blocks and Investigations curricula and the award-winning Turtle Math. Her latest book is *Early Childhood Mathematics Education Research: Learning Trajectories for Young Children.*

WILLIAM TEALE is Professor of Education at the University of Illinois at Chicago. Author of over one hundred publications on early literacy learning, the intersection of technology and literacy education, and children's literature, he helped pioneer research in emergent literacy. Dr. Teale has worked in the area of early childhood education with schools, libraries, and other organizations across the country and internationally. He has also directed three U.S. Department of Education-funded Early Reading First projects that involve developing model preschool literacy curricula for four-year-old children from urban, low-income settings in Chicago.

Contributing Authors

Kimberly Brenneman, PhD, is an Assistant Research Professor of Psychology at Rutgers University. She is also affiliated with the Rutgers Center for Cognitive Science (RuCCS) and the National Institute for Early Education Research (NIEER). Brenneman is co-author of *Preschool Pathways to Science (PrePS): Facilitating Scientific Ways of Thinking, Talking, Doing, and Understanding* and is an educational advisor for PBS's *Sid the Science Kid* television show and website. Research interests include the development of scientific reasoning and methods to improve instructional practices that support science and mathematics learning in preschool.

Peggy Cerna is an independent Early Childhood Consultant. She was a bilingual teacher for 15 years and then served as principal of the Rosita Valley Literacy Academy, a Pre-Kindergarten through Grade 1 school in Eagle Pass, Texas. Cerna then opened Lucy Read Pre-Kindergarten Demonstration School in Austin, Texas, which had 600 Pre-Kindergarten students. During her principalship at Lucy Read, Cerna built a strong parental community with the collaboration of the University of Texas, AmeriCorps, and Austin Community College. Her passion for early literacy drove her to create book clubs where parents were taught how to read books to their children.

Dan Cieloha is an educator with more than 30 years' experience in creating, implementing, and evaluating experientially based learning materials, experiences, and environments for young children. He believes that all learners must be actively and equitably involved in constructing, evaluating, and sharing what they learn. He has spearheaded the creation and field-testing of a variety of learning materials including *You & Me: Building Social Skills in Young Children*. He is also president of the Partnership for Interactive Learning, a leading nonprofit organization dedicated to the development of children's social and thinking skills.

Paula A. Jones, M.Ed., is an Early Childhood Consultant at the state and national levels. As a former Early Childhood Director for the Lubbock Independent School District, she served as the Head Start Director and co-founded three of their four Early Childhood campuses which also became a model design and Best Practices Program for the Texas Education Agency. She was a contributing author for the first Texas Prekindergarten Guidelines, served as president for the Texas Association of Administrators and Supervisors of Programs for Young Children, and is a 2010 United Way Champions for Children Award winner.

Bobbie Sparks is a retired educator who has taught biology and middle school science as well as being the K-12 district science consultant for a suburban district. At Harris County Department of Education she served as the K-12 science consultant in Professional Development. During her career as K-12 science consultant, Sparks worked with teachers at all grade levels to revamp curriculum to meet the Texas science standards. She served on Texas state committees to develop the TEKS standards as well as committees to develop items for tests for teacher certification in science.

Opening Routines

Below are a few suggested routines to use for beginning your day with your class. You can rotate through them, or use one for a while before trying a new approach. You may wish to develop your own routines by mixing and matching ideas from the suggestions given.

1. Days of the Week

Ask children what day of the week it is. When they respond, tell them that you are going to write a sentence that tells everyone what day of the week it is. Print "Today is Monday." on the board. If you have a helper chart, have children assist you in finding the name of the day's helper. Print: "Today's helper is Miguel." Ask the helper to come forward and find the Letter Tiles or ABC Picture Cards that spell his or her name.

As the year progresses, you might want to have the helper find the letters that spell the day of the week. Eventually some children may be able to copy the entire sentence with Letter Tiles or ABC Picture Cards.

2. Calendar Search

Print "Today is _____." on the board. Ask children to help you fill in the blank. Print the day of the week in the blank. Invite children to look at the calendar to determine today's date. Write the date under the sentence that tells what day of the week it is. Invite children to clap out the syllables of both the sentence and the date.

Review the days of the week and the months of the year using the "Days of the Week Song"/"Canción de los dias de la semana" and the "Months of the year"/ "Los meses del año."

Ask children what day of the week it was yesterday. When they respond, ask them what day it is today. Place a seasonal sticker on today's date. Have children follow your lead and recite "Yesterday was Monday, September 12. Today is Tuesday, September 13. Tomorrow will be Wednesday, September 14."

3. Feelings

Make happy- and sad-faced puppets for each child by cutting yellow circles from construction paper and drawing happy and sad faces on them. Laminate the faces, and glue them to tongue depressors. Cover two large coffee cans. On one can glue a happy face, and write the sentence "I feel happy today." Glue the sad face to the second can, and write the sentence "I feel sad today."

Give each child a happy- and a sad-faced puppet. Encourage children to tell how they feel today and to hold up the appropriate puppet. Encourage children to come forward and place their puppets in the can that represents their feelings. Later in the year you can add puppets to represent other emotions.

You can vary this activity by using a graph titled "How I Feel Today"/"Como me siento hoy." Have children place their puppets in the appropriate column on the graph instead of in the cans.

4. Pledge of Allegiance/ Moment of Silence

Have children locate the United States flag. Recite the Pledge of Allegiance to the U.S. flag. Then allow a minute for a moment of silence.

Discuss these activities with children, allowing them to volunteer reasons the Pledge of Allegiance is said and other places they have seen the Pledge recited.

5. Coming to Circle

Talk with children about being part of a class family. Tell children that as part of a class family they will work together, learn together, respect each other, help each other, and play together. Explain that families have rules so that jobs get done and everyone stays safe. Let children know they will learn rules for their classroom. One of those rules is how they will come together for circle. Sing "This is the Way We Come to Circle" (to the tune of "This is the Way We Wash Our Clothes").

This is the way we come to circle.
Come to circle, come to circle.
This is the way we come to circle,
So early in the morning.

This is the way we sit right down,
Sit right down, sit right down.
This is the way we sit right down,
So early in the morning.

This is the way we fold our hands,
Fold our hands, fold our hands.
This is the way we fold our hands,
So early in the morning.

Transition Tips

Sing songs or chants such as those listed below while transitioning between activities:

1. I Am Now in Pre-K

To the tune of "I'm a Little Teapot"

I am now in Pre-K,
I can learn.
I can listen. I can take a turn.
When the teacher says so,
I can play.
Choose a center and together we'll play.

2. Did You Clean Up?

To the tune of "Are You Sleeping, Are You Sleeping, Brother John?"

Did you clean up?
Did you clean up?
Please make sure.
Please make sure.
Everything is picked up.
Everything is picked up.
Please. Thank you!
Please. Thank you!

Chant: Red, Yellow, Green
Red, yellow, green
Stop, change, go
Red, yellow, green
Stop, change, go
Green says yes.
And red says no.
Yellow says everybody wait in a row.
Red, yellow, green
Stop, change, go
Red, yellow, green
Stop, change, go

3. The Five Senses Song

To the tune of "If You're Happy and You Know It"

I can see with my eyes every day (clap clap)
I can see with my eyes every day (clap clap)
I can see with my eyes
I can see with my eyes
I can see with my eyes every day (clap clap)
(Repeat with smell with my nose, hear with my ears, feel with my hands, and taste with my mouth.)

4. Eat More Vegetables

To the tune of "Row, Row, Row Your Boat"

Eat, eat, eat more,
Eat more vegetables.
Carrots, carrots, carrots, carrots
Eat more vegetables.
(Repeat with broccoli, lettuce, celery, and spinach.)

5. Circle Time

To the tune of "Here We Go 'Round the Mulberry Bush"

This is the way we come to circle
Come to circle, come to circle.
This is the way we come to circle
So early in the morning.

This is the way we sit right down,
Sit right down, sit right down.
This is the way we sit right down,
So early in the morning.

Play a short game such as one of the following to focus children's attention:

Name That Fruit!

Say: *It's red on the outside and white on the inside. It rhymes with chapel!*

Children answer, "Apple!" and then repeat twice, "Apple/Chapel."

Repeat with other fruits, such as cherry and banana.

I Spy

Use a flashlight to focus on different letters and words in the classroom. Have children identify them.

Monkey See Monkey Do

Choose one child to be the monkey leader. He or she will act out a motion such as twist, jump, clap, or raise hand, and the rest of the monkeys say the word and copy the motion.

Let's Play Pairs

Distribute one *ABC Picture Card* to each child. Draw letters from an additional set of cards. The child who has the matching letter identifies it and goes to the center of his or her choice.

That's My Friend!

Take children's name cards with their pictures from the wall and distribute making sure no one gets his or her own name. When you call a child's name, she or he has to say something positive about the child on the card and end with "That's my friend!"

Name Game

Say: *If your name begins with ____, you may choose a center.* Have the child say his or her name as he or she gets up. Repeat the child's name, emphasizing the beginning sound.

Center Management

Learning Centers provide children with additional opportunities to practice or extend each lesson's skills and concepts either individually or in small groups. The activities and materials that are explored in the centers not only promote oral language but also help develop children's social skills as they work together. The use of these Learning Centers encourage children to explore their surroundings and make their own choices.

Teacher's Role

The Learning Centers allow time for you to:

- Observe children's exploration of the centers.

- Assess children's understanding of the skills and concepts being taught.

- Provide additional support and encouragement to children who might be having difficulty with specific concepts or skills. If a child is having difficulty, model the correct approach.

Classroom Setup

The materials and activities in the centers should support what children are learning. Multiple experiences are necessary for children's comprehension. The centers should also engage them in learning by providing hands-on experiences. Every time children visit a center and practice skills or extend concepts being taught in the lessons, they are likely to broaden their understanding or discover something new.

In order to support children's learning, the materials and activities in the Learning Centers should change every week. It is important that all the children have a chance to explore every center throughout each week. Be sure they rotate to different centers and do not focus on only one activity. You might also consider adding new materials to the centers as the week progresses. This will encourage children to expand on their past work. Modify or add activities or materials based on your classroom needs.

It is crucial that children know what is expected of them in each center. To help children understand the expectation at each center, display an "I can" statement with an illustration or photograph of a student completing the activity. Discuss these expectations with children in advance, and reinforce them as needed. These discussions might include reviewing your typical classroom rules and talking about the limited number of children allowed in each center. Remind them that they may work individually or in small groups.

Library and Listening Center

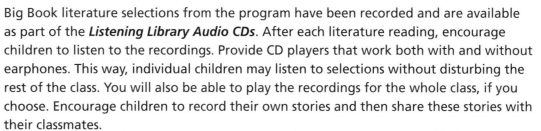

Children should feel free throughout the day to explore books and other printed materials. Create a comfortable reading area in the room, and fill it with as many children's books as possible. Include a number of informational books that tell why things happen and books of rhymes, poems, and songs, as well as storybooks and simple alphabet books.

Before beginning each unit in the program, bring in books about the specific concepts or themes in a unit. Encourage children to bring in books they have enjoyed and would like to share with classmates. Even though they may not be actually reading, have children visit the area often. Here they can practice their book handling, apply their growing knowledge of print awareness, and look at pictures and talk about them. Have them read the books to you or to classmates.

Big Book literature selections from the program have been recorded and are available as part of the *Listening Library Audio CDs*. After each literature reading, encourage children to listen to the recordings. Provide CD players that work both with and without earphones. This way, individual children may listen to selections without disturbing the rest of the class. You will also be able to play the recordings for the whole class, if you choose. Encourage children to record their own stories and then share these stories with their classmates.

As you set up the Learning Centers, here are a few ideas you might want to implement in your classroom.

- Create a separate Workshop Center sign-up chart for children to use when choosing a center to explore.

- Provide an area for children who want to be alone to read or to simply reflect on the day's activities.

- Separate loud areas and quiet areas.

- Hang posters or art at eye level for the children.

- Place on shelves materials, such as books or art supplies, that are easily accessible to the children.

English Language Learners

Teaching the English Language Learner

Stages of English-Language Proficiency

An effective learning environment is an important goal of all educators. In a supportive environment, all English learners have the opportunity to participate and to learn. The materials in this guide are designed to support children while they are acquiring English, allowing them to develop English-language reading skills and the fluency they need to achieve in the core content areas as well.

This guide provides direction in supporting children in four stages of English proficiency: Beginning, Intermediate, Advanced, and Advanced-High. While children at a beginning level by definition know little English and will probably have difficulty comprehending English, by the time they progress to the intermediate or early advanced levels of English acquisition, their skills in understanding more complex language structures will have increased. These stages can be described in general terms as follows:

BEGINNING AND INTERMEDIATE Children identified at these levels of English-language proficiency demonstrate dramatic growth. During these stages, children progress from having no receptive or productive English to possessing a basic command of English. They are learning to comprehend and produce one- or two-word responses to questions, are moving to phrases and simple sentences using concrete and immediate topics, and are learning to interact in a limited fashion with text that has been taught. They progress to responding with increasing ease to more varied communication tasks using learned material, comprehending a sequence of information on familiar topics, producing basic statements and asking questions on familiar subjects, and interacting with a variety of print. Some basic errors are found in their use of English syntax and grammar.

ADVANCED Children who have reached the Advanced level of English-language proficiency have good comprehension of overall meaning and are beginning to demonstrate increased comprehension of specific details and concepts. They are learning to respond in expanded sentences, are interacting more independently with a variety of text, and in using newly acquired English vocabulary to communicate ideas orally and in writing. They demonstrate fewer errors in English grammar and syntax than at the beginning and early intermediate levels.

ADVANCED-HIGH Children who are identified at this level of English-language proficiency demonstrate consistent comprehension of meaning, including implied and nuanced meaning, and are learning the use of idiomatic and figurative language. They are increasingly able to respond using detail in compound and complex sentences and sustain conversation in English. They are able to use standard grammar with few errors and show an understanding of conventions of formal and informal usage.

It is important to provide an instructional scaffold for phonemic awareness, phonics, words structure, language structures, comprehension strategies and skills, and grammar, usage, and mechanics so that children can successfully learn to read while advancing along the continuum of English acquisition. For example, at the Beginning level, you might ask children for *yes* or *no* answers when answering questions about selection comprehension or grammar. Children at the Advanced-High level should be asked to provide answers in complete and expanded sentences. By the time children achieve an Advanced level, their knowledge of English will be more sophisticated because they are becoming more adept at comprehending English and using techniques such as making inferences or using persuasive language.

The following charts illustrate how to use sentence stems with children at each level of English-language proficiency:

Teaching Sentence Stems

- Write the sentence stems on the board, chart paper, or sentence strips. Choose stems that are appropriate for the four general levels of English proficiency.

- Model using the sentence stem(s) for the comprehension strategy or skill.

- Read each phrase as you insert the appropriate words to express an idea. Have children repeat the sentences after you. For Beginning and Intermediate children, use the stems within the questions you ask them.

Linguistic Pattern: *I predict that* _____.

Beginning	Intermediate	Advanced	Advanced-High
Simple questions about the text. Yes-or-no responses or responses that allow children to point to an object or picture.	Simple questions about the text which allow for one- or two-word responses or give children two options for a response to select from.	Questions that elicit a short response or a complete simple sentence using the linguistic pattern.	Have children make predictions on their own. Children should use the linguistic pattern and respond with a complete complex sentence.

Practicing Sentence Stems

- To give children multiple opportunities to generate the language they have just been taught, have them work in pairs or small groups and utilize cooperative learning participation strategies to facilitate this communicative practice.

- Pair children one level of proficiency above or below the other. For example, have Beginning children work with Intermediate level children.

- Use differentiated prompts to elicit the responses that incorporate the linguistic patterns and structures for the different proficiency levels. See the following sample of prompts and responses.

Beginning	Intermediate	Advanced	Advanced-High
Do you predict _____? Yes/No	Do you predict _____ or _____? *I predict* _____.	What do you predict _____? *I predict* _____.	Give a prediction about _____. *I predict* _____.

- Select some common cooperative learning participation strategies to teach to children. Once they have learned some language practice activities, they can move quickly into the various routines. See the examples on the next page.

English Language Learners

My Turn, Your Turn

Children work in pairs.

1. The teacher models a sentence and the whole group repeats, or echoes it.

2. One child generates an oral phrase, and the partner echoes it.

3. Partners switch and alternate roles so that each child has a chance to both generate and repeat phrases.

Talking Stick

Children work in small groups. This strategy allows every child to have an opportunity to speak several times and encourages more reflective or reticent participants to take a turn. Children can "pass" only one time.

1. The teacher charts sentence graphic organizers and linguistic patterns children will use in their responses.

2. The teacher models use of linguistic patterns from the lesson.

3. The teacher asks a question or gives a prompt, and then passes a stick, eraser, stuffed animal, or any other designated object to one child.

4. A child speaks, everyone listens, and then the child passes the object on to the person next to him or her.

5. The next child speaks, everyone listens, and the process continues until the teacher or facilitator gives a signal to return the object.

Think-Pair-Share

This strategy allows children time for processing ideas by building in sufficient wait time to process the question and frame an answer. It is an appropriate strategy to use during small- or large-group discussions or lessons, giving all children a chance to organize their thoughts and have a turn sharing their responses with a partner. It also allows for small group verbal interaction to practice language before sharing with the larger group.

1. After reading or listening to a section of text, the teacher presents a question or task. It is helpful to guide with a specific prompt, modeling the language to be used in the response.

2. Children think about their responses for a brief, designated amount of time.

3. Partners share and discuss their responses with each other.

4. An adaptation can be to have each child share his or her partner's response within a small group to promote active listening.

Teaching Vocabulary

Building the background knowledge and a context for children to learn new words is critical in helping children understand new vocabulary. Primary language can be a valuable tool for preteaching, concept development, and vocabulary. Cognates, or words similar in English counterparts, often provide an opportunity for bridging the primary language and English. Also, children who have background knowledge about a topic can more easily connect the new information they are learning with what they already know than children without a similar context from which to work. Therefore, giving children background information and encouraging them to make as many connections as possible with the new vocabulary word they encounter will help them better understand the selection they are about to read.

In addition to building background knowledge, visual displays such as pictures, graphs, charts, maps, models, or other strategies offer unambiguous access to new content. They provide a clear and parallel correspondence between the visual objects and the new vocabulary to be learned. Thus, because the correlation is clear, the negotiation of meaning is established. Additionally, this process must be constant and reciprocal between you and each child if the child is to succeed in effectively interacting with language.

Included in this guide is a routine for teaching vocabulary words. In addition to this routine, more detailed explanations of the ways to teach vocabulary are as follows:

REAL OBJECTS AND REALIA: Because of the immediate result visuals have on learning language, when explaining a word such as *car,* the best approach is simply to show a real car. As an alternative to the real object, you can show realia. Realia are toy versions of real things, such as plastic eggs to substitute for real eggs, or in this case, a toy car to signify a real car. A large, clear picture of an automobile can also work if it is absolutely recognizable.

If, however, the child has had no experience with the item in the picture, more explanation might be needed. For example, if the word you are explaining is a zoo animal such as an *ocelot,* and children are not familiar with this animal, one picture might be insufficient. They might confuse this animal with a cat or any one of the feline species. Seeing several clear pictures, then, of each individual type of common feline and comparing their similarities and differences might help clarify meaning in this particular instance. When children make a connection between their prior knowledge of the word *cat* with the new word *ocelot,* it validates their newly acquired knowledge, and thus they process learning more quickly.

PICTURES: Supplement story illustrations with visuals such as those found in the **Photo Library CD, ABC Picture Cards,** magazine pictures, and picture dictionaries. Videos, especially those that demonstrate an entire setting such as a farm or zoo, or videos where different animals are highlighted in the natural habitat, for instance, might be helpful. You might also wish to turn off the soundtrack to avoid a flood of language that children might not be able to understand. This way children can concentrate on the visual-word meaning correlation.

PANTOMIME: Language is learned through modeling within a communicative context. Pantomiming is one example of such a framework of communication. Some words, such as *run* and *jump,* are appropriate for pantomiming. Throughout this guide, you will find suggestions for pantomiming words like *sick* by coughing, sneezing, and holding your stomach. If children understand what you are trying to pantomime, they will more easily engage in the task of learning.

Letter Formation Guide

A Starting point, slanting down left
Starting point, slanting down right
Starting point, across the middle: capital *A*

a Starting point, around left all the way
Starting point, straight down,
touching the circle: small *a*

B Starting point, straight down
Starting point, around right and in
at the middle, around right and in
at the bottom: capital *B*

b Starting point, straight down, back
up, around right all the way: small *b*

C Starting point, around left to
stopping place: capital *C*

c Starting point, around left to
stopping place: small *c*

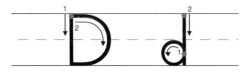

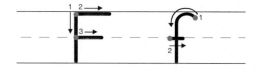

D Starting point, straight down
Starting point, around right and in
at the bottom: capital *D*

d Starting point, around left all the way
Starting point, straight down, touching
the circle: small *d*

E Starting point, straight down
Starting point, straight out
Starting point, straight out
Starting point, straight out: capital *E*

e Starting point, straight out, up and
around to the left, curving down
and around to the right: small *e*

F Starting point, straight down
Starting point, straight out
Starting point, straight out: capital *F*

f Starting point, around left and straight down
Starting point, straight across: small *f*

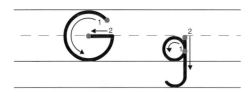

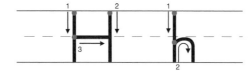

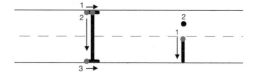

G Starting point, around left, curving up and
around
Straight in: capital *G*

g Starting point, around left all the way
Starting point, straight down, touching the
circle, around left to stopping place: small *g*

H Starting point, straight down
Starting point, straight down
Starting point, across the middle: capital *H*

h Starting point, straight down, back
up, around right, and straight down: small *h*

I Starting point, across
Starting point, straight down
Starting point, across: capital *I*

i Starting point, straight down
Dot exactly above: small *i*

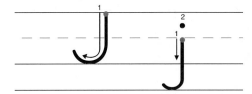

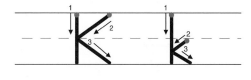

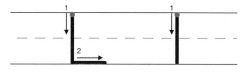

J Starting point, straight down, around left to stopping place: capital *J*

j Starting point, straight down, around left to stopping place Dot exactly above: small *j*

K Starting point, straight down Starting point, slanting down left, touching the line, slanting down right: capital *K*

k Starting point, straight down Starting point, slanting down left, touching the line, slanting down right: small *k*

L Starting point, straight down, straight out: capital *L*

l Starting point, straight down: small *l*

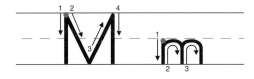

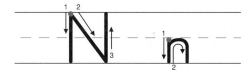

M Starting point, straight down Starting point, slanting down right to the point, slanting back up to the right, straight down: capital *M*

m Starting point, straight down, back up, around right, straight down, back up, around right, straight down: small *m*

N Starting point, straight down Starting point, slanting down right, straight back up: capital *N*

n Starting point, straight down, back up, around right, straight down: small *n*

O Starting point, around left all the way: capital *O*

o Starting point, around left all the way: small *o*

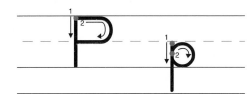

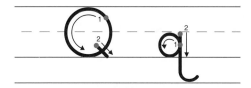

P Starting point, straight down Starting point, around right and in at the middle: capital *P*

p Starting point, straight down Starting point, around right all the way, touching the line: small *p*

Q Starting point, around left all the way Starting point, slanting down right: capital *Q*

q Starting point, around left all the way Starting point, straight down, touching the circle, curving up right to stopping place: small *q*

R Starting point, straight down Starting point, around right and in at the middle, touching the line, slanting down right: capital *R*

r Starting point, straight down, back up, curving around right to stopping place: small *r*

Letter Formation Guide

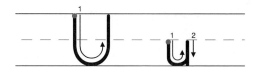

S Starting point, around left, curving right and down around right, curving left and up: capital *S*

s Starting point, around left, curving right and down around right, curving left and up to stopping place: small *s*

T Starting point, straight across
Starting point, straight down: capital *T*

t Starting point, straight down
Starting point, across short: small *t*

U Starting point, straight down, curving around right and up, straight up: capital *U*

u Starting point, straight down, curving around right and up, straight up, straight back down: small *u*

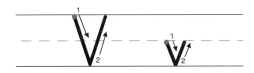

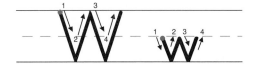

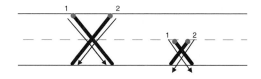

V Starting point, slanting down right, slanting up right: capital *V*

v Starting point, slanting down right, slanting up right: small *v*

W Starting point, slanting down right, slanting up right, slanting down right, slanting up right: capital *W*

w Starting point, slanting down right, slanting up right, slanting down right, slanting up right: small *w*

X Starting point, slanting down right
Starting point, slanting down left: capital *X*

x Starting point, slanting down right
Starting point, slanting down left: small *x*

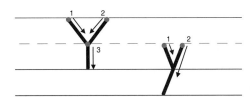

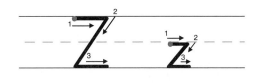

Y Starting point, slanting down right, stop
Starting point, slanting down left, stop
Starting point, straight down: capital *Y*

y Starting point, slanting down right Starting point, slanting down left, connecting the lines: small *y*

Z Starting point, straight across, slanting down left, straight across: capital *Z*

z Starting point, straight across, slanting down left, straight across: small *z*

Number Formation Guide

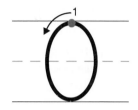

0 Starting point, curving left all the way around to starting point: *0*

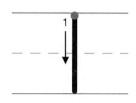

1 Starting point, straight down: *1*

2 Starting point, around right, slanting left and straight across right: *2*

3 Starting point, around right, in at the middle, around right: *3*

4 Starting point, straight down
Straight across right
Starting point, straight down, crossing line: *4*

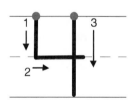

5 Starting point, straight down, curving around right and up
Starting point, straight across right: *5*

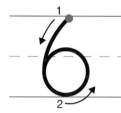

6 Starting point, slanting left, around the bottom curving up, around right and into the curve: *6*

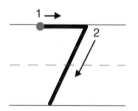

7 Starting point, straight across right, slanting down left: *7*

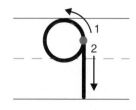

8 Starting point, curving left, curving down and around right, slanting up right to starting point: *8*

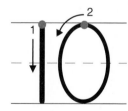

9 Starting point, curving around left all the way, straight down: *9*

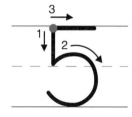

10 Starting point, straight down
Starting point, curving left all the way around to starting point: *10*

Vocabulary Development

Vocabulary development is a key part of **The DLM Early Childhood Express**. Children learn new words through exposure during reading and class discussion. They build language and vocabulary through activities using key words and phrases and by exploring selected vocabulary. After vocabulary words have been introduced, encourage children to use the words in sentences. Again, providing linguistic structures gives children a context for using new vocabulary and building oral language and gives you the opportunity to assess children's understanding of new words. For example, use sentence patterns such as the following:

- A _____ can _____.
- A _____ is a _____.
  (Use this for classification activities. *A tulip is a flower. A rabbit is an animal.*)
- The _____ is _____.
  (Use for describing. *The rabbit is soft.*)

Define words in ways children in your class can understand. When possible, show pictures of objects or actions to help clarify the meanings of words. Provide examples or comparisons to help reinforce the meanings of words and to connect new words to previously learned words. For example, say *The rabbit's FUR is soft like COTTON.* Connect words to categories. For example, say: *Pears are fruits. Are apples fruits? What else is a fruit?* Demonstrate the meaning of words when possible.

During reading, be sure children feel comfortable asking questions and sharing their reactions to what you are reading. Encourage children to share explanations, make predictions, compare and contrast ideas, sequence story events, and describe what you are reading. Encourage children's engagement by modeling reactions and responses while reading. For example, say *I like the part where _____ did _____.* or *This story is about _____.* Support children who are reluctant to speak by using linguistic structures that encourage them to talk about stories and use vocabulary words. You might use the following linguistic structures:

- This story is about _____.
- First _____.
- Next _____.
- Last _____. (Use this for retelling stories.)
- The _____ is the same as _____.
- The _____ is different from _____.
- We read about _____.

Model asking questions before, during, and after reading:

- I wonder what this story is going to be about.
- Who is _____?
- What is _____?
- What did _____ do?
- Why did _____ do _____?
- What happened first? Middle? Last?

Be sure to ask open-ended questions. Unlike questions that simply require a *yes* or *no* or one-word answer, open-ended questions encourage children to think about responses and use new vocabulary in sentences.

Throughout the day, create opportunities for children to talk to each other as they share daily experiences, discuss and explain what they are doing, and talk abut what they are learning.

Vocabulary Words by Topic

Animals

alligator/caimán
ant/horminga
anteater/oso hormiguero
bat/murciélago
bear/oso
beaver/castor
bee/abeja
beetle/escarabajo
bobcat/lince
butterfly/mariposa
camel/camello
cat/gato
chicken/gallina/pollo
chipmunk/ardilla
cow/vaca
crab/cangrejo
deer/venado/ciervo
dog/perro
dolphin/delfin
donkey/burro
dragonfly/libélula
duck/pato
eagle/águila
elephant/elefante
flamingo/flamingo
fly/mosca
fox/zorro
frog/rana
giraffe/jirafa
goat/cabra
gorilla/
grasshopper/saltamontes
hamster/hámster
hippopotamus/hipopótamo
horse/caballo
kangaroo/canguro
koala/coala

ladybug/catarina
leopard/leopardo
lion/león
llama/llama
lobster/langosta
monkey/mono
moose/alce
mosquito/mosquito
mouse/ratón
octopus/pulpo
opossum/zarigüeya
owl/búho
panda/oso panda
parakeet/periquito
peacock/pavo real
pelican/pelicano
penguin/pingüino
pig/cerdo
polar bear/oso polar
porcupine/puerco espín
rabbit/conejo
raccoon/mapache
rhinoceros/rinoceronte
robin/petirrojo
salamander/salamandra
sea horse/caballo de mar
shark/tiburón
sheep/oveja
skunk/mofeta/zorrillo
snake/serpiente
squirrel/ardilla
starfish/estrella de mar
swan/cisne
tiger/tigre
toad/sapo
turkey/pavo
turtle/tortuga
walrus/morsa

whale/ballena
zebra/cebra

Colors and Shapes

blue/azul
green/verde
red/rojo
yellow/amarillo
circle/círculo azul
diamond/diamante
oval/óvalo
rectangle/rectángulo
square/cuadrado
triangle/triángulo

Signs

deer crossing/cruce de venado
handicapped parking/
    estacionamiento para inválidos
railroad crossing/paso del tren
school crossing/cruce escolar
speed limit/limite de velocidad
stop sign/señal de alto
traffic light/semáforo
yield sign/señal de ceder el paso

Earth

beach/playa
blizzard/tormenta de nieve
cloud/nube
coral reef/arrecife de coral
desert/desierto
dry season/temporada seca
fall/otoño
fog/niebla
forest/bosque
geyser/géiser
glacier/glaciar

hail/granizo
hurricane/huracán
ice/hielo
island/isla
lake/lago
lightning/relámpago
mountain/montaña
ocean/océano
plain/llano
rain/lluvia
rain forest/selva tropical
rainy season/temporada de lluvias
rapids/rápidos
river/río
snow/nieve
spring/primavera
stream/arroyo
summer/verano
sun/sol
tornado/tornado
tundra/tundra
volcano/volcán
waterfall/cascada
wind/viento
winter/invierno

Human Body

ankle/tobillo
arm/brazo
body/cuerpo
ear/oreja
elbow/codo
eyes/ojos
feet/pies
fingers/dedos
hair/pelo
hands/manos

Vocabulary Words by Topic

head/cabeza
hearing/oído
heel/talón
hips/caderas
knee/rodilla
legs/piernas
mouth/boca
nose/nariz
sense/sentido
shoulders/hombros
sight/vista
smell/olfato
taste/gusto
teeth/dientes
toes/dedos de los pies
touch/ tacto

Plants

cactus/cactus
carrot/zanahoria
clover/trébol
cornstalk/planta de maíz
dandelion/diente de león
fern/helecho
grapevine/parra
grass/hierba
lettuce/lechuga
lilac bush/lila de monte
marigold/caléndula
moss/musgo
oak tree/árbol de roble
onion/cebolla
orange tree/naranjo
palm tree/palma
pine tree/pino
poison ivy/hiedra venenosa
rice/arroz
rose/rosa

seaweed/alga marina
sunflower/girasol
tomato/tomate
tulip/tulipán
water lily/nenúfar
wheat/trigo

Clothing

belt/cinturón
blouse/blusa
boots/botas
boy's swimsuit/traje de baño para
    niños
coat/abrigo
dress/vestido
earmuffs/orejeras
girl's swimsuit/traje de baño para
    niñas
gloves/guantes
hat/sombrero
jacket/chaqueta
jeans/pantalones vaqueros
mittens/manoplas
pajamas/pijama
pants/pantalones
raincoat/impermeable
robe/bata
scarf/bufanda
shirt/camisa
shoes/zapatos
shorts/pantalones cortos
skirt/falda
slippers/pantuflas
socks/calcetines
sweat suit/chandal
sweater/suéter
tie/corbata
vest/chaleco

Food

apples/manzanas
bacon/tocino
bagels/roscas de pan
bananas/plátanos
beans/frijoles
beef/carne
beets/betabel
blueberries/arándanos
bread/pan
broccoli/brécol
butter/mantequilla
cake/pastel
cantaloupe/cantalupo
carrots/zanahoria
cauliflower/coliflor
celery/apio
cereal/cereal
cheese/queso
cherries/cerezas
chicken/pollo
clams/almejas
cookies/galletas
corn/maíz
cottage cheese/requesón
crackers/galletas saladas
cream cheese/queso crema
cucumbers/pepinos
eggs/huevos
figs/higos
fish/pescado
grapefruit/toronja
grapes/uvas
green peppers/pimientos verdes
ham/jamón
ice-cream cone/cono de helado
jelly/gelatina
lemons/limones

lettuce/lechuga
limes/limas
macaroni/macarrones
milk/leche
mushrooms/champiñones
nuts/nueces
onions/cebollas
orange juice/jugo de naranja
oranges/naranjas
peaches/duraznos
peanut butter/crema de cacahuete
pears/peras
peas/guisantes
pie/tarta
pineapples/piñas
plums/ciruelas
pork chop/chuleta de puerco
potatoes/papas
radishes/rábanos
raisins/pasas
rice/arroz
rolls/panecillos
salad/ensalada
sausage/salchicha
shrimp/camarón
soup/sopa
spaghetti/espaguetis
squash/calabaza
strawberries/fresas
sweet potatoes/camotes
tomatoes/tomates
watermelon/sandía
yogurt/yogur

Recreation

archery/tiro el arco
badminton/bádminton
baseball/béisbol
basketball/baloncesto
biking/ciclismo
boating/paseo en bote
bowling/boliche
canoeing/piragüismo
climbing/montañismo
croquet/croquet
discus/disco
diving/buceo
fishing/pesca
football/fútbol
golf/golf
gymnastics/gimnasia
hiking/excursionismo
hockey/hockey
horseback riding/equitación
ice-skating/patinaje sobre hielo
in-line skating/patines en línea
lacrosse/lacrosse
pole-vaulting/salto con pértiga
running/atletismo
scuba diving/buceo
shot put/lanzamiento de peso
skiing/esquí
soccer/fútbol
surfing/surfing
swimming/natación
T-ball/T-ball
tennis/tenis
volleyball/voleibol
walking/caminar
waterskiing/esquí acuático
weight lifting/levantamiento

School

auditorium/auditorio
book/libro
cafeteria/cafetería
cafeteria table/mesa de cafetería
calculator/calculadora
chair/silla
chalk/tiza
chalkboard/pizarrón
chart paper/rotafolio
classroom/aula
computer/omputadora
construction paper/papel para
    construir
crayons/crayones
desk/escritorio
easel/caballete
eraser/borrador
globe/globo
glue/pegamento
gym/gimnasio
hallway/vestíbulo
janitor's room/conserjería
learning center/centro de
    aprendizaje
library/biblioteca
markers/marcadores
music room/salón de música
notebook paper/papel de cuaderno
nurse's office/enfermería
paint/pintura
paintbrush/pincel
pen/pluma
pencil/lápiz
pencil sharpener/sacapuntas
playground/patio de recreo
principal's office/oficina del
    director

ruler/regla
science room/salón de ciencias
scissors/tijeras
stairs/escaleras
stapler/grapadora
supply room/almacén
tape/cinta adhesiva

Toys

ball/pelota
balloons/globos
bike/bicicleta
blocks/cubos
clay/arcilla
coloring book/libro para colorear
doll/muñeca
doll carriage/careola de muñecas
dollhouse/casa de muñecas
farm set/juego de la granja
game/juego
grocery cart/carro de compras
hats/sombreros
in-line skates/patines
instruments/instrumentos
jump rope/cuerda para saltar
kite/cometa
magnets/imanes
marbles/canicas
puppet/títere
puzzle/rompecabezas
scooter/motoneta
skateboard/patineta
slide/tobogán
stuffed animals/peluches
tape recorder/grabadora
top/trompo
toy cars/carro de juguete
toy trucks/camión de juguete

train set/juego de tren
tricycle/triciclo
wagon/vagón
yo-yo/yó-yó

Equipment

baggage cart/carro para equipaje
baseball/béisbol
bat/bate
mitt/manopla
basketball/pelota de baloncesto
basketball net/canasta
blueprints/planos
computer/computadora
drafting tools/borradores
bow/arco
arrow/flecha
bowling ball/pelota de boliche
bowling pin/bolos de boliche
bridle/freno
saddle/silla de montar
saddle pad/montura
broom/escoba
bulldozer/aplanadora
canoe/canoa
paddle/paleta
cash register/caja registradora
computer/computadora
crane/grúa
dishwasher/lavaplatos
drill/taladro
drum/tambor
drumsticks/palillos
dryer/secadora
dustpan/recogedor
figure skates/patinaje artistico

Vocabulary Words by Topic

football/balón
shoulder pads/hombreras
football helmet/casco
goggles/gafas
golf ball/pelota de golf
golf clubs/palo de golf
tee/tee
hammer/martillo
handcuffs/esposas
badge/placa
hat/gorra
hockey stick/palo de hockey
hockey puck/disco de hockey
ice skates/patines
hoe/azadón
hose/manguera
coat/chaqueta
hat/sombrero
sprinkler/rociador
iron/plancha
ironing board/tabla de planchar
lawn mower/cortacéspedes
mail pouch/bolsa de correo
mirror/espejo
probe/sonda
pick/pico
mop/estropajo
paintbrush/brocha de pintar
piano/piano
pliers/alicates
rake/rastrillo
roller skates/patines
saw/sierra
screwdriver/desarmador
scuba tank/tanque de buceo
mask/máscara
flippers/aletas
shovel/pala

sketch pad/cuaderno para dibujo
palette/paleta
skis/esquís
ski boots/botas para esquiar
poles/palos
soccer ball/balón de fútbol
shoes/zapatos de tenis
stepladder/escalera doble
stethoscope/estetoscopio
surfboard/tabla de surf
tennis ball/pelota de tenis
tennis racket/raqueta de tenis
tractor/tractor
vacuum cleaner/aspiradora
washer/lavadora
water skis/esquís acuáticos
rope/cuerda
life jacket/chaleco salvavidas
watering can/regadera
wheelbarrow/carretilla
wrench/llave inglesa

Home

basement/sótano
bathroom/baño
bathroom sink/lavabo
bathtub/bañera
bed/cama
bedroom/recámara/habitación
blanket/cobija/manta
chair/silla
circuit breaker/cortocircuito
dresser/cómoda
electrical outlet/enchufe
end table/mesa auxiliar
fireplace/chimenea
furnace/horno
kitchen/cocina

kitchen chair/silla de cocina
kitchen sink/fregadero
kitchen table/mesa de cocina
lamp/lámpara
light switch/interruptor de la luz
living room/sala
medicine cabinet/botiquín
nightstand/mesilla de noche
pillow/almohada
refrigerator/refrigerador
shower/ducha
smoke alarm/alarma de incendios
sofa/sofá
stove/estufa
thermostat/termostato
toilet/el baño
water heater/calentador de agua

Occupations

administrative assistant/asistente
administrativo
air traffic controller/controlador
aéreo
airline pilot/piloto
architect/arquitecto
artist/artista
astronaut/astronauta
athlete/atleta
author/autor
ballerina/bailarina
banker/banquero
bus driver/conductor de autobús
camera operator/operador de
cámara
carpenter/carpintero
cashier/cajero
chef/jefe de cocina
computer technician/técnico en

computación
cosmetologist/cosmetólogo
dancer/bailarín
dentist/dentista
doctor/doctor
electrician/electricista
engineer/ingeniero
farmer/granjero
firefighter/bombero
forest ranger/guardabosques
lawyer/abogado
manicurist/manicurista
musician/músico
nurse/enfermera
paramedic/paramédico
photographer/fotógrafo
police officer/policía
postal worker/empleado postal
real estate agent/corridor de
bienes raíces
refuse collector/recolector de
basura
reporter/reportero
school crossing guard/guarda
escolar
server/mesero
ship captain/capitán de barco
singer/cantante
skater/patinador
teacher/maestro
truck driver/conductor de camión
veterinarian/veterinario
weaver/tejedora

Structures

adobe/casa de adobe
airplane hangar/hangar de avión
airport/aeropuerto
apartment building/edificio de
    departamentos/edificio de pisos
arena/arena
art museum/museo de arte
bakery/panadería
bank/banco
barn/granero
bridge/peunte
bus shelter/parada cubierta
city hall/ayuntamiento
clothing store/tienda de ropa
condominium/condominio
courthouse/tribunal
covered bridge/puente cubierto
dam/presa
dock/muelle
drawbridge/puente levadizo
duplex/dúplex
fire station/estación de bomberos
flower shop/floristeria
garage/garaje
gas station/gasolinera
gazebo/mirador
grain elevator/elevador de granos
grocery store/supermercado
hospital/hospital
house/casa
library/biblioteca
log cabin/cabaña de madera
marina/marina
monument/monumento
movie theater/cine
opera house/teatro de la ópera
palace/palacio

parking garage/estacionamiento
pizza shop/pizzaría
police station/estación de policía
power plant/central eléctrica
pyramid/pirámide
restaurant/restaurante
school/escuela
shelter house/albergue
shopping mall/centro comercial
skyscraper/rascacielos
stadium/estadio
swimming pool/alberca/piscina
tent/tienda
toy store/juguetería
train station/estación del tren
windmills/molino de viento

Transportation

airplane/avión
bicycle/bicicleta
bus/autobús
canoe/canoa
car/coche
four-wheel-drive vehicle/coche con
    doble tracción
helicopter/helicóptero
hot air balloon/globo de aire
    caliente
kayak/kayac
moped/ciclomotor
motor home/casa motora
motorboat/lancha motora
motorcycle/motocicleta
pickup truck/camioneta
rowboat/bote de remos
sailboat/velero
school bus/camión escolar

semitrailer truck/camión con semi-
    remolque
ship/barco
submarine/submarino
subway/metro
taxi/taxi
train/tren
van/furgoneta

Learning Trajectories for Math

Children follow natural developmental progressions in learning. Curriculum research has revealed sequences of activities that are effective in guiding children through these levels of thinking. These developmental paths are the basis for *Building Blocks* learning trajectories.

Learning Trajectories for Primary Grades Mathematics

Learning trajectories have three parts: a mathematical goal, a developmental path along which children develop to reach that goal, and a set of activities matched to each of the levels of thinking in that path that help children develop the next higher level of thinking. The **Building Blocks** learning trajectories give simple labels, descriptions, and examples of each level. Complete learning trajectories describe the goals of learning, the thinking and learning processes of children at various levels, and the learning activities in which they might engage. This document provides only the developmental levels.

The following provides the developmental levels from the first signs of development in different strands of mathematics through approximately age 8. Research shows that when teachers understand how children develop mathematics understanding, they are more effective in questioning, analyzing, and providing activities that further children's development than teachers who are unaware of the development process. Consequently, children have a much richer and more successful math experience in the primary grades.

Each of the following tables, such as "Counting," represents a main developmental progression that underlies the learning trajectory for that topic.

For some topics, there are "subtrajectories"—strands within the topic. In most cases, the names make this clear. For example, in Comparing and Ordering, some levels are "Composer" levels and others involve building a "Mental Number Line." Similarly, the related subtrajectories of "Composition" and "Decomposition" are easy to distinguish. Sometimes, for clarification, subtrajectories are indicated with a note in italics after the title. For example, Parts and Representing are subtrajectories within the Shape Trajectory.

Frequently Asked Questions (FAQ)

1. Why use learning trajectories? Learning trajectories allow teachers to build the mathematics of children—the thinking of children as it develops naturally. So, we know that all the goals and activities are within the developmental capacities of children. Finally, we know that the activities provide the mathematical building blocks for success.

2. When are children "at" a level? Children are at a certain level when most of their behaviors reflect the thinking—ideas and skills—of that level. Most levels are levels of thinking. However, some are merely "levels of attainment" and indicate a child has gained knowledge. For example, children must learn to name or write more numerals, but knowing more numerals does not require more complex thinking.

3. Can children work at more than one level at the same time? Yes, although most children work mainly at one level or in transition between two levels. Levels are not "absolute stages." They are "benchmarks" of complex growth that represent distinct ways of thinking.

4. Can children jump ahead? Yes, especially if there are separate subtopics. For example, we have combined many counting competencies into one "Counting" sequence with subtopics, such as verbal counting skills. Some children learn to count to 100 at age 6 after learning to count objects to 10 or more, some may learn that verbal skill earlier. The subtopic of verbal counting skills would still be followed.

5. How do these developmental levels support teaching and learning? The levels help teachers, as well as curriculum developers, assess, teach, and sequence activities. Through planned teaching and encouraging informal, incidental mathematics, teachers help children learn at an appropriate and deep level.

6. Should I plan to help children develop just the levels that correspond to my children's ages? No! The ages in the table are typical ages children develop these ideas. (These are rough guides only.) These are "starting levels" not goals. We have found that children who are provided high-quality mathematics experiences are capable of developing to levels one or more years beyond their peers.

Developmental Levels for Counting

The ability to count with confidence develops over the course of several years. Beginning in infancy, children show signs of understanding numbers. With instruction and number experience, most children can count fluently by age 8, with much progress in counting occurring in kindergarten and first grade. Most children follow a natural developmental progression in learning to count with recognizable stages or levels. This developmental path can be described as part of a learning trajectory.

Age Range	Level Name	Level	Description
1–2	Precounter	1	At the earliest level a child shows no verbal counting. The child may name some number words with no sequence.
1–2	Chanter	2	At this level, a child may sing-song or chant indistinguishable number words.
2	Reciter	3	At this level, the child may verbally count with separate words, but not necessarily in the correct order.
3	Reciter (10)	4	A child at this level may verbally count to 10 with some correspondence with objects. He or she may point to objects to count a few items, but then lose track.
3	Corresponder	5	At this level, a child may keep one-to-one correspondence between counting words and objects—at least for small groups of objects laid in a line. A corresponder may answer "how many" by recounting the objects.
4	Counter (Small Numbers)	6	At around 4 years of age, the child may begin to count meaningfully. He or she may accurately count objects in a line to 5 and answer the "how many" question with the last number counted. When objects are visible, and especially with small numbers, the child begins to understand cardinality (that numbers tell how many).
4	Producer (Small Numbers)	7	The next level after counting small numbers is to count out objects to 5. When asked to show four of something, for example, this child may give four objects.
4	Counter (10)	8	This child may count structured arrangements of objects to 10. He or she may be able to write or draw to represent 1–10. A child at this level may be able to tell the number just after or just before another number, but only by counting up from 1.
5	Counter and Producer—Counter to (10+)	9	Around 5 years of age, a child may begin to count out objects accurately to 10 and then beyond to 30. He or she has explicit understanding of cardinality (that numbers tell how many). The child may keep track of objects that have and have not been counted, even in different arrangements. He or she may write or draw to represent 1 to 10 and then 20 and 30, and may give the next number to 20 or 30. The child also begins to recognize errors in others' counting and is able to eliminate most errors in his or her own counting.

Age Range	Level Name	Level	Description
5	Counter Backward from 10	10	Another milestone at about age 5 is being able to count backward from 10 to 1, verbally, or when removing objects from a group.
6	Counter from N (N+1, N–1)	11	Around 6 years of age, the child may begin to count on, counting verbally and with objects from numbers other than 1. Another noticeable accomplishment is that a child may determine the number immediately before or after another number without having to start back at 1.
6	Skip Counting by 10s to 100	12	A child at this level may count by 10s to 100 or beyond with understanding.
6	Counter to 100	13	A child at this level may count by 1s to 100. He or she can make decade transitions (for example, from 29 to 30) starting at any number.
6	Counter On Using Patterns	14	At this level, a child may keep track of a few counting acts by using numerical patterns, such as tapping as he or she counts.
6	Skip Counter	15	At this level, the child can count by 5s and 2s with understanding.
6	Counter of Imagined Items	16	At this level, a child may count mental images of hidden objects to answer, for example, "how many" when 5 objects are visible and 3 are hidden.
6	Counter On Keeping Track	17	A child at this level may keep track of counting acts numerically, first with objects, then by counting counts. He or she counts up one to four more from a given number.
6	Counter of Quantitative Units	18	At this level, a child can count unusual units, such as "wholes" when shown combinations of wholes and parts. For example, when shown three whole plastic eggs and four halves, a child at this level will say there are five whole eggs.
6	Counter to 200	19	At this level, a child may count accurately to 200 and beyond, recognizing the patterns of ones, tens, and hundreds.
7	Number Conserver	20	A major milestone around age 7 is the ability to conserve number. A child who conserves number understands that a number is unchanged even if a group of objects is rearranged. For example, if there is a row of ten buttons, the child understands there are still ten without recounting, even if they are rearranged in a long row or a circle.
7	Counter Forward and Back	21	A child at this level may count in either direction and recognize that sequence of decades mirrors single-digit sequence.

Learning Trajectories for Math

Developmental Levels for Comparing and Ordering Numbers

Comparing and ordering sets is a critical skill for children as they determine whether one set is larger than another in order to make sure sets are equal and "fair." Prekindergartners can learn to use matching to compare collections or to create equivalent collections. Finding out how many more or fewer in one collection is more demanding than simply comparing two collections. The ability to compare and order sets with fluency develops over the course of several years. With instruction and number experience, most children develop foundational understanding of number relationships and place value at ages four and five. Most children follow a natural developmental progression in learning to compare and order numbers with recognizable stages or levels. This developmental path can be described as part of a learning trajectory.

Age Range	Level Name	Level	Description
2	Object Corresponder	1	At this early level, a child puts objects into one-to-one correspondence, but may not fully understand that this creates equal groups. For example, a child may know that each carton has a straw, but does not necessarily know there are the same numbers of straws and cartons.
2	Perceptual Comparer	2	At this level, a child can compare collections that are quite different in size (for example, one is at least twice the other) and know that one has more than the other. If the collections are similar, the child can compare very small collections.
3	First-Second Ordinal Counter	3	At this level the child can identify the "first" and often "second" object in a sequence.
3	Nonverbal Comparer of Similar Items	4	At this level, a child can identify that different organizations of the same number are equal and different from other sets (1–4 items). For example, a child can identify ••• and •‌•• as equal and different from •• or •‌•.
4	Nonverbal Comparer of Dissimilar Items	5	At this level, a child can match small, equal collections of dissimilar items, such as shells and dots, and show that they are the same number.
4	Matching Comparer	6	As children progress, they begin to compare groups of 1–6 by matching. For example, a child gives one toy bone to every dog and says there are the same number of dogs and bones.

Age Range	Level Name	Level	Description
4	Knows-to-Count Comparer	7	A significant step occurs when the child begins to count collections to compare. At the early levels, children are not always accurate when a larger collection's objects are smaller in size than the objects in the smaller collection. For example, a child at this level may accurately count two equal collections, but when asked, says the collection of larger blocks has more.
4	Counting Comparer (Same Size)	8	At this level, children make accurate comparisons via counting, but only when objects are about the same size and groups are small (about 1–5 items).
5	Counting Comparer (5)	9	As children develop their ability to compare sets, they compare accurately by counting, even when a larger collection's objects are smaller. A child at this level can figure out how many more or less.
5	Ordinal Counter	10	At this level, a child identifies and uses ordinal numbers from "first" to "tenth." For example, the child can identify who is "third in line."
6	Counting Comparer (10)	11	This level can be observed when the child compares sets by counting, even when a larger collection's objects are smaller, up to 10. A child at this level can accurately count two collections of 9 items each, and says they have the same number, even if one collection has larger blocks.
6	Mental Number Line to 10	12	As children move into this level, they begin to use mental images and knowledge of number relationships to determine relative size and position. For example, a child at this level can answer which number is closer to 6, 4 or 9 without counting physical objects.
6	Serial Orderer to 6+	13	At this level, the child orders lengths marked into units (1–6, then beyond). For example, given towers of cubes, this child can put them in order, 1 to 6.
7	Place Value Comparer	14	Further development is made when a child begins to compare numbers with place value understanding. For example, a child at this level can explain that "63 is more than 59 because six tens is more than five tens, even if there are more than three ones."
7	Mental Number Line to 100	15	Children demonstrate the next level when they can use mental images and knowledge of number relationships, including ones embedded in tens, to determine relative size and position. For example, when asked, "Which is closer to 45, 30 or 50?" a child at this level may say "45 is right next to 50, but 30 isn't."
8+	Mental Number Line to 1,000s	16	At about age 8, children may begin to use mental images of numbers up to 1,000 and knowledge of number relationships, including place value, to determine relative size and position. For example, when asked, "Which is closer to 3,500—2,000 or 7,000?" a child at this level may say "70 is double 35, but 20 is only fifteen from 35, so twenty hundreds, 2,000, is closer."

Developmental Levels for Recognizing Number and Subitizing (Instantly Recognizing)

The ability to recognize number values develops over the course of several years and is a foundational part of number sense. Beginning at about age two, children begin to name groups of objects. The ability to instantly know how many are in a group, called *subitizing,* begins at about age three. By age eight, with instruction and number experience, most children can identify groups of items and use place values and multiplication skills to count them. Most children follow a natural developmental progression in learning to count with recognizable stages or levels. This developmental path can be described as part of a learning trajectory.

Age Range	Level Name	Level	Description
2	Small Collection Namer	1	The first sign occurs when the child can name groups of 1 to 2, sometimes 3. For example, when shown a pair of shoes, this young child says, "two shoes."
3	Maker of Small Collections	2	At this level, a child can nonverbally make a small collection (no more than 4, usually 1 to 3) with the same number as another collection. For example, when shown a collection of 3, the child makes another collection of 3.
4	Perceptual Subitizer to 4	3	Progress is made when a child instantly recognizes collections up to 4 and verbally names the number of items. For example, when shown 4 objects briefly, the child says "4."
5	Perceptual Subitizer to 5	4	This level is the ability to instantly recognize collections up to 5 and verbally name the number of items. For example, when shown 5 objects briefly, the child says "5."
5	Conceptual Subitizer to 51	5	At this level, the child can verbally label all arrangements to about 5, when shown only briefly. For example, a child at this level might say, "I saw 2 and 2, and so I saw 4."
5	Conceptual Subitizer to 10	6	This step is when the child can verbally label most arrangements to 6 shown briefly, then up to 10, using groups. For example, a child at this level might say, "In my mind, I made 2 groups of 3 and 1 more, so 7."
6	Conceptual Subitizer to 20	7	Next, a child can verbally label structured arrangements up to 20 shown briefly, using groups. For example, the child may say, "I saw 3 fives, so 5, 10, 15."
7	Conceptual Subitizer with Place Value and Skip Counting	8	At this level, a child is able to use groups, skip counting, and place value to verbally label structured arrangements shown briefly. For example, the child may say, "I saw groups of tens and twos, so 10, 20, 30, 40, 42, 44, 46...46!"
8+	Conceptual Subitizer with Place Value and Multiplication	9	As children develop their ability to subitize, they use groups, multiplication, and place value to verbally label structured arrangements shown briefly. At this level, a child may say, "I saw groups of tens and threes, so I thought, 5 tens is 50 and 4 threes is 12, so 62 in all."

Learning Trajectories for Math

Developmental Levels for Composing (Knowing Combinations of Numbers)

Composing and decomposing are combining and separating operations that allow children to build concepts of "parts" and "wholes." Most prekindergartners can "see" that two items and one item make three items. Later, children learn to separate a group into parts in various ways and then to count to produce all of the number "partners" of a given number. Eventually children think of a number and know the different addition facts that make that number. Most children follow a natural developmental progression in learning to compose and decompose numbers with recognizable stages or levels. This developmental path can be described as part of a learning trajectory.

Age Range	Level Name	Level	Description
4	Pre-Part-Whole Recognizer	1	At the earliest levels of composing, a child only nonverbally recognizes parts and wholes. For example, when shown 4 red blocks and 2 blue blocks, a young child may intuitively appreciate that "all the blocks" includes the red and blue blocks, but when asked how many there are in all, the child may name a small number, such as 1.
5	Inexact Part-Whole Recognizer	2	A sign of development is that the child knows a whole is bigger than parts, but does not accurately quantify. For example, when shown 4 red blocks and 2 blue blocks and asked how many there are in all, the child may name a "large number," such as 5 or 10.
5	Composer to 4, then 5	3	At this level, a child knows number combinations. A child at this level quickly names parts of any whole, or the whole given the parts. For example, when shown 4, then 1 is secretly hidden, and then shown the 3 remaining, the child may quickly say "1" is hidden.
6	Composer to 7	4	The next sign of development is when a child knows number combinations to totals of 7. A child at this level quickly names parts of any whole, or the whole when given parts, and can double numbers to 10. For example, when shown 6, then 4 are secretly hidden, and then shown the 2 remaining, the child may quickly say "4" are hidden.
6	Composer to 10	5	This level is when a child knows number combinations to totals of 10. A child at this level may quickly name parts of any whole, or the whole when given parts, and can double numbers to 20. For example, this child would be able to say "9 and 9 is 18."
7	Composer with Tens and Ones	6	At this level, the child understands two-digit numbers as tens and ones, can count with dimes and pennies, and can perform two-digit addition with regrouping. For example, a child at this level may explain, "17 and 36 is like 17 and 3, which is 20, and 33, which is 53."

Developmental Levels for Adding and Subtracting

Single-digit addition and subtraction are generally characterized as "math facts." It is assumed children must memorize these facts, yet research has shown that addition and subtraction have their roots in counting, counting on, number sense, the ability to compose and decompose numbers, and place value. Research has also shown that learning methods for addition and subtraction with understanding is much more effective than rote memorization of seemingly isolated facts. Most children follow an observable developmental progression in learning to add and subtract numbers with recognizable stages or levels. This developmental path can be described as part of a learning trajectory.

Age Range	Level Name	Level	Description
1	Pre +/−	1	At the earliest level, a child shows no sign of being able to add or subtract.
3	Nonverbal +/−	2	The first sign is when a child can add and subtract very small collections nonverbally. For example, when shown 2 objects, then 1 object being hidden under a napkin, the child identifies or makes a set of 3 objects to "match."
4	Small Number +/−	3	This level is when a child can find sums for joining problems up to 3 1 2 by counting with objects. For example, when asked, "You have 2 balls and get 1 more. How many in all?" the child may count out 2, then count out 1 more, then count all 3: "1, 2, 3, 3!"
5	Find Result +/−	4	**Addition** Evidence of this level in addition is when a child can find sums for joining (you had 3 apples and get 3 more; how many do you have in all?) and part-part-whole (there are 6 girls and 5 boys on the playground; how many children were there in all?) problems by direct modeling, counting all, with objects. For example, when asked, "You have 2 red balls and 3 blue balls. How many in all?" the child may count out 2 red, then count out 3 blue, then count all 5. **Subtraction** In subtraction, a child can also solve take-away problems by separating with objects. For example, when asked, "You have 5 balls and give 2 to Tom. How many do you have left?" the child may count out 5 balls, then take away 2, and then count the remaining 3.

Age Range	Level Name	Level	Description
5	Find Change +/–	5	**Addition** At this level, a child can find the missing addend (5 + _ =7) by adding on objects. For example, when asked, "You have 5 balls and then get some more. Now you have 7 in all. How many did you get?" The child may count out 5, then count those 5 again starting at 1, then add more, counting "6, 7," then count the balls added to find the answer, 2. **Subtraction** A child can compare by matching in simple situations. For example, when asked, "Here are 6 dogs and 4 balls. If we give a ball to each dog, how many dogs will not get a ball?" a child at this level may count out 6 dogs, match 4 balls to 4 of them, then count the 2 dogs that have no ball.
5	Make It +/–	6	A significant advancement occurs when a child is able to count on. This child can add on objects to make one number into another without counting from 1. For example, when told, "This puppet has 4 balls, but she should have 6. Make it 6," the child may put up 4 fingers on one hand, immediately count up from 4 while putting up 2 fingers on the other hand, saying, "5, 6," and then count or recognize the 2 fingers.
6	Counting Strategies +/–	7	This level occurs when a child can find sums for joining (you had 8 apples and get 3 more…) and part-part-whole (6 girls and 5 boys…) problems with finger patterns or by adding on objects or counting on. For example, when asked "How much is 4 and 3 more?" the child may answer "4…5, 6, 7. 7!" Children at this level can also solve missing addend (3 + _ = 7) or compare problems by counting on. When asked, for example, "You have 6 balls. How many more would you need to have 8?" the child may say, "6, 7 [puts up first finger], 8 [puts up second finger]. 2!"
6	Part-Whole +/–	8	Further development has occurred when the child has part-whole understanding. This child can solve problems using flexible strategies and some derived facts (for example, "5 + 5 is 10, so 5 + 6 is 11"), can sometimes do start-unknown problems (_ + 6 = 11), but only by trial and error. When asked, "You had some balls. Then you get 6 more. Now you have 11 balls. How many did you start with?" this child may lay out 6, then 3, count, and get 9. The child may put 1 more, say 10, then put 1 more. The child may count up from 6 to 11, then recount the group added, and say, "5!"

Age Range	Level Name	Level	Description
6	Numbers-in-Numbers +/–	9	Evidence of this level is when a child recognizes that a number is part of a whole and can solve problems when the start is unknown (_ + 4 = 9) with counting strategies. For example, when asked, "You have some balls, then you get 4 more balls, now you have 9. How many did you have to start with?" this child may count, putting up fingers, "5, 6, 7, 8, 9." The child may then look at his or her fingers and say, "5!"
7	Deriver +/–	10	At this level, a child can use flexible strategies and derived combinations (for example, "7 + 7 is 14, so 7 + 8 is 15") to solve all types of problems. For example, when asked, "What's 7 plus 8?" this child thinks: 7 + 8 = 7 [7 + 1] = [7 +7] + 1 = 14 + 1 = 15. The child can also solve multidigit problems by incrementing or combining 10s and 1s. For example, when asked "What's 28 + 35?" this child may think: 20 + 30 = 50; + 8 = 58; 2 more is 60, and 3 more is 63. He or she can also combine 10s and 1s: 20 + 30 = 50. 8 + 5 is like 8 plus 2 and 3 more, so it is 13. 50 and 13 is 63.
8+	Problem Solver +/–	11	As children develop their addition and subtraction abilities, they can solve by using flexible strategies and many known combinations. For example, when asked, "If I have 13 and you have 9, how could we have the same number?" this child may say, "9 and 1 is 10, then 3 more makes 13. 1 and 3 is 4. I need 4 more!"
8+	Multidigit +/–	12	Further development is shown when children can use composition of 10s and all previous strategies to solve multidigit +/– problems. For example, when asked, "What's 37 − 18?" this child may say, "Take 1 ten off the 3 tens; that's 2 tens. Take 7 off the 7. That's 2 tens and 0…20. I have one more to take off. That's 19." Or, when asked, "What's 28 + 35?" this child may think, 30 + 35 would be 65. But it's 28, so it's 2 less…63.

Learning Trajectories for Math

Developmental Levels for Multiplying and Dividing

Multiplication and division build on addition and subtraction understanding and are dependent upon counting and place-value concepts. As children begin to learn to multiply, they make equal groups and count them all. They then learn skip counting and derive related products from products they know. Finding and using patterns aid in learning multiplication and division facts with understanding. Children typically follow an observable developmental progression in learning to multiply and divide numbers with recognizable stages or levels. This developmental path can be described as part of a learning trajectory.

Age Range	Level Name	Level	Description
2	Non-quantitative Sharer "Dumper"	1	Multiplication and division concepts begin very early with the problem of sharing. Early evidence of these concepts can be observed when a child dumps out blocks and gives some (not an equal number) to each person.
3	Beginning Grouper and Distributive Sharer	2	Progression to this level can be observed when a child is able to make small groups (fewer than 5). This child can share by "dealing out," but often only between 2 people, although he or she may not appreciate the numerical result. For example, to share 4 blocks, this child may give each person a block, check that each person has one, and repeat this.
4	Grouper and Distributive Sharer	3	The next level occurs when a child makes small equal groups (fewer than 6). This child can deal out equally between 2 or more recipients, but may not understand that equal quantities are produced. For example, the child may share 6 blocks by dealing out blocks to herself and a friend one at a time.
5	Concrete Modeler ×/÷	4	As children develop, they are able to solve small-number multiplying problems by grouping—making each group and counting all. At this level, a child can solve division/sharing problems with informal strategies, using concrete objects—up to 20 objects and 2 to 5 people—although the child may not understand equivalence of groups. For example, the child may distribute 20 objects by dealing out 2 blocks to each of 5 people, then 1 to each, until the blocks are gone.
6	Parts and Wholes ×/÷	5	A new level is evidenced when the child understands the inverse relation between divisor and quotient. For example, this child may understand "If you share with more people, each person gets fewer."

Age Range	Level Name	Level	Description
7	Skip Counter ×/÷	6	As children develop understanding in multiplication and division, they begin to use skip counting for multiplication and for measurement division (finding out how many groups). For example, given 20 blocks, 4 to each person, and asked how many people, the children may skip count by 4, holding up 1 finger for each count of 4. A child at this level may also use trial and error for partitive division (finding out how many in each group). For example, given 20 blocks, 5 people, and asked how many each should get, this child may give 3 to each, and then 1 more.
8+	Deriver ×/÷	7	At this level, children use strategies and derived combinations to solve multidigit problems by operating on tens and ones separately. For example, a child at this level may explain "7 × 6, five 7s is 35, so 7 more is 42."
8+	Array Quantifier	8	Further development can be observed when a child begins to work with arrays. For example, given 7 × 4 with most of 5 × 4 covered, a child at this level may say, "There are 8 in these 2 rows, and 5 rows of 4 is 20, so 28 in all."
8+	Partitive Divisor	9	This level can be observed when a child is able to figure out how many are in each group. For example, given 20 blocks, 5 people, and asked how many each should get, a child at this level may say, "4, because 5 groups of 4 is 20."
8+	Multidigit ×/÷	10	As children progress, they begin to use multiple strategies for multiplication and division, from compensating to paper-and-pencil procedures. For example, a child becoming fluent in multiplication might explain that "19 times 5 is 95, because 20 fives is 100, and 1 less five is 95."

Developmental Levels for Measuring

Measurement is one of the main real-world applications of mathematics. Counting is a type of measurement which determines how many items are in a collection. Measurement also involves assigning a number to attributes of length, area, and weight. Prekindergarten children know that mass, weight, and length exist, but they do not know how to reason about these or to accurately measure them. As children develop their understanding of measurement, they begin to use tools to measure and understand the need for standard units of measure. Children typically follow an observable developmental progression in learning to measure with recognizable stages or levels. This developmental path can be described as part of a learning trajectory.

Age Range	Level Name	Level	Description
3	Length Quantity Recognizer	1	At the earliest level, children can identify length as an attribute. For example, they might say, "I'm tall, see?"
4	Length Direct Comparer	2	In this level, children can physically align 2 objects to determine which is longer or if they are the same length. For example, they can stand 2 sticks up next to each other on a table and say, "This one's bigger."
5	Indirect Length Comparer	3	A sign of further development is when a child can compare the length of 2 objects by representing them with a third object. For example, a child might compare the length of 2 objects with a piece of string. Additional evidence of this level is that when asked to measure, the child may assign a length by guessing or moving along a length while counting (without equal-length units). For example, the child may move a finger along a line segment, saying 10, 20, 30, 31, 32.
6	Serial Orderer to 6+	4	At this level, a child can order lengths, marked in 1 to 6 units. For example, given towers of cubes, a child at this level may put them in order, 1 to 6.
6	End-to-End Length Measurer	5	At this level, the child can lay units end-to-end, although he or she may not see the need for equal-length units. For example, a child might lay 9-inch cubes in a line beside a book to measure how long it is.
7	Length Unit Iterater	6	A significant change occurs when a child iterates a single unit to measure. He or she sees the need for identical units. The child uses rulers with help.
7	Length Unit Relater	7	At this level, a child can relate size and number of units. For example, the child may explain, "If you measure with centimeters instead of inches, you'll need more of them because each one is smaller."
8+	Length Measurer	8	As a child develops measurement ability, they begin to measure, knowing the need for identical units, the relationships between different units, partitions of unit, and the zero point on rulers. At this level, the child also begins to estimate. The children may explain, "I used a meterstick 3 times, then there was a little left over. So, I lined it up from 0 and found 14 centimeters. So, it's 3 meters, 14 centimeters in all."
8+	Conceptual Ruler Measurer	9	Further development in measurement is evidenced when a child possesses an "internal" measurement tool. At this level, the child mentally moves along an object, segmenting it, and counting the segments. This child also uses arithmetic to measure and estimates with accuracy. For example, a child at this level may explain, "I imagine one meterstick after another along the edge of the room. That's how I estimated the room's length to be 9 meters."

Learning Trajectories for Math

Developmental Levels for Recognizing Geometric Shapes

Geometric shapes can be used to represent and understand objects. Analyzing, comparing, and classifying shapes help create new knowledge of shapes and their relationships. Shapes can be decomposed or composed into other shapes. Through their everyday activities, children build both intuitive and explicit knowledge of geometric figures. Most children can recognize and name basic two-dimensional shapes at four years of age. However, young children can learn richer concepts about shape if they have varied examples and nonexamples of shape, discussions about shapes and their characteristics, a wide variety of shape classes, and interesting tasks. Children typically follow an observable developmental progression in learning about shapes with recognizable stages or levels. This developmental path can be described as part of a learning trajectory.

Age Range	Level Name	Level	Description
2	Shape Matcher—Identical	1	The earliest sign of understanding shape is when a child can match basic shapes (circle, square, typical triangle) with the same size and orientation.
2	Shape Matcher—Sizes	2	A sign of development is when a child can match basic shapes with different sizes.
2	Shape Matcher—Orientations	3	This level of development is when a child can match basic shapes with different orientations.
3	Shape Recognizer—Typical	4	A sign of development is when a child can recognize and name a prototypical circle, square, and, less often, a typical triangle. For example, the child names this a square. Some children may name different sizes, shapes, and orientations of rectangles, but also accept some shapes that look rectangular but are not rectangles. Children name these shapes "rectangles" (including the nonrectangular parallelogram).
3	Shape Matcher—More Shapes	5	As children develop understanding of shape, they can match a wider variety of shapes with the same size and orientation.
3	Shape Matcher—Sizes and Orientations	6	The child matches a wider variety of shapes with different sizes and orientations.
3	Shape Matcher—Combinations	7	The child matches combinations of shapes to each other.
4	Shape Recognizer—Circles, Squares, and Triangles	8	This sign of development is when a child can recognize some nonprototypical squares and triangles and may recognize some rectangles, but usually not rhombi (diamonds). Often, the child does not differentiate sides/corners. The child at this level may name these as triangles.
4	Constructor of Shapes from Parts—Looks Like *Representing*	9	A significant sign of development is when a child represents a shape by making a shape "look like" a goal shape. For example, when asked to make a triangle with sticks, the child may create the following: △.

Age Range	Level Name	Level	Description
5	Shape Recognizer— All Rectangles	10	As children develop understanding of shape, they recognize more rectangle sizes, shapes, and orientations of rectangles. For example, a child at this level may correctly name these shapes "rectangles."
5	Side Recognizer *Parts*	11	A sign of development is when a child recognizes parts of shapes and identifies sides as distinct geometric objects. For example, when asked what this shape is, the child may say it is a quadrilateral (or has 4 sides) after counting and running a finger along the length of each side.
5	Angle Recognizer *Parts*	12	At this level, a child can recognize angles as separate geometric objects. For example, when asked, "Why is this a triangle," the child may say, "It has three angles" and count them, pointing clearly to each vertex (point at the corner).
5	Shape Recognizer— More Shapes	13	As children develop, they are able to recognize most basic shapes and prototypical examples of other shapes, such as hexagon, rhombus (diamond), and trapezoid. For example, a child can correctly identify and name all the following shapes:
6	Shape Identifier	14	At this level, the child can name most common shapes, including rhombi, without making mistakes such as calling ovals circles. A child at this level implicitly recognizes right angles, so distinguishes between a rectangle and a parallelogram without right angles. A child may correctly name all the following shapes:
6	Angle Matcher *Parts*	15	A sign of development is when the child can match angles concretely. For example, given several triangles, the child may find two with the same angles by laying the angles on top of one another.

Age Range	Level Name	Level	Description
7	Parts of Shapes Identifier	16	At this level, the child can identify shapes in terms of their components. For example, the child may say, "No matter how skinny it looks, that's a triangle because it has 3 sides and 3 angles."
7	Constructor of Shapes from Parts—Exact Representing	17	A significant step is when the child can represent a shape with completely correct construction, based on knowledge of components and relationships. For example, when asked to make a triangle with sticks, the child may create the following:
8	Shape Class Identifier	18	As children develop, they begin to use class membership (for example, to sort) not explicitly based on properties. For example, a child at this level may say, "I put the triangles over here, and the quadrilaterals, including squares, rectangles, rhombi, and trapezoids, over there."
8	Shape Property Identifier	19	At this level, a child can use properties explicitly. For example, a child may say, "I put the shapes with opposite sides that are parallel over here, and those with 4 sides but not both pairs of sides parallel over there."
8	Angle Size Comparer	20	The next sign of development is when a child can separate and compare angle sizes. For example, the child may say, "I put all the shapes that have right angles here, and all the ones that have bigger or smaller angles over there."
8	Angle Measurer	21	A significant step in development is when a child can use a protractor to measure angles.
8	Property Class Identifier	22	The next sign of development is when a child can use class membership for shapes (for example, to sort or consider shapes "similar") explicitly based on properties, including angle measure. For example, the child may say, "I put the equilateral triangles over here, and the right triangles over here."
8	Angle Synthesizer	23	As children develop understanding of shape, they can combine various meanings of angle (turn, corner, slant). For example, a child at this level could explain, "This ramp is at a 45° angle to the ground."

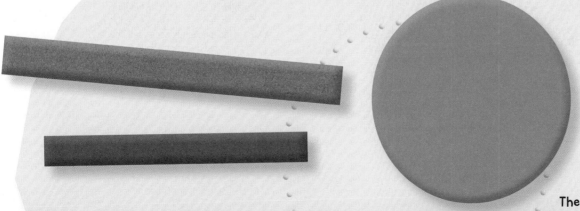

Learning Trajectories for Math

Developmental Levels for Composing Geometric Shapes

Children move through levels in the composition and decomposition of two-dimensional figures. Very young children cannot compose shapes but then gain ability to combine shapes into pictures, synthesize combinations of shapes into new shapes, and eventually substitute and build different kinds of shapes. Children typically follow an observable developmental progression in learning to compose shapes with recognizable stages or levels. This developmental path can be described as part of a learning trajectory.

Age Range	Level Name	Level	Description
2	Pre-Composer	1	The earliest sign of development is when a child can manipulate shapes as individuals, but is unable to combine them to compose a larger shape.
3	Pre-Decomposer	2	At this level, a child can decompose shapes, but only by trial and error.
4	Piece Assembler	3	Around age 4, a child can begin to make pictures in which each shape represents a unique role (for example, one shape for each body part) and shapes touch. A child at this level can fill simple outline puzzles using trial and error.
5	Picture Maker	4	As children develop, they are able to put several shapes together to make one part of a picture (for example, 2 shapes for 1 arm). A child at this level uses trial and error and does not anticipate creation of the new geometric shape. The children can choose shapes using "general shape" or side length, and fill "easy" outline puzzles that suggest the placement of each shape (but note that the child is trying to put a square in the puzzle where its right angles will not fit).
5	Simple Decomposer	5	A significant step occurs when the child is able to decompose ("take apart" into smaller shapes) simple shapes that have obvious clues as to their decomposition.

Age Range	Level Name	Level	Description
5	Shape Composer	6	A sign of development is when a child composes shapes with anticipation ("I know what will fit!"). A child at this level chooses shapes using angles as well as side lengths. Rotation and flipping are used intentionally to select and place shapes.
6	Substitution Composer	7	A sign of development is when a child is able to make new shapes out of smaller shapes and uses trial and error to substitute groups of shapes for other shapes in order to create new shapes in different ways. For example, the child can substitute shapes to fill outline puzzles in different ways.
6	Shape Decomposer (with Help)	8	As children develop, they can decompose shapes by using imagery that is suggested and supported by the task or environment.
7	Shape Composite Repeater	9	This level is demonstrated when the child can construct and duplicate units of units (shapes made from other shapes) intentionally, and understands each as being both multiple, small shapes and one larger shape. For example, the child may continue a pattern of shapes that leads to tiling.
7	Shape Decomposer with Imagery	10	A significant sign of development is when a child is able to decompose shapes flexibly by using independently generated imagery.
8	Shape Composer—Units of Units	11	Children demonstrate further understanding when they are able to build and apply units of units (shapes made from other shapes). For example, in constructing spatial patterns, the child can extend patterning activity to create a tiling with a new unit shape—a unit of unit shapes that he or she recognizes and consciously constructs. For example, the child may build Ts out of 4 squares, use 4 Ts to build squares, and use squares to tile a rectangle.
8	Shape Decomposer — Units of Units	12	As children develop understanding of shape, they can decompose shapes flexibly by using independently generated imagery and planned decompositions of shapes that themselves are decompositions.

Developmental Levels for Comparing Geometric Shapes

As early as four years of age, children can create and use strategies, such as moving shapes to compare their parts or to place one on top of the other, for judging whether two figures are the same shape. From Pre-K to Grade 2, they can develop sophisticated and accurate mathematical procedures for comparing geometric shapes. Children typically follow an observable developmental progression in learning about how shapes are the same and different with recognizable stages or levels. This developmental path can be described as part of a learning trajectory.

Age Range	Level Name	Level	Description
3	"Same Thing" Comparer	1	The first sign of understanding is when the child can compare real-world objects. For example, the children may say two pictures of houses are the same or different.
4	"Similar" Comparer	2	This sign of development occurs when the child judges two shapes to be the same if they are more visually similar than different. For example, the child may say, "These are the same. They are pointy at the top."
4	Part Comparer	3	At this level, a child can say that two shapes are the same after matching one side on each. For example, a child may say, "These are the same" (matching the two sides).
4	Some Attributes Comparer	4	As children develop, they look for differences in attributes, but may examine only part of a shape. For example, a child at this level may say, "These are the same" (indicating the top halves of the shapes are similar by laying them on top of each other).
5	Most Attributes Comparer	5	At this level, the child looks for differences in attributes, examining full shapes, but may ignore some spatial relationships. For example, a child may say, "These are the same."
7	Congruence Determiner	6	A sign of development is when a child determines congruence by comparing all attributes and all spatial relationships. For example, a child at this level may say that two shapes are the same shape and the same size after comparing every one of their sides and angles.
7	Congruence Superposer	7	As children develop understanding, they can move and place objects on top of each other to determine congruence. For example, a child at this level may say that two shapes are the same shape and the same size after laying them on top of each other.
8+	Congruence Representer	8	Continued development is evidenced as children refer to geometric properties and explain with transformations. For example, a child at this level may say, "These must be congruent because they have equal sides, all square corners, and I can move them on top of each other exactly."

Developmental Levels for Spatial Sense and Motions

Infants and toddlers spend a great deal of time learning about the properties and relations of objects in space. Very young children know and use the shape of their environment in navigation activities. With guidance they can learn to "mathematize" this knowledge. They can learn about direction, perspective, distance, symbolization, location, and coordinates. Children typically follow an observable developmental progression in developing spatial sense with recognizable stages or levels. This developmental path can be described as part of a learning trajectory.

Age Range	Level Name	Level	Description
4	Simple Turner	1	An early sign of spatial sense is when a child mentally turns an object to perform easy tasks. For example, given a shape with the top marked with color, the child may correctly identify which of three shapes it would look like if it were turned "like this" (90 degree turn demonstrated), before physically moving the shape.
5	Beginning Slider, Flipper, Turner	2	This sign of development occurs when a child can use the correct motions, but is not always accurate in direction and amount. For example, a child at this level may know a shape has to be flipped to match another shape, but flips it in the wrong direction.
6	Slider, Flipper, Turner	3	As children develop spatial sense, they can perform slides and flips, often only horizontal and vertical, by using manipulatives. For example, a child at this level may perform turns of 45, 90, and 180 degrees. For example, a child knows a shape must be turned 90 degrees to the right to fit into a puzzle.
7	Diagonal Mover	4	A sign of development is when a child can perform diagonal slides and flips. For example, children at this level may know a shape must be turned or flipped over an oblique line (45 degree orientation) to fit into a puzzle.
8	Mental Mover	5	Further signs of development occur when a child can predict results of moving shapes using mental images. A child at this level may say, "If you turned this 120 degrees, it would be just like this one."

Learning Trajectories for Math

Developmental Levels for Patterning and Early Algebra

Algebra begins with a search for patterns. Identifying patterns helps bring order, cohesion, and predictability to seemingly unorganized situations and allows one to make generalizations beyond the information directly available. The recognition and analysis of patterns are important components of young children's intellectual development because they provide a foundation for the development of algebraic thinking. Although prekindergarten children engage in pattern-related activities and recognize patterns in their everyday environment, research has revealed that an abstract understanding of patterns develops gradually during the early childhood years. Children typically follow an observable developmental progression in learning about patterns with recognizable stages or levels. This developmental path can be described as part of a learning trajectory.

Age Range	Level Name	Level	Description
2	Pre-Patterner	1	A child at the earliest level does not recognize patterns. For example, a child may name a striped shirt with no repeating unit a "pattern."
3	Pattern Recognizer	2	At this level, the child can recognize a simple pattern. For example, a child at this level may say, "I'm wearing a pattern" about a shirt with black and white stripes.
4	Pattern Fixer	3	At this level the child fills in missing elements of a pattern, first with ABABAB patterns. When given items in a row with an item missing, such as ABAB_BAB, the child identifies and fills in the missing element (A).
4	Pattern Duplicator AB	4	A sign of development is when the child can duplicate an ABABAB pattern, although the children may have to work alongside the model pattern. For example, given objects in a row, ABABAB, the child may make his or her own ABABAB row in a different location.
4	Pattern Extender AB	5	At this level the child extends AB repeating patterns. For example, given items in a row—ABABAB—the child adds ABAB to the end of the row.
4	Pattern Duplicator	6	At this level, the child is able to duplicate simple patterns (not just alongside the model pattern). For example, given objects in a row, ABBABBABB, the child may make his or her own ABBABBABB row in a different location.
5	Pattern Extender	7	A sign of development is when the child can extend simple patterns. For example, given objects in a row, ABBABBABB, he or she may add ABBABB to the end of the row.
7	Pattern Unit Recognizer	8	At this level, a child can identify the smallest unit of a pattern. For example, given objects in a row with one missing, ABBAB_ABB, he or she may identify and fill in the missing element.

Developmental Levels for Classifying and Analyzing Data

Data analysis contains one big idea: classifying, organizing, representing, and using information to ask and answer questions. The developmental continuum for data analysis includes growth in classifying and counting to sort objects and quantify their groups. Children eventually become capable of simultaneously classifying and counting; for example, counting the number of colors in a group of objects. Children typically follow an observable developmental progression in learning about patterns with recognizable stages or levels. This developmental path can be described as part of a learning trajectory.

Age Range	Level Name	Level	Description
2	Similarity Recognizer	1	The first sign that a child can classify is when he or she recognizes, intuitively, two or more objects as "similar" in some way. For example, "that's another doggie."
2	Informal Sorter	2	A sign of development is when a child places objects that are alike in some attribute together, but switches criteria and may use functional relationships as the basis for sorting. A child at this level might stack blocks of the same shape or put a cup with its saucer.
3	Attribute Identifier	3	The next level is when the child names attributes of objects and places objects together with a given attribute, but cannot then move to sorting by a new rule. For example, the child may say, "These are both red."
4	Attribute Sorter	4	At the next level the child sorts objects according to given attributes, forming categories, but may switch attributes during the sorting. A child at this stage can switch rules for sorting if guided. For example, the child might start putting red beads on a string, but switches to spheres of different colors.
5	Consistent Sorter	5	A sign of development is when the child can sort consistently by a given attribute. For example, the child might put several identical blocks together.
6	Exhaustive Sorter	6	At the next level, the child can sort consistently and exhaustively by an attribute, given or created. This child can use terms "some" and "all" meaningfully. For example, a child at this stage would be able to find all the attribute blocks of a certain size and color.

Age Range	Level Name	Level	Description
6	Multiple Attribute Sorter	7	A sign of development is when the child can sort consistently and exhaustively by more than one attribute, sequentially. For example, a child at this level can put all the attribute blocks together by color, then by shape.
7	Classifier and Counter	8	At the next level, the child is capable of simultaneously classifying and counting. For example, the child counts the number of colors in a group of objects.
7	List Grapher	9	In the early stage of graphing, the child graphs by simply listing all cases. For example, the child may list each child in the class and each child's response to a question.
8+	Multiple Attribute Classifier	10	A sign of development is when the child can intentionally sort according to multiple attributes, naming and relating the attributes. This child understands that objects could belong to more than one group. For example, the child can complete a two-dimensional classification matrix or form subgroups within groups.
8+	Classifying Grapher	11	At the next level the child can graph by classifying data (e.g., responses) and represent it according to categories. For example, the child can take a survey, classify the responses, and graph the result.
8+	Classifier	12	A sign of development is when the child creates complete, conscious classifications logically connected to a specific property. For example, a child at this level gives a definition of a class in terms of a more general class and one or more specific differences and begins to understand the inclusion relation.
8+	Hierarchical Classifier	13	At the next level, the child can perform hierarchical classifications. For example, the child recognizes that all squares are rectangles, but not all rectangles are squares.
8+	Data Representer	14	Signs of development are when the child organizes and displays data through both simple numerical summaries such as counts, tables, and tallies, and graphical displays, including picture graphs, line plots, and bar graphs. At this level the child creates graphs and tables, compares parts of the data, makes statements about the data as a whole, and determines whether the graphs answer the questions posed initially.